No-Fault Divorce

No-Fault Divorce

What Went Wrong?

Allen M. Parkman

Westview Press

BOULDER • SAN FRANCISCO • OXFORD

Copyright © 1992 by Westview Press, Inc.

Published in 1992 in the United States of America by Westview Press, Inc., 5500 Central Avenue, Boulder, Colorado 80301-2847, and in the United Kingdom by Westview Press, 36 Lonsdale Road, Summertown, Oxford OX2 7EW

Library of Congress Cataloging-in-Publication Data
Parkman, Allen M.
  No-fault divorce : what went wrong? / Allen M. Parkman.
    p. cm.
  Includes bibliographical references (p.   ) and index.
  ISBN 0-8133-1433-X
  1. Divorce—Economic aspects. 2. No-fault divorce—Economic aspects—United States. I. Title.
HQ814.P37 1992
306.89—dc20   92-5560
                                                                                 CIP

Printed and bound in the United States of America

The paper used in this publication meets the requirements
of the American National Standard for Permanence of Paper
for Printed Library Materials Z39.48-1984.

10   9   8   7   6   5   4   3   2   1

To Amy, Ian, and Andrew

Contents

List of Tables and Figures   ix
Preface   xi
Acknowledgments   xv

1 Introduction   1

The Effects of No-Fault, 1
An Economic Perspective, 3
The Book, 8
Notes, 8

2 Marriage and Divorce Laws   13

Marriage Laws, 13
Divorce Laws, 16
Matrimonial Property, 18
Conclusion, 22
Notes, 22

3 The Economics of Marriage and Divorce   25

The Role of Economic Analysis, 25
The Economic Approach to Marriage, 27
The Economics of Divorce, 35
The Effect of Marriage on Wealth, 38
The Economics of the Political Process, 43
The Economics of Negotiation and Litigation, 44
The Economics of the Second Best, 46
Conclusion, 47
Notes, 47

4 The Introduction of No-Fault Divorce Statutes   53

Case Law Versus Statutory Law, 53
No-Fault in California, 54
The Economic Perspective on the Introduction
  of No-Fault, 58

Conclusion, 66
Notes, 66

5 The Impact of No-Fault Divorce   71

The Divorce Rate, 72
The Financial Condition of Divorced Women, 79
Property, 88
The Incentive to Marry, 94
The Labor Force Participation Rate of Married Women, 96
Education, 98
The Quality of Life for Married Women, 99
The Quality of Family Life, 101
Conclusion, 104
Notes, 104

6 The Reform of No-Fault Divorce   111

The Recognition of the Problem, 112
The Emphasis on Property Settlements, 113
The Goal of Reform, 120
A Program for the Reform of Divorce, 123
Mutual Consent Divorce, 137
Concerns About Using Human Capital in
   Property Settlements, 140
Conclusion, 143
Notes, 144

Appendix   151
References   153
About the Book and Author   161
Index   163

Tables and Figures

Tables

5.1	Divorce Rates and Related Data	73
5.2	Marriage Rates and Related Data	95
5.3	Labor Force Participation Rates for Married Women	97

Figures

3.1	The Advantages of Specialization	30
3.2	A Relationship Without Specialization	34

Preface

In this book I address the repercussions of no-fault divorce, first identifying the problems that have been created by no-fault and then offering a program for divorce law reform. I first became aware of these problems a decade ago when I was asked to appraise the professional goodwill of an orthopedic surgeon for his divorce settlement. The courts in a number of states, including New Mexico, had held that the goodwill of a professional individual was marital property subject to division at divorce. Although I was familiar with business goodwill, an intangible asset of a smoothly functioning business, professional goodwill was something new to me.

The appraisal of professional goodwill presented many difficult questions. What was professional goodwill worth? The usual procedure for estimating the value of goodwill is to compare the income of an ongoing business to that of a similar, but new, business that has not yet had time to acquire goodwill. Applying this concept to professionals is difficult. Because of differences in characteristics such as intelligence, ambition, and willingness to accept risk, it is virtually impossible to identify the proportion of professional income attributable to goodwill.

When was professional goodwill acquired? Because property must be allocated between the separate property that existed at the time of marriage and the marital property created during the marriage, the timing of the acquisition of property can be important at divorce. Although the date a business was established usually can be determined, it is difficult, if not impossible, to establish when a professional career was initiated. A professional's income is the result of investments made throughout his or her life. Efforts during high school and college often make professional school possible. These investments may have been made by the professional, parents, taxpayers, or a spouse. Therefore, even if the value of professional goodwill can be estimated, its allocation between the separate property of the professional and the marital property of the couple may be unclear. I eventually reached the conclusion that the determination and allocation of professional goodwill at divorce was an extremely arbitrary process. So why had the concept developed? As I thought about that question, the answer became clear: no-fault divorce.

The courts were attempting to mitigate the dire financial situations of many divorced women that resulted from the no-fault divorce laws that became common in the 1970s. These laws replaced the fault grounds for divorce, such as adultery, cruelty, and desertion, with the no-fault grounds of "incompatibility" or "irretrievable breakdown." Under fault divorce, the spouse seeking the divorce had to prove that the other spouse was guilty of a prohibited activity. That was usually not easy, so fabricated testimony was common. If one spouse did not want a divorce, the other spouse had to provide compensation to induce him or her to be the plaintiff and to provide the required testimony that established the fault grounds.

The fault grounds for divorce thus afforded the spouse who wanted to continue the marriage with substantial negotiating power. Alternatively, the no-fault grounds often provided for divorce based on the desire of only one spouse, removing the need to negotiate with an uncooperative spouse and shifting the financial arrangements at divorce to the legal standards. These legal standards, which were especially unfair to wives who had accommodated the career of their husbands, had not been subjected to close scrutiny under fault divorce because of the prevalence of negotiated settlements. The courts reacted to this situation by creating ad hoc concepts such as professional goodwill in an attempt to correct for the limited funds provided older women under the new divorce laws.

The case of the surgeon's wife is a common one. She was a middle-aged woman who had committed herself to being a housewife and mother. The couple had lived well on the surgeon's comfortable income, but they had accumulated only a limited amount of marital property. Their children had grown and left the home. At divorce, the wife faced a very gloomy future. Her share of the limited community property did not amount to much. There would be no child support. In the spirit of fairness and equality, the courts had moved toward short-term, rehabilitative spousal support instead of long-term alimony. The wife had limited employment prospects, but her husband was leaving the marriage with his income intact. The provision of professional goodwill created an additional source of funds for her.

The more I investigated how society was reacting to the no-fault grounds for divorce, the more I became convinced that no-fault divorce was creating many problems. It sanctioned socially undesirable divorces. It encouraged family members to make decisions that were not in the best interests of the other family members. It impoverished many divorced women and the children of divorced parents. Furthermore, I became convinced that an important reason the literature on no-fault didn't deal adequately with these problems was largely due to a failure to consider the insights available from an economic perspective. Economics studies the choices that people make in an environment in which wants exceed resources, so they must weigh the benefits and costs of the alternatives.

Although love and sexual attraction are appropriately associated with marriage and divorce, the benefit/cost framework of economics can provide valuable additional insights about how people decide to marry or to end a marriage. Marriage is one of the most important decisions that people make. The decision by an individual to marry another precludes--at least temporarily--the person's remaining single or marrying anyone else. From an economic perspective, that individual is presumed to consider the benefits of the marriage to exceed those of any alternate arrangement. The foregone benefits of the alternative arrangements are among the costs of the marriage. So long as the benefits of marriage exceed the costs for both spouses, the couple stays married. When the costs exceed the benefits for one spouse, that spouse may seek a divorce. The divorce laws influence the costs of dissolving a marriage. For example, no-fault reduced the costs of divorce for many spouses who wanted to dissolve their marriage.

It appeared that my background in economics and law provided me with a perspective on the problems and the reform of no-fault divorce that was unique among the people analyzing that subject. The primary problem with no-fault divorce is its potential for encouraging divorce when the financial and psychological benefits to all the persons involved do not exceed the costs. Because a divorce can be acquired in most states based on the desire of just one spouse, the gain experienced by the divorcing spouse can be less than the loss experienced by the other members of the family. These divorces reduce social welfare. In addition, no-fault laws encourage the members of families to make other social-welfare-reducing decisions such as working outside the home and pursuing additional education during marriage, not to benefit the family, but to protect themselves from the adverse effects of divorce.

A major reform of the no-fault divorce laws would recognize individuals' earning capacities, which economists call human capital, as property. During marriage, some spouses, such as professionals, may acquire human capital, while other spouses, such as housewives, may lose human capital. Recognizing the effect of marriage on the spouses' human capital would more accurately align the legal costs of divorce with the true costs. Even with this reform, no-fault divorce would not force the spouses, especially the divorcing spouse, to recognize all the costs of divorce.

The incapacity of no-fault divorce to force the divorcing spouse to recognize all the costs of divorce is a fundamental flaw that leads me to conclude that social welfare would be improved if the grounds for divorce were changed to require the consent of both spouses for a divorce. Requiring mutual consent as the normal requirement for divorce might appear to be a radical step, but it is in effect a return to the conditions under fault divorce--without the hypocritical grounds that prevailed. In fact, negotiated divorces were common under fault divorce, and mutual consent would again require the spouses to consider the benefits and costs of divorce to all the parties. Given the importance of the family to all its members and to society at large, it is essential that the divorce laws create incentives for people to make social-welfare-enhancing decisions.

Allen M. Parkman
Albuquerque, New Mexico

Acknowledgments

This book would not have been possible without the assistance of many individuals and organizations. The University of New Mexico gave me a sabbatical during the spring term of 1991 to work on this project, and the Anderson Schools of Management Foundation provided financial support through a summer research grant. June Carbone, Ron Johnson, Tom Oldham, and Barbara Shapiro contributed valuable comments on the first draft. Mona Mason, Peg Merrell, Patti Reis, and Darlene Trujillo provided research and editorial assistance during this project. The people at Westview Press have been a consistent source of support: Spencer Carr assisted in the early phase of the project, Mary Kay Scott guided the project through its various stages, and Stephanie Hoppe copyedited the manuscript into a readable form.

A.M.P.

1

Introduction

Just over twenty years ago, California adopted the first unequivocal no-fault divorce statute in the United States.[1] Over the following fifteen years, all the other states and the District of Columbia enacted similar statutes establishing "irretrievable breakdown" or "incompatibility" as the only grounds for divorce or adding these to the preexisting fault grounds.[2] The new provisions were viewed as a major, and desirable, reform of the statutes in effect through most of the history of the United States, under which a divorce, when permitted at all, could only be obtained on grounds such as adultery, cruelty, or desertion,[3] with the assumption that one of the spouses was responsible for the failure of the marriage. Most no-fault divorce statutes removed the consideration of marital fault from the grounds for divorce, the award of spousal support, and the division of property.

The Effects of No-Fault

The no-fault divorce laws have had dramatic and often unexpected financial effects on families in general and women in particular in dismantling a system that had been based essentially on mutual consent. This system had protected parties who had relied on their marriage continuing, but no-fault divorce reduced this protection and the resulting negotiating power of the spouse who did not want to dissolve the marriage,[4] usually the wife.[5] The loss of negotiating power has unfortunately reduced the incentive for spouses to make certain contributions to their family such as the contributions of married women who committed themselves to a career that accommodated that of their husband.

Today, both women and families are worse off. No-fault divorce has resulted in a decline in the welfare of divorced women and the children of divorced parents.[6] Lenore Weitzman reported, for example, that divorced women and their children experience a 73 percent decline in their standard of living during the first year after a divorce.[7] Elizabeth Peters showed that in 1979 women who were divorced in no-fault divorce states received less alimony and child support than in fault divorce states.[8]

Less obvious, but also substantial, has been the effect of no-fault divorce on families that stay married. The fault grounds for divorce had the effect of providing some protection against the potential costs of divorce for married women who chose to be housewives and mothers. No-fault grounds for divorce have forced married women to seek other forms of protection. Reduced incentives for women to be housewives and mothers and increased incentives for them to work outside the home and seek additional education to maintain their human capital--their income-earning capacity--have often reduced the welfare of their families.

These are not the results expected by the proponents of no-fault divorce. Fault divorce was attacked by many reformers because of the hypocritical procedures used by many people to obtain divorces.[9] The fault divorce system was predicated on the belief that unless the breakdown of a marriage could be attributed solely to the wrongdoing of a single, identifiable spouse, divorce was not permitted. In most states, a divorce was not permitted if both spouses were at fault. The procedures used under fault divorce encouraged perjury and brought an adversarial process to situations often calling for conciliation. Normally only the innocent spouse could ask for a divorce and a guilty spouse who wanted a divorce found it very difficult to obtain a divorce without the cooperation of the other spouse. Many men argued that the result was not the protection of innocent wives but the requirement that husbands buy their way out of marriage.[10] Some reformers felt that a reform of the divorce process could reverse the trend toward higher divorce rates that had been observed during most of this century.[11] In either case, the solution was obvious: remove the fault grounds from the requirements for a divorce.

I will argue that the primary problem with the no-fault divorce laws has been the ignoring of many of the costs associated with divorce resulting in undesirable decisions being made during marriage and at divorce. Central among the ignored costs is the effect of marriage on the income-earning capacities of the spouses--their human capital. Incorporating considerations of human capital into financial settlements under no-fault divorce would increase the welfare of families and society. Other costs of divorce to the spouses and children are more difficult to estimate and they may require a shift to mutual consent as the basis for divorce. The failure to grapple with the adverse effects of no-fault divorce has resulted in numerous adverse effects on society: In the two decades since the introduction of no-fault divorce, we have probably seen more changes in the structure and stability of the U. S. family than in any other period in U. S. history.[12]

An Economic Perspective

Marriage and divorce have long been active areas for analysis and discussion by sociologists and lawyers,[13] but I believe the general absence of an economic perspective has obscured some problems. Economics is the study of choice:[14] the choices that people make, or rationally should make, in an environment in which the array of goods and activities available to individuals exceeds their resources of income and time. My analysis here includes an investigation of the reasons why no-fault divorce statutes were introduced and why they have had a detrimental effect on U. S. families with particular attention to the deterioration in the financial welfare of divorced women and children of divorced parents.

Economic analysis, based on society's preference for efficient outcomes, provides an alternate explanation to the moralistic one given for the introduction of no-fault divorce. We live in a world in which wants--financial and psychological--exceed the available resources. Choices have to be made. Efficient outcomes occur when choices are made for which the benefits exceed the costs. Efficient outcomes increase social welfare. As the benefits and costs of activities change, the efficient choices change. Economists view the decision to marry and, sometimes, to divorce as based on the benefits and the costs associated with those choices. Over time, the costs and benefits of marriage and divorce can change and then the incentives to marry and to stay married change. Economists have argued that changes that have occurred since World War II, such as the expanded employment opportunities for women and the availability of improved forms of contraception, have reduced both the benefit of marriage and the cost of divorce for some people.[15] Under those circumstances, we would expect to observe fewer marriages and more divorces. If the legal system conflicts with people's new preferences, especially for more flexible grounds for divorce, they will work to change that legal environment.[16] Thus, social change created pressures to modify the fault grounds for divorce because in a changed society they were no longer efficient for some individuals.

Whatever the acknowledged need for change, actual changes that occur are the result of the political process. Many political analysts assign a public interest motive to legislators. Economists, however, taking a more cynical view see politicians basing their decisions on self-interest. Their primary goal normally is to be reelected. With that goal, they are particularly sensitive to the preferences of vocal pressure groups who provide verbal and financial support.[17] In California, for example, the reform process was dominated by men, although they had the support of many women's groups.[18] Sometimes the self-interest of politicians can be more narrowly focused. The assemblyman primarily responsible for the passage of no-fault divorce in California was going through a divorce at the time. It did not take a conspiracy for a male-dominated legislature to enact no-fault divorce legislation that seemed appropriate from their perspective and was based on the information that they had been provided. This is especially true when few of the proponents of divorce reform, male or female, were arguing that no-fault divorce would be a disaster, especially for divorced women and their children. The California Family Law Act of 1969,[19] which began the no-fault divorce revolution and set the standard for the statutes enacted in the other states, was passed by a male dominated legislature.[20]

Much was made of the hypocrisy that occurred under the fault divorce laws, but it was evidence of the change in society's preferences, not the cause. There are many laws on the books, such as highway speed limits, that are hypocritical and these laws can remain on the books for indefinite periods, especially if they are not enforced. It takes both new circumstances and undesirable enforcement of existing laws to change laws. Certainly enforcement of the fault divorce laws was hypocritical, but an increase in the demand for simpler procedures for dissolving marriages was an important impetus for no-fault divorce legislation. The male-dominated reform process, together with the absence of a clear understanding of the repercussions of the legislation, resulted in the enactment of the specific no-fault divorce laws now in existence.

Economics can provide insights about why no-fault divorce resulted in the deterioration of the financial situation of divorced women and the children of divorced parents identified by Weitzman and Peters.[21] Many of the reformers appear to have been so preoccupied with reducing the hypocrisy of the fault divorce system that few of them thought about the consequences of the new system--consequences that included a decline in the bargaining power of married women at divorce and, therefore, in their financial situations after divorce.[22] The California Governor's Commission on the Family that initiated the fault divorce debate in that state did not include any economists or financial analysts.

When marriage was a more stable institution and the laws determining the grounds for divorce were strictly enforced, there were only a few divorces and the laws that controlled the financial repercussions at divorce were of secondary importance. As the demand for divorce by some spouses increased, these individuals found that the legal grounds for divorce were more restrictive than they wished. They also found the financial repercussions of divorce prescribed by the law unacceptable. The parties could fabricate evidence to establish the grounds for divorce and then, in theory, the courts would decide on property settlements based on legal standards.[23] In fact, under the fault divorce laws, most divorcing couples with significant wealth chose to negotiate a settlement rather than to rely on the courts' allocation.[24] Often one party did not want a divorce and a more generous financial settlement and custody of any children was necessary to induce that party to initiate the lawsuit and provide the obligatory testimony.[25] The innocent party had to be the plaintiff, so that a contested divorce was difficult under the fault divorce laws.[26] Even if both parties wanted a divorce, they had reasons to reject the legal financial arrangements as inequitable. Most women who had pursued the traditional roles as housewives and mothers knew that short-term alimony, limited child support, and the property allocation provided by law would leave them in a precarious financial position, especially compared to the financial condition of their husband.

Interrelated Laws

Problems developed with no-fault divorce because the reformers did not recognize the interrelationship among laws concerning the grounds for divorce, parental rights, and the financial condition of the spouses. Changing one set of rules without changing the others destroyed a delicate balance. Under the fault divorce statutes, the custodial and financial settlements were commonly based on the negotiations of the parties, with the spouse who did not want to dissolve the marriage having substantial power over the outcome. With no-fault divorce eliminating negotiations to establish the grounds for divorce, the previously disregarded laws that governed the custodial and financial repercussions of divorce became much more important--the financial condition of divorced women and children of divorced parents deteriorated.

In some states, eliminating the fault grounds for divorce was accompanied by the removal of fault as a factor in the other aspects of divorce such as property settlements and alimony. No-fault divorce eliminated the presumption that couples had an obligation to remain married and removed any reason for the party seeking the divorce to compensate the other spouse. California, for example, required an equal division of marital property. Another problem arose from the legal definitions of property failing to conform to basic financial principles. This discrepancy had little practical effect when most divorces were settled with only minimal reference to the applicable laws. But that all changed with the introduction of no-fault divorce.

Because marriage consists of two people coming together to participate in a collective action, economists view the financial aspects of the relationship much as a business partnership: If the marriage is dissolved, the parties should share the gains or losses of the partnership, but assets acquired outside marriage are not part of this distribution. Based on this framework, economic analysis would support a strict application of the principles of community property, in which each spouse has a half interest in property created during the marriage by their collective activities. From a statutory perspective, marital property is all property that is not defined as either spouse's separate property, while separate property is property that the parties brought into the marriage and property that came to them during the marriage by will, bequest, or devise. Strict community property concepts are the basis of property divisions at the dissolution of marriages in only a minority of the states, but there has been a trend in all states to move toward an equal distribution of marital property at divorce.[27] As we will see, the problem with this distribution of property at divorce is not the definitions of separate and marital property, but the underlying definition of property itself.

What Is Property?

The statutes that defined how property was to be allocated at divorce, under fault and no-fault, did not define what is property.[28] That task has been left to the courts, which tend to recognize only items for which there is tangible evidence as property. These items include houses and cars as well as shares of stock or bonds. What the courts have historically called "property" should be just another name for the items that economists have identified as assets. From an economic perspective, assets exist and have value because they can provide a stream of future income or services; these items include houses and shares of common stock as well as individuals themselves. From a practical perspective, the actual property settlements under fault divorce had been part of the larger issue of financial settlements with the allocation between property and alimony often driven by tax considerations rather than definitions. With no-fault divorce, it became more likely than under fault divorce that statutes determined the allocation of property. Still, because the definition of property has been too restricted, the items considered in the financial allocations at divorce have also tended to be too restricted.

Human Capital

Financial allocations at divorce tend to ignore the most valuable asset owned by most people--their income-earning capacities or human capital. Human capital exists because of prior investments, and its value is based on the expected future earnings of the individual. Depending on when critical investments occurred, it can be marital or separate property. Human capital, which has not been recognized by the legal system in a systematic way as property subject to division at divorce,[29] represents a major difference in the assets identified by the legal system and economists.

Shortly after the introduction of no-fault divorce, state legislatures and the courts recognized that something was amiss with the finances of divorced women and the children of divorced parents. They groped for a way to increase financial awards to women. One way was ad hoc adjustments to the definition of property based not on the realization that the definition was conceptually wrong, but instead on a desire to expand the funds available to women and children.[30] The definition of property has been expanded in some jurisdictions to include such obvious assets as pensions and business goodwill. Courts and legislatures also have considered whether intangible items such as degrees, licenses, and the goodwill of professionals should be added to the list of property. Still, the definition of property has not been expanded systematically to cover human capital, and I argue that the failure to incorporate the effects of marriage on the human capital of the spouses into the financial arrangements at divorce in any systematic way is a major cause for divorced women suffering a substantial reduction in their welfare.[31]

The incorporation of an adjustment for the effect of a divorce on the human capital of the parties would compensate a spouse in the often-cited situation in which one spouse has provided financial support while the other spouse was in graduate school. The recognition of human capital is, however, probably even more important in the situation in which the husband and the wife have decided that the family would benefit from one spouse, usually the wife, pursuing activities that accommodate the career of the other, usually the husband. This decision often reduces the wife's human capital compared to the position that she would be in if either she had never married or the marriage had accommodated her career rather than that of the husband.

Economic analysis of the effect of divorce on the spouses' human capital also requires an adjustment in child support awards. The cost of child custody is not just the direct outlays to maintain the children but also the reduction of income from the presence of children limiting the custodial parent's employment and remarrying opportunities. Children can be an encumbrance that reduces income and opportunities for those who rear them, translating into a reduced human capital at divorce. Economics can provide a framework for evaluating these effects, producing a more systematic and equitable outcome to divorce and correcting for the deteriorating financial condition of divorced women and the children of divorced parents.

The Subjective Costs of Divorce

The effect of marriage on the spouses' human capital can be estimated with reasonable accuracy, but other costs of divorce are more difficult to measure. These costs, which can be financial as well as psychological, are associated with the loss of the companionship of a particular individual, the search for a new mate or social situation, and the impact on the children. The spouse being divorced will often still care about the divorcing spouse, and the loss of this companionship due to the dissolution of the marriage imposes a cost on the divorced spouse. To begin with, the marriage resulted from a search process by the parties. At divorce, the divorcing spouse has decided that he or she is willing to incur the costs, if any, of a new search for another living situation, which often will result in a new mate--and also, unilaterally, imposes search costs on the divorced spouse. If the divorced spouse wants a new mate, this cost can be very high, because many divorced people, especially older women, never remarry. Even if the divorced spouse has no desire to remarry, he or she incurs costs in establishing a new social situation. Last, the divorce can impose costs on the children of the couple. Often these costs are ignored by the divorcing spouse; the failure of no-fault divorce to require the parties to consider these costs directly when considering divorce contributes to the unsatisfactory outcomes of present-day divorce. By forcing the spouses to recognize these costs when considering divorce, mutual consent divorce might increase social welfare.

The Book

In this book I investigate why no-fault divorce has not lived up to the expectations of its proponents. First, in the next chapter, the evolution of the marriage and divorce laws that ultimately resulted in no-fault divorce will be presented. In Chapter 3, I introduce the economic perspective as it applies to marriage, divorce, and property. This material on the economic framework is followed by a chapter that traces the development of the California no-fault divorce statute, with an emphasis on the economic reasons why the statute was introduced. Economic analysis then is used to evaluate the impact of no-fault divorce on individual decisions. It will be observed that the introduction of no-fault divorce has had numerous effects, including changes in the divorce rate and the financial situation of the parties as well as other areas of human behavior such as when people marry and whether married women work outside the house. I conclude with an economic analysis particularizing the reforms that could lessen the social and individual costs of no-fault divorce.

Notes

1. Family Law Act, ch. 1608, §§ 1-32, 1969 Cal. Stat. 3312. The first "pure" no-fault statute was enacted in California in 1969. The California statute has been described as "pure" because it based divorce exclusively on the factual breakdown of the marriage. See Herma Hill Kay, "Equality and Difference: A Perspective on No-Fault Divorce and Its Aftermath," *University of Cincinnati Law Review,* Vol. 56, 1987, pp. 1-90. Several states already had "no-fault" grounds for divorce, such as incompatibility of temperament, voluntary separation for a period of time, or incurable insanity; by the mid-1960s, eighteen states, Puerto Rico, and the District of Columbia permitted a divorce based on the parties living apart. See Glenda Riley, *Divorce: An American Tradition* (New York: Oxford University Press, 1991), p. 162. By 1985, all the states had some form of no-fault divorce, either exclusively no-fault grounds or with no-fault

grounds added to the fault grounds. For data on the current status of divorce laws, see Doris J. Freed and Timothy B. Walker, "Family Law in the Fifty States: An Overview," *Family Law Quarterly*, Vol. 23, No. 4, Winter 1990, pp. 495-608.

2. No-fault divorce statutes rapidly were enacted by the states. Iowa passed its no-fault divorce statute in 1971. By August 1977, only three states retained essentially fault grounds for divorce. See Doris J. Freed and Henry H. Foster, Jr., "Divorce in the Fifty States: An Overview," *Family Law Quarterly*, Vol. 11, No. 3, Fall 1977, pp. 297-313.

3. Lawrence M. Friedman, *A History of American Law* (New York: Simon and Schuster, 1973), pp. 179-184, 434-440.

4. Mary Ann Glendon notes, "The fault-oriented divorce law of the recent past furnished opportunities for one spouse (usually the wife) to obtain a settlement more generous than a court might have awarded in exchange for cooperation in obtaining or expediting the divorce or as the price of avoiding the embarrassing publicity or a contested divorce." Mary Ann Glendon, *The New Family and the New Property* (Toronto: Butterworths, 1981), p. 61.

5. No-fault divorce statutes reduced the bargaining power of the spouse who did not want to dissolve the marriage. The evidence is that spouse tended to be the wife. This occurred because women usually are worse off after divorce than are men. Women in marriages of long duration were particularly vulnerable. See Lenore J. Weitzman, *The Divorce Revolution* (New York: Free Press, 1985). The vulnerability of women after lengthy marriage has been explained by the timing of the contributions of men and women to marriage. The contributions of married women are often front-end loaded relative to married men: Married women have traditionally placed a special emphasis on child rearing that occurs early in a marriage, but the income-earning contribution of the husband tends to increase over the duration of the marriage. When the children leave the home, the contribution of the wife to the marriage can fall, although the contribution of the husband continues to grow. Without the protection of a long-term arrangement such as was provided to a certain extent by fault divorce, some husbands may conclude that they are better off divorced. This is especially true when the financial obligations incurred by the husband to the wife due to the divorce are modest. See Lloyd Cohen, "Marriage, Divorce, and Quasi Rents; or 'I Gave Him the Best Years of My Life,'" *Journal of Legal Studies*, Vol. 16, June 1987, pp. 267-304.

It will be assumed here that the wife has the most to lose if the marriage is dissolved, and therefore is more likely to want to continue the marriage, but certainly many men used fault divorce to continue marriages that their wives wanted to dissolve. Under fault divorce, most negotiated divorce actions desired by men were filed by women because the defendant had to be the party who was at fault. See B. G. Gunter and Doyle Johnson, "Divorce Filing as Role Behavior: Effect of No-Fault Law on Divorce Filing Patterns," *Journal of Marriage and the Family*, Vol. 40, August 1978, pp. 571-574.

6. This conclusion is documented in Weitzman, *Divorce Revolution*, and H. Elizabeth Peters, "Marriage and Divorce: Informational Constraints and Private Contracting," *American Economic Review*, Vol. 76, No. 3, June 1986, pp. 437-454. The conclusions and methodology of Weitzman have been challenged by a number of authors, including Herbert Jacob, "Faulting No-Fault," in Howard S. Erlanger, ed.,

"Review Symposium on Weitzman's *Divorce Revolution,*" *American Bar Foundation Research Journal,* Vol. 1986, No. 4, Fall 1986, pp. 773-780; Herbert Jacob, *Silent Revolution: The Transformation of Divorce Law in the United States* (Chicago: University of Chicago Press, 1988); Herbert Jacob, "Another Look at No-Fault Divorce and the Post-Divorce Finances of Women," *Law and Society Review,* Vol. 23, No. 1, 1989, pp. 95-115; Marygold S. Melli, "Constructing a Social Problem: The Post-Divorce Plight of Women and Children," in Erlanger, ed., "Review Symposium on Weitzman's *Divorce Revolution,*" pp. 759-772; Jana B. Singer, "Divorce Reform and Gender Justice," *North Carolina Law Review,* Vol. 67, 1989, pp. 1103-1121; Marsha Garrison, "The Economics of Divorce: Changing Rules, Changing Results," in Stephen D. Sugarman and Herma Hill Kay, eds., *Divorce Reform at the Crossroads* (New Haven, CT: Yale University Press, 1990), pp. 75-101; and Stephen D. Sugarman, "Dividing Financial Interests in Divorce," in Sugarman and Kay, eds., *Divorce Reform at the Crossroads,* pp. 130-165.

7. Weitzman, *Divorce Revolution,* p. 323.

8. Peters, "Marriage and Divorce," p. 449.

9. Michael Wheeler, *No-Fault Divorce* (Boston: Beacon, 1974), p. 8 and Lynne Carol Halem, *Divorce Reform* (New York: Free Press, 1980), p. 238.

10. Wheeler, *No-Fault,* p. 15.

11. Weitzman, *Divorce Revolution,* p. 16, cites Judge Roger Pfaff, who pioneered the use of conciliation courts in Los Angeles, arguing that the trend toward higher divorce rates could be reversed by California adopting premarital and predivorce conciliation procedures.

12. Gary S. Becker, *A Treatise of the Family* (Cambridge, MA: Harvard University Press, 1981), p. 245, notes that between 1950 and 1977, the legitimate birth rate declined by about one-third, the divorce rate more than doubled, the labor force participation rate of married women with young children more than tripled, and the percent of households headed by women with dependent children also almost tripled. Between 1970 and 1984, the percent of males and females eighteen years old and over that were married fell from 75.3 percent and 68.5 percent to 65.8 percent and 60.8 percent, respectively. Meanwhile, the percent of males and females eighteen years old and over that were divorced rose from 2.5 percent and 3.9 percent to 6.1 percent and 8.3 percent, respectively. *Statistical Abstract of the United States, 1986* (Washington, DC: Government Printing Office, 1986), Table 44, p. 35.

13. For example, see Andrew J. Cherlin, *Marriage, Divorce, Remarriage* (Cambridge, MA: Harvard University Press, 1981); Kingsley Davis, ed., *Contemporary Marriage: Comparative Perspectives on a Changing Institution* (New York: Russell Sage, 1985); Halem, *Divorce Reform;* Max Rheinstein, *Marriage Stability, Divorce and the Law* (Chicago: University of Chicago Press, 1972); and Weitzman, *Divorce Revolution.*

14. Paul A. Samuelson and William D. Nordhaus, *Economics,* 13th ed. (New York: McGraw-Hill, 1989), p. 5.

15. Gary S. Becker, William Landes, and Robert Michael, "An Analysis of Marital Instability," *Journal of Political Economy,* Vol. 85, No. 6, 1977, p. 1184, concludes that the divorce rate, which accelerated after 1960, can be explained in part by "the decline over time in the number of children, the growth in labor force participation and earnings power of women, the growth in the breadth of the remarriage market as more

persons become divorced and perhaps also the growth in legal access to divorce, illegitimacy, and public transfer payments."

16. Victor R. Fuchs, *Women's Quest for Economic Equality* (Cambridge, MA: Harvard University Press, 1988), p. 29, notes that it is less likely that legislation alters behavior than that changes in behavior initiate changes in legislation--legislators tend to be attuned to basic socioeconomic forces and to respond to the legislative demands created by the new behavior.

17. Gary S. Becker, "A Theory of Competition Among Pressure Groups for Political Influence," *Quarterly Journal of Economics,* Vol. 98, 1983, pp. 371-400.

18. The California Governor's Commission on the Family consisted of individuals from male-dominated professions, including two state senators, one assemblyman, five judges, six attorneys, two law school professors, one social worker, four physicians, and one clergymen. See Halem, *Divorce Reform,* p. 240. Fourteen of the fifteen members of the public who testified before the commission were men and ten men identified themselves as divorced. The California Commission on the Status of Women supported the removal of fault from divorce. "Report of the Advisory Commission of the Status of Women," *California Women,* 1969, pp. 79-80.

19. Family Law Act, ch. 1608, §§ 1-32, 1969 Cal. Stat. 3312.

20. In 1970, the Uniform Marriage and Divorce Act was approved by the National Conference of Commissioners on Uniform State Laws. The uniform act adopted as the sole ground for divorce "that the marriage is irretrievably broken." 9A *Uniform Laws Annotated* 91(1979). Homer H. Clark, Jr., *The Law of Domestic Relations in the United States,* 2d ed. (St. Paul, MN: West, 1988), p. 411.

21. Lenore J. Weitzman, "The Economics of Divorce: Social and Economic Consequences of Property, Alimony and Child Support Awards," *UCLA Law Review,* Vol 28, 1981, pp. 1181-1268; Weitzman, *Divorce Revolution,* and Peters, "Marriage and Divorce."

22. Weitzman, *Divorce Revolution,* p. 19.

23. Max Rheinstein notes that collusive practices and migratory divorce had been common in the United States under fault divorce. See Max Rheinstein, *Marriage Stability,* pp. 247-260 and "A Survey of Mental Cruelty as a Ground for Divorce," *De Paul Law Review,* Vol. 15, 1965, pp. 159 and 163.

24. Under fault divorce, approximately 90 percent of divorces were uncontested. This figure understates the percent that probably were uncontested as those divorces in which the defendant filed an answer or offered any evidence in opposition to the divorce were counted as contested. See Rheinstein, *Marriage Stability,* p. 248. The "Report of the Governor's Commission on the Family," Sacramento, CA, December, 1966, pp. 30-31, estimated that 94 percent of divorce hearings in California were uncontested and, p. 119, n. 23, that they were granted with pro forma testimony as to fault.

25. This is supported by evidence that there was an increase in the proportion of men filing for divorce after the introduction of no-fault. Gunter and Johnson, "Divorce Filing," pp. 571-574.

26. Harry D. Krause, *Family Law,* 2d ed. (St. Paul, MN: West, 1986).

27. Ibid., p. 102.

28. Clark, *Domestic Relations,* p. 595.

29. Mary Ann Glendon, "Family Law Reform in the 1980's," *Louisiana Law Review,* Vol. 44, No. 6, July 1984, p. 1559, expresses the commonly accepted view that the only significant property of a young couple was a house and its contents. She does not recognize that the spouses have their individual human capital that can be valuable and may have been affected by the marriage. See Allen M. Parkman, "Human Capital as Property in Divorce Settlements," *Arkansas Law Review,* Vol 40, No. 3, 1987, pp. 439-467.

30. There are problems associated with a concept called "professional goodwill" that was one of the attempts by the courts to create property to allocate to wives. See Allen M. Parkman, "The Treatment of Professional Goodwill in Divorce Proceedings," *Family Law Quarterly,* Vol. 18, No. 2, Summer 1984, pp. 213-224.

31. The principles developed here are relevant for both men and women. The situation that normally requires an adjustment in the property settlement to incorporate the effect of the marriage on the human capital of the spouses is one spouse making major sacrifices in his or her employment opportunities to accommodate the other spouse. Generally, wives are the spouses that adjust, but as the economic opportunities of women increase, we would expect to find more men making these sacrifices. In this book, I assume the spouse who makes the adjustments is the wife.

2

Marriage and Divorce Laws

The laws that govern people's options to marry and divorce have changed over time. From within a given legal environment, it is often difficult to envision the legal rules that applied at other times and places--especially for matters as pervasive and private as marriage. Not long ago, marriage was a very different institution.[1] Society, rather than the parties, defined marriage roles. The expectation was that once begun, marriage would continue for the joint lives of the parties. Divorce could be granted only if one party failed in a very fundamental way to live up to the standards expected by society. That party was held to be at fault for the failure of the marriage. In many states, husband and wife were required to live together at a place chosen by the husband if his choice was a safe and reasonable location. The husband, if able, was required to provide for the support of his wife and children. The stability of marriage was important both for the individuals involved and for society.[2] By removing fault and recognizing the preferences of the parties as preeminent to the dictates of society, no-fault divorce caused a revolution in the family law that had existed for most of the history of the United States. To place no-fault divorce in perspective, we will look in this chapter at the evolution of marriage and divorce laws both as they establish the procedures and grounds for marriage and divorce and as they also affect the property of the parties.

Marriage Laws

The topic of this book is divorce, but marriage is a necessary precondition to divorce, and a society's approach to divorce often is reflected in its laws governing marriage. Every society has had its own idea of marriage.[3] Among early civilizations, marriage was considered a social contract to which the state was not a party. These groups often did not have the nuclear family structure that dominates modern U.S. society, as they operated with extended families or clans. Marriage was not so much a transaction between the two people immediately concerned as between their respective parents or chiefs. Under Roman law, it was possible to initiate a marriage without a ceremony or at least without a ceremony prescribed by law. Christianity changed the regulation of marriage: Marriage as we know it today was formalized by the Catholic church. The canon law of the Catholic church was the only law governing matrimonial relations between Christians in Western Europe until the Reformation in the sixteenth century and it retains considerable authority in Roman Catholic countries.

The influence of the church over marriage was asserted gradually, beginning with restrictions on the parties that could marry, such as the marriages between near relatives that had been common until that time. Marriage became monogamous and indissoluble.[4] The doctrine of indissolubility was given special significance by its being combined with the dogma of the sacramental nature of marriage: In the eyes of the church, a marriage could only be dissolved by God through death or by the church through annulment.

The introduction of indissolubility created the need to precisely define what it was that could not be dissolved. In other words, what was a marriage? The church desired, and later demanded, that an act of such deep religious significance as marriage could only be performed with the blessing of the church. It thus became customary that parties planning to be married would meet at the door of the church with the parish priest, who would bestow his blessing on them, although the actual creation of the married state remained the private transaction of the parties. When followed by carnal consummation, their expression of desire to be married matured into the sacrament and the marriage became indissoluble. The church attempted to require that marriages be blessed by a priest, but the violation of this command did not invalidate the marriage. This informal process continued until the time of the Council of Trent in 1563, which formalized marriage rules and established that a valid marriage required a ceremony performed by a priest in the presence of at least two witnesses.

The procedures created by the Council of Trent resulted from more than religious concerns. The recognition of clandestine marriages could enable strangers to marry into wealthy families without prior parental approval. At the Council of Trent, the same bishops who were the chief proponents of compulsory marriage ceremonies also tried to make parental consent an ecclesiastical marriage requirement. A minister's presence at the wedding was made mandatory in some German states at the time of the Reformation and these states often required couples to obtain the consent of their parents before they could marry.[5]

From the sixteenth to the eighteenth century, in many parts of Western Europe, the Catholic church lost its jurisdiction over marriage. England, under Henry VIII, broke from the Catholic church in 1534. In Protestant regions, this separation occurred because of the Reformation, and in France it accompanied the assertion of national power by the monarchy. As the power of the church waned, the states assumed control over marriage by default, generally continuing the rules that had been generated by the church. The reformers objected to the power of the church, but not to Christianity, and although some rejected the notion that marriage was a sacrament, most assumed that secular marriage regulations should conform to Christian teachings.

With the dual influences of the Reformation and the Enlightenment, the idea of marriage as a contract took a new turn. Voluntary consent between the parties with or without a ceremony had been the essence of marriage under canon law, but the trend toward codification of the law throughout Europe in the eighteenth century resulted in a more formal regulation of marriage. In France, the desire for legislative regulation during this period caused the development of two important modern institutions affecting the family: the compulsory civil marriage ceremony and public registration of marriages. The civil marriage ceremony became mandatory in France in 1792.

England followed a somewhat different path. Replacing the Catholic church, the Church of England retained control of marriage laws until the middle of the nineteenth century. Informal marriages remained valid in England until 1753, when Lord Hardwicke's reform of the marriage laws made a church ceremony compulsory and required publication of the vows for a legal marriage, but cohabitation rather than marriage was the norm until the Victorian era.[6]

The marriage laws in the United States evolved out of the laws that had developed in Europe. In England, marriage was based on individual decisions and was generally a life-long commitment. Because of the realities of the frontier life and the shortage of clergymen, Lord Hardwicke's reforms were not implemented in the American colonies and informal or "common law" marriages remained legal even after 1753.[7] In New England, the Puritans maintained as a religious doctrine the contractual character of marriage in contrast to the church doctrine of its sacramental character. The U.S. Constitution gave jurisdiction over matrimonial matters to the states, which enacted a variety of statutes. By the end of the nineteenth century, many states abolished informal marriages, but even today common law marriage is possible in many states.

Despite attacks on the marriage laws in the United States by homosexual couples and the religious groups that advocate polygamy, marriage in the United States has been standardized as a monogamous union between two individuals of opposite sex who are not closely related by blood. People often choose a religious ceremony for their marriage, but the key requirements are secular and most states require compliance with specific formalities to establish a valid marriage.

Divorce Laws

The regulation of divorce has tended to parallel the regulation of marriage: So long as the regulation of marriage remained outside the purview of church authorities or the state, the regulation of divorce was also outside their jurisdiction. The usual result was that marriage could easily be dissolved, either by mutual consent or by unilateral repudiation, sometimes with the payment of a penalty. In the case of arranged marriages the same parties that arranged them could dissolve them. At the time of Jesus, under Hebrew law a marriage could be dissolved whenever the husband desired, although no corresponding power existed for the wife.

As the legal regulation of divorce developed, it assumed two forms.[8] Divorce *a mensa et thoro*--from bed and board--provided a legal separation with all of the other obligations of marriage continuing; neither party could remarry. Alternatively, divorce *a vinculo matrimonii*--from the bonds of matrimony--enabled remarriage. Under pressure from early Christians, the sixth-century emperor Justinian enacted a code strictly regulating the dissolution of marriage in Rome with adultery being the only major ground.

As the Catholic church asserted control over marriage, it also established rules for divorce, which dominated the legal requirements for the dissolution of marriage in Europe for the next thousand years. The canon law applied two main principles to divorce. First, there could be no divorce *a vinculo matrimonii* that resulted in the parties, after once marrying, being free to remarry. Second, no divorce could be obtained at the will of the parties, but only by the decision of an ecclesiastical court. Annulments were used during this period by influential persons to dissolve a marriage--the declaration that the marriage had never existed left the parties free to remarry. For example, the marriage of Eleanor of Aquitaine to Louis VII of France was annulled in 1152 after fourteen years and the birth of two daughters.[9]

At the time of the Reformation, there were thus two remedies for persons dissatisfied with their marriage.[10] They could argue that the marriage had never been valid due to some technicality; if this claim was successful, the marriage was annulled and the parties were both free to remarry. Alternatively, they could seek a divorce *a mensa et thoro* based on one spouse's actions. These divorces were based on fault, with the grounds including adultery, serious mistreatment, and desertion. Divorce was only available to the innocent party and did not permit either party to remarry. If both parties were at fault, neither could be released from the marriage.[11]

Divorce became more flexible after the Reformation. Both Martin Luther and John Calvin cast doubt on the sacramental nature of marriage and its indissolubility and their followers did not feel bound by canon law. Divorce became more common on the Continent as secular laws and courts replaced the canon laws and the ecclesiastical courts. England followed a different course. The Church of England had replaced the Catholic church in that country in 1534[12] and ecclesiastical courts continued to exercise jurisdiction over matrimonial matters in England until the passage of the Matrimonial Causes Act of 1857. After 1602, no divorces were granted by those courts.[13] The only absolute divorces were obtained by the costly procedure of a private act of Parliament and until the middle of the nineteenth century when a new and more flexible divorce law was introduced, only 317 divorces were granted by Parliament.[14] The Matrimonial Causes Act of 1857 permitted divorce primarily on the ground of adultery, but additional grounds have been added over the years.

Divorce was more common in the British colonies in North America than in England. The Puritan leaders permitted divorce for excessive marital incompatibility.[15] In New England and the Middle Atlantic colonies, divorce was available on a sporadic basis, although in the southern colonies, divorce was as restricted as in England. With the adoption of the U.S. Constitution, the states assumed responsibility for the regulation of divorce. In those areas that had been settled by Protestants, there were divorce laws from before statehood, but in areas with a strong Anglican influence, especially in the South, there were often no provisions for divorce. A variety of statutes were enacted with grounds ranging from adultery to separation for a statutory period. Over time, the number of grounds grew in most states. Cruelty, defined in a variety of ways, was a ground in most states, and its use became increasingly common. A critical characteristic of the grounds was the requirement that one party had to be at fault, and therefore a divorce could not be obtained easily. During the period for which national data is available, the number of divorces rose dramatically-- from 56,000 in 1900 to 1,213,000 in 1981.[16]

The western states took a more liberal approach to divorce, so that by the middle of the nineteenth century the migratory divorce was already part of the American scene. Migrating temporarily to a state with more liberal standards for a divorce and establishing a domicile in that state, people could receive a divorce more easily than in the state in which they normally resided. The possibility of the migratory divorce had existed since the signing of the Constitution, but it did not become an issue of much concern until the twentieth century. In 1942 in Williams v. North Carolina,[17] the U.S. Supreme Court upheld the validity of a divorce that had been obtained in Nevada, where only six weeks were required to create domicile and jurisdiction for a divorce decree. The increased use of migratory divorces, which were only available to those who could afford to travel, created pressures for uniform divorce laws throughout the United States.

The pressures for change accelerated after World War II as more and more people were divorcing. The fault grounds for divorce usually required the plaintiff in the divorce suit to be an innocent party, resulting in pressure for the couple to negotiate a settlement with the party requesting the divorce assuming the role of the defendant. Thus, the party who had not initially wanted the divorce was often the person who actually filed the lawsuit. The common ground for divorce was some form of cruelty, which many couples used perjured testimony to establish. This hypocrisy increased pressure to change the divorce statutes and gradually some small states added no-fault grounds to the existing statutes.[18] In 1970, California became the first state to introduce unequivocal no-fault grounds for divorce. Between 1970 and 1985, all the states enacted no-fault divorce statutes or added no-fault grounds to the existing fault grounds. Initially, the courts retained the right to determine if the no-fault grounds had been established by the parties, but as the new grounds for divorce became more familiar to the courts, they have come to acknowledge that the parties' views about their marriage have to be taken at face value.[19] From being almost impossible without evidence of fault or the agreement of one's spouse, divorce has become essentially unilateral in many states.

Matrimonial Property

Marriage in the modern era is based on the attraction between the parties, but it is also a decision with substantial financial consequences--consequences that become particularly apparent if the marriage is dissolved. Laws regulating the effect of marriage and divorce on the property of the parties sometimes can be preempted by premarital and postmarital agreements or negotiated settlements. Negotiated settlements, in particular, often were important under fault divorce as an inducement for an otherwise unwilling spouse. The introduction of no-fault divorce reemphasized the preexisting legal standards for property settlement, support, and custody. Understanding the impact of marriage and divorce on property requires a review of those laws.

The effect of marriage on the properties of the parties has a long history, especially among the wealthy. When marriage was primarily a private arrangement, the effect of the marriage on the parties' properties was also private. Marriage contracts could provide for desired effects of marriage and divorce on property. In Europe, it was traditional for these relationships to be arranged, within certain limits, by private agreements. U.S. courts have been less willing to accept private contracts that define the financial effects of divorce on the parties. Outside private agreements, statutes determine the effects of marriage on property brought into the marriage or acquired during the marriage. In much of Europe, such laws were introduced when the secular governments assumed control over marriage after the Reformation. As early as the thirteenth century, however, laws existed, for example, in Spain to maintain estates, which consisted primarily of land.[20] To make sure that estates would remain in a family, they were passed from generation to generation through the male bloodline. The estate remained the separate property of the husband and a wife never acquired any rights in the property while there was an heir.

With the spread of wealth after the Reformation, governments assumed more control over the regulation of the effect of marriage on the title to property. By the time of the Industrial Revolution, the regulation of family economic affairs was similar in all the major Western European countries: The husband had the power to manage all the family property, including the property and earnings of the wife. He was also expected to provide for the maintenance of the members of the household. He was limited by a fiduciary responsibility to manage any property brought into the marriage by the wife.

Matrimonial Property in the United States

In the United States, two different legal systems developed that addressed matrimonial property, one based on the common law of England and the other on the civil law of continental Europe as it developed in Mexico. These legal systems define the items that are the separate properties of the individual spouses and those that are their collective marital property and specify rules to allocate property between the spouses if they divorce.

Common Law. In most of the states, marital property law derives from the English common law, under which all the wife's real and personal property came under the husband's control upon marriage. Her property was returned to her, if she lived longer than her husband and she had certain limited rights in her husband's property if he predeceased her, but the general conclusion has been that the common law system favored the husband's interests.

To avoid the harsher aspects of the common law, most states passed Married Women's Property acts during the nineteenth century.[21] These laws ended the husband's assumption of the wife's property at the time of the marriage. She was permitted to own, sell, and otherwise act on her behalf with respect to her property, and she could sue her husband over property-related issues, enter into contracts, and assume full rights over her earnings. On their face, these laws approached equal treatment, entitling husband and wife to their separate properties and to their earnings. But the spouses were equal only in a strict formal sense: The properties of the spouses were often commingled so the separate properties were treated as joint property, and because the husband was the principal wage earner, the bulk of the assets acquired during the marriage were in his name. These reforms were thus of little value to women who did not come into the marriage with separate property or did not work outside the home during the marriage.

The rules in most common law states attempted to make a distinction between the separate property of the spouses and their marital property, normally based on title. Following the example of the Uniform Marriage and Divorce Act, as it was amended in 1973,[22] nearly all the common law states have replaced their fixed rules for determining how property is allocated after a divorce with "equitable distribution" statutes. These statutes give judges broad discretion to distribute all property, both separate and marital, in a way that they consider to be fair.[23] Judges have had a difficult time with the fairness concept resulting in the predictable pattern that courts usually return the parties' separate properties and divide the martial property equally.

Community Property. Some western states use a property system based on the civil law system of Mexico.[24] In these jurisdictions, each spouse has a one-half interest in all marital, or community, property. As noted earlier, community property is all property that is not the separate property of the spouses. Separate property is, in turn, defined by statute as the property that the parties brought into the marriage or that came to them during the marriage by will, bequest, or devise. The states regard the management of the community property during the marriage in a variety of ways. Some states give the idea of community property broad play, and in other states the spouses control their property and earnings more directly. Some community property states require a strict equal division of marital property; in others the courts are given some discretion. The usual effect at divorce, however, is that each spouse keeps his or her separate property and the community property is divided equally between the spouses.

Traditionally the two systems produced different results, but recent reforms have moved the common law and community property states closer together with an emphasis on community property principles. The Uniform Marital Property Act created in 1983,[25] if it were enacted by the states, would effectively create a nationwide system of community property. The act makes the spouses equal owners of property acquired during marriage, except those items that have traditionally been treated as separate property, such as gifts and inheritance. The act says nothing about how property shall be divided upon divorce or death, however, which is when the issue of ownership becomes critical. The act does provide for premarital and postmarital property agreements, with the courts scrutinizing postmarital agreements more closely than premarital agreements.[26] If the enforcement of an agreement would result in one spouse going on public assistance, the courts may require the other spouse to contribute enough support so that public assistance is avoided. Thus, both common law and community property systems establish rights of spouses in property, but neither provides a clear definition of the items that are property.

Premarital Agreements

Where the laws of a given jurisdiction do not define or allocate property at divorce or death in a way that meets the particular needs of the parties, a private contract has offered an alternative. Such private contracts, often premarital agreements, are coming into wider use because of changes in marital patterns. By the early 1980s, men and women over thirty years of age accounted for 41 percent and 32 percent, respectively, of new marriages.[27] Not only are these people older and therefore more aware of the potential problems associated with marriage, they also bring more assets to their marriages. The increasing divorce rate also results in ever more people marrying more than once. For example, in 45 percent of new marriages at least one party has been married before.[28]

In most civil law jurisdictions in Europe, the marriage contract is an established institution,[29] but it has not been looked on favorably by the courts in the United States.[30] Concerns include fears that premarital determinations of the consequences of divorce will encourage divorce against public policy and that no contract could adequately deal with all the circumstances that could confront the parties in a marriage of long duration.[31] Nevertheless, many courts now uphold premarital agreements, especially when strict standards of fairness are met or in the case of a second marriage. The courts ask whether there was a fair disclosure of the parties' wealth at the time of the contract, how the provisions of the contract compare with the legal support obligations that they would replace, and whether enforcement of the contract would make one spouse a burden on society.[32]

The Uniform Marriage and Divorce Act, which has been enacted in some states, makes a premarital contract only one factor to be used by the court in determining whether the division of the spouses' property is equitable. The trend of court decisions is more supportive of agreements relating to property settlements than of agreements affecting support obligations, support being deemed more essential to marriage than are matters of property. The difference between support and property at the time of a divorce has been clouded by practical concerns, for example, about taxes. Premarital agreements that seek to define or waive support obligations and other essential duties of marriage still tend to be declared invalid as against public policy. One attempt to clarify these issues is the Uniform Premarital Agreement Act of 1983.[33]

In the current legal environment, the enforcement of premarital agreements is sufficiently uncertain that they do not offer a clear alternative to the legally defined allocation of property at divorce. When the no-fault divorce statutes removed most of the negotiating power of married women, premarital and postmarital agreements did not offer an attractive option. Women who were married or considering marriage were confronted with an environment in which their marriage often could be dissolved unilaterally without compensation in any significant manner for any financial losses they might suffer from being housewives and mothers during the marriage.

Conclusion

Marriage laws have changed over the years, with a shift toward secular control and legal formality, but they have been stable compared to divorce laws. Until the middle of the nineteenth century, a divorce was difficult to obtain in the United States. The parties who committed themselves to the obligations of marriage were protected by the fault grounds for divorce. Gradually, the grounds for divorce were expanded, and the courts became more willing to accept questionable testimony to establish the legal grounds for divorce. Still, it was difficult for one spouse to divorce without the cooperation of the other spouse. When a spouse could not establish the grounds, but wanted a divorce, the usual outcome was negotiations, often resulting in the initially unwilling party--usually the wife--accepting compensation that made her willing to accept the divorce. The solution was a wealth transfer and the fabrication of evidence to establish the necessary grounds. This situation took a dramatic turn in 1970 with the adoption of no-fault divorce statutes. No-fault not only changed the grounds for divorce, it also increased the importance of the legal rules that define and allocate property at divorce.

In the next chapter, I offer an economic analysis of marriage, divorce, and property to aid in understanding why people marry, how they select their spouses, why they sometimes decide that they no longer want to be married, and what is property.

Notes

1. "Marriage" in *Collier's Encyclopedia* (New York: Macmillan, 1989) Vol. 15, p. 440.
2. Margaret F. Brinig and June Carbone, "The Reliance Interest in Marriage and Divorce," *Tulane Law Review,* Vol. 62, No. 5, May 1988, p. 860.
3. The history of marriage law in Europe and the United States is available from numerous sources. For example, see Max Rheinstein, *Marriage Stability, Divorce and the Law* (Chicago: University of Chicago Press, 1972) and Mary Ann Glendon, *The Transformation of Family Law* (Chicago: University of Chicago Press, 1989).
4. Marriage only became indissoluble when the Catholic church gained jurisdiction over marital matters for its own courts. Rheinstein, *Marriage Stability,* pp. 7-28.
5. Glendon, *Transformation,* p. 29.
6. Ibid., p. 33.
7. Homer H. Clark, Jr., *The Law of Domestic Relations in the United States,* 2d ed. (St. Paul, MN: West, 1988), p. 23.
8. Brinig and Carbone, "Reliance Interest," pp. 860-861.

9. "Divorce" in *Encyclopedia Britannica* (Chicago: *Encyclopedia Britannica*, 1967), Vol. 7, p. 514.

10. O'Connell, "Alimony After No-Fault," p. 449.

11. Brinig and Carbone, "Reliance Interest," p. 861.

12. The establishment of the Church of England was in part a response to the Pope's refusal to grant an annulment to Henry VIII's marriage to Catherine of Aragon. Clark, *Domestic Relations,* p. 407.

13. *Encyclopedia Britannica,* p. 515.

14. Ibid.

15. Glenda Riley, *Divorce: An American Tradition* (Oxford, UK: Oxford University Press, 1991), p. 9.

16. The number then fell to a slightly lower level for the remainder of the decade. The rate per 1,000 married females rose from 8 in 1920 to 22.6 in 1981. *Historical Statistics of the United States* (Washington: Government Printing Office, 1975), Series B 216-220, p. 64, and *Statistical Abstract of the United States, 1990* (Washington, DC: Government Printing Office, 1990), Table 126, p. 86.

17. 317 U.S. 287(1942).

18. Riley, *Divorce,* p. 162.

19. Clark, *Domestic Relations,* p. 517.

20. William A. Reppy, Jr., "Major Events in the Evolution of American Community Property Law and Their Import to Equitable Distribution States," *Family Law Quarterly,* Vol. 23, No. 2, Summer 1989, pp. 163-192.

21. Lawrence M. Friedman, *A History of American Law* (New York: Simon and Schuster, 1973), pp. 184-186.

22. Uniform Marriage and Divorce Act, § 307, alternative A, 9A *Uniform Laws Annotated* 142-143 (1973).

23. For a discussion of this process and a description of the statutes, see Mary Ann Glendon, *The New Family and the New Property* (Toronto: Butterworths, 1981), pp. 57-68. Glendon argues that the "equitable distribution" statutes have resulted in too much ambiguity. See Mary Ann Glendon, "Family Law Reform in the 1980's," *Louisiana Law Review,* Vol. 44, 1984, pp. 1553-1573.

24. These states include Arizona, California, Idaho, Louisiana, Nevada, New Mexico, Texas, and Washington.

25. Uniform Marital Property Act(UMPA), § 10(b), 9A *Uniform Laws Annotated* 35 (Supp. 1983).

26. UMPA, §§ 3, 10(c)(3)-(4).

27. *Vital Statistics of the United States, 1983, 3, Marriage and Divorce* (Hyattsville, MD: National Center for Health Statistics, 1987), Table 1-13, p. 1-15.

28. Ibid., Table 1-14, p. 1-16.

29. Max Rheinstein and Mary Ann Glendon, "Interspousal Relations," in A. Chloros, ed., *International Encyclopedia of Comparative Law* (Tubingen, Germany: Mohr, 1980), Vol. 4, Chapter 4.

30. Homer H. Clark, Jr., "Antenuptial Contracts," *University of Colorado Law Review,* Vol. 50, No. 2, Winter 1979, pp. 141-164. Dawley v. Dawley, 551 P.2d 323(Cal. 1976), rejected the traditional public policy objections and accepted that prenuptial agreements can serve a useful purpose as a planning device when there is recognition of the possibility of dissolution.

31. Harry D. Krause, *Family Law,* 2d ed. (St. Paul, MN: West, 1986), p. 79.
32. Glendon, *Transformation,* p. 137.
33. Uniform Premarital Agreements Act, *Family Law Report (BNA),* Vol. 201, March 13, 1984, p. 121.

3

The Economics of Marriage
and Divorce

During the last few decades, the use of economic analysis has been expanded to many nonmarket activities, including marriage, divorce, education, and crime.[1] As marriage and divorce can affect the financial welfare of the parties, it is not difficult to understand that economics has some relevance to the analysis of the effects of marriage and divorce. I will show here that economics can provide insights about marriage and divorce that go far beyond the valuation of property affected by marriage and divorce.

The Role of Economic Analysis

On a general level, economics is the study of the choices individuals make. The economic perspective fundamentally assumes that resources are scarce compared to human wants, that these resources can be put to alternative uses, and that people have diverse wants, not all of which can be satisfied. It follows that the basic economic problem of every society--and of every individual--is to allocate the available resources in the most efficient manner to satisfy wants. Especially in the United States, where legal marriage is a monogamous relationship, the need for a person to make a choice when selecting a spouse is obvious: Here economic analysis goes far beyond the comparison of alternatives according to prices denominated in dollars.

Ever since Adam Smith's day, social scientists have been using the economic framework to gain a better understanding of why people make the choices that they make. Much of the power of economics to explain human behavior is rooted in the following set of assumptions:

1. People are constantly confronted with the necessity of making choices in their roles, for example, as consumers, workers, and lovers. Many alternatives are mutually exclusive.
2. In making these choices, people try to improve rather than reduce their welfare. The choices are made by comparing the costs and benefits of the alternatives in a context of constraints such as laws, time, abilities, and income.
3. Choices are influenced by the relative sacrifices, or "prices," involved with the different alternatives; these sacrifices can involve money, time, and psychic costs.
4. These "economic" decisions are made in an environment that is influenced by a range of other factors such as religion, social class, and physical and psychological needs. Economists have traditionally assumed that these environmental factors change slowly.[2]

When we observe systematic changes in human behavior, we would be well advised to investigate whether there has been a change in the constraints or the relative prices confronting the individuals. People will usually buy less of a good if their incomes fall or if the price of the good rises. Economists assume that tastes and preferences change less quickly than do the prices and the constraints that individuals face. At the same time, different groups can have preferences for different commodities and activities. Irish-Americans might eat more corned beef and cabbage than persons of other ethnic groups, but all consumers would be expected to buy less corned beef if its price rose.

But divorce is our primary topic here. People must marry before they can divorce, so first we will analyze why people marry. The decision to marry consists of two steps: the decision that the individual will be better off married than single and the choice of a particular person as spouse. Although the sequence is not predetermined, both choices have to be made before someone marries.

An understanding of why people marry is important because the incentives that induce people to marry can change so that they no longer want to be married. The result is often a divorce. Economics provides a foundation for understanding why people rationally choose to marry and why some of these people, also rationally, choose to dissolve their marriages. As marriage and divorce have effects on the financial and psychological condition of the parties, economics can be particularly relevant for analyzing the effect of marriage and divorce on their wealth. It also can be used to evaluate whether marriage and divorce decisions have the capacity to improve social welfare. Last, economics can provide insights about other issues concerning divorce: Why do the spouses litigate the divorce instead of negotiating a settlement? Why does the political process produce particular laws affecting divorce? Why is only one step toward the reform of the fault divorce laws potentially worse for society than no reform at all?

The Economic Approach to Marriage

One has to wonder why it took economists so long to turn their attention to the analysis of marriage. As the study of choice, economics should be a valuable tool for analyzing one of the most important decisions made by individuals. It was not until the 1960s, however, that economists started to develop a concerted interest in decision making outside markets,[3] including marriage. Marriage in the United States has characteristics that are similar to the other transactions that economists observe. First, marriage is voluntary, and therefore it can be assumed that the parties expect that decision to raise their individual welfare above the level that they could attain if they remained single. Second, the parties compete in markets for the best mates. Gary Becker argued that the economic approach can be used to explain the variety of marriage patterns around the world.[4] Although economics also can provide insights about homosexual unions and heterosexual relationships that do not result in legal marriage, here I focus on why a man and a woman in the United States choose to marry.

The Decision to Marry

First, the individual must decide that he or she wants to marry. Second, he or she must select a particular mate. These decisions are not necessarily sequential, but will be addressed sequentially here with first a look at why people marry. The process by which individuals choose their preferred mate will be discussed in the economic analysis of divorce.

Men and women date, enter sexual relationships, and live together; but why do they go a step further and marry? The economic analysis of the decision to marry focuses on the parties' expectation that marriage will increase their individual welfare--that marriage will expand the "commodities" available to them compared with those available if they remained single.[5] Of course, love and physical attraction are important factors when selecting the preferred person to marry.

The Production of Commodities

Individual welfare is increased through the acquisition or production of commodities. Economic analysis of consumer behavior traditionally focused on the acquisition of goods and services, but economists have come to recognize that individuals do not necessarily receive enjoyment from just the acquisition of goods and services--enjoyment comes from combining goods and services with time to produce commodities.[6] A given commodity can be produced using a variety of combinations of money and time. A meal, for example, can consist of a dinner at an elegant restaurant costing many dollars and several hours of time. Alternatively, a meal can consist of a picnic in the country costing less money but more time. The enjoyment does not come from just buying the food, but from combining the food with time. Commodities produced at home can be an important component of individual welfare; these commodities tend to be time intensive, including home-cooked meals, an attractive lawn, and activities associated with raising children.

The production of these commodities benefits from specialization. We often observe that businesses increase their output and profits by specialization. Businesses gain from specialization that reduces the time lost as workers move between activities and that permits employees to develop the unique skills necessary to perform specific tasks faster. The same principle is appropriate for the production of commodities by consumers. When people specialize, they can become more efficient in the production of commodities. When people cook more frequently, they become better cooks.

The activities in which people specialize tend to be based on comparative advantage. Comparative advantage exists when two people have levels of productivity that vary among activities. The most important of these activities for marriage have, traditionally, been income earning and child raising. On average, men have earned and continue to earn higher incomes than women.[7] Only women can give birth to children, however, and women therefore have an absolute advantage in delivering if not raising children. Based on this limited, but critical, array of activities, it can be concluded that men have a comparative advantage in earning income compared with giving birth to children. Women have an advantage in giving birth to children compared with producing income. Psychological reasons are often given for couples preferring the mother to be the parent with primary responsibility for child rearing, but women's lower earnings also make them the lower-cost parent to provide those services. Within marriage in the United States, men have tended to specialize in income earning and women have tended to specialize in home-based activities. This specialization is not absolute: Married men often provide services around the house, and many married women work outside the home. During marriage, however, men and women have tended to increase their specialization compared with when they were single. The comparative advantages of men and women, and therefore their roles during marriage, are not permanent. Over the past few decades, the earnings of women have increased relative to those of men, and the importance of children, measured by the number of children per family, has decreased. These two trends reduce the comparative advantages of both men and women, in turn altering the roles of men and women during marriage and diminishing the incentive for people to marry.

The reason comparative advantage provides an incentive for men and women to marry is illustrated in Figure 3.1. Economists assume that subject to the constraints they face, people attempt to obtain the bundle of commodities that provides them with the highest level of welfare.[8] For simplicity, assume that there are only two types of commodities: market commodities, which are income intensive, such as automobiles and houses, and household commodities, which are time intensive, such as children and meals. Let us denominate the values of these commodities in dollars. Say the man has the potential by himself to produce either $50 of market commodities, $20 of household commodities, or a combination of the two; the woman has the potential by herself to produce either $20 of market commodities, $50 of household commodities, or a combination of the two. These combinations are called their *production possibility frontiers*. The man has a comparative advantage in the production of market commodities relative to household commodities and the reverse is true for the woman.

By working together and specializing in production, a man and a woman can increase their output beyond the level that is available to each functioning alone. If they specialize, their combined output is illustrated in Figure 3.1 by the line labeled "Combined Output." They can produce $70 of market commodities, $70 of household commodities, or a combination of the two commodities. Because of specialization, the combined production possibility frontier is no longer a straight line. It is kinked. If the woman specializes in the production of household commodities and the man specializes in the production of market commodities, they can produce $50 of market commodities and $50 of household commodities, B_c.

So far this example has illustrated production possibilities. To determine the actual production of the individuals on their own, we need to know their preferences. If it is assumed that both have approximately equal preferences for the two types of commodities, they would choose bundles that lie in approximately the middle of their production possibility frontiers at B_m and B_w. For example, the man's bundle, B_m, could be $20 of market commodities and $12 of household commodities. The woman's bundle, B_w, could be $12 of market commodities and $20 of household commodities. If each lives alone, they are forced to produce the commodities for which they have a comparative advantage as well as the commodities for which they have a comparative disadvantage.

They can both increase their welfare by specializing in production. To show how this occurs, Figure 3.1 includes a line that represents one-half their combined output. Between the bundles on their individual production possibility frontiers and the bundles on the line representing one-half the combined output are the bundles of the commodities that are available to each member of a couple that are not available to them as individuals. If

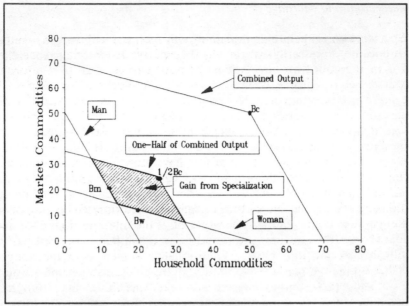

Figure 3.1 The Advantages of Specialization

the couple has approximately equal preferences for market commodities and household commodities, they might choose to specialize completely and produce $50 of each, B_c. An equal division of that output between the man and the woman results in their each having $25 of each commodity, $1/2B_c$. One-half the combined output is more of both commodities than they each can produce if they live alone. They are both better off if they specialize in production and then exchange their outputs.[9]

The discussion here assumes that men and women specialize in the production of either only market commodities or only household commodities during marriage. Marriage is still attractive for many people when they each produce both market and household commodities, so long as they specialize more than they would if they were single. By reducing the extent to which they specialize, however, they also may reduce the gains from marriage. For example, if the two people described above considered marriage, but expected to continue to produce the same bundles of commodities as before marriage, their combined output would be $32 of market commodities and $32 of household commodities. An equal division of this output would be $16 of each, which is less than the $25 of each that would be available to each of them through specialization. The man would have more household commodities than before marriage, but fewer market commodities; the reverse would be true for the woman, leaving them uncertain whether they would be better off married than single.

Specialization and Marriage

Specialization is helpful in explaining why men and women live together, but it does not necessarily explain why they marry. Even though specialization is in the collective best interest of both parties while a relationship lasts, it can be revealed as costly if the relationship ends. This is especially true for a relationship of long duration. If the man specializes in the production of market commodities that involve earning income, that skill will be intact if the relationship ends. He would lose his share of the household commodities provided by the woman, but these commodities may have decreased in value after any children have grown up and left the home. During the relationship, the woman may have developed skills producing household commodities that do not have substantial value outside the relationship and her income-earning capacity has deteriorated because of her working only at home. She may be worse off if the relationship is dissolved, compared with the situation she would be in if she had never entered the relationship in the first place. Traditionally, women were reluctant to specialize unless they had the expectation of the relationship being of a long duration and marriage was associated with that expectation. Since both men and women benefited from specialization, they both had an incentive to marry.

Children. The pressure for a couple to specialize within a relationship grows when they have children. The specialization in rearing children and the associated costs for the parent who assumes primary responsibility for that role increases the incentive for the parents to marry. The arrival of children usually results in one party, usually the woman, increasing the emphasis that she places on household production. The parents may be tempted to share the responsibility for child rearing, but usually it will be less costly to the couple for just one parent to alter his or her employment than for both to alter their employment. The lower average wages available to women make the mother the lower-cost provider of child rearing. Because that specialization may reduce her potential earnings later, the mother would rationally want a long-term agreement to protect herself from the potential costs of that decision. Although there are a variety of reasons why men and women live together, the desire for children is one of the primary reasons they marry.

The Timing of Contributions. The incentive for couples to marry can be reinforced by the timing of their contributions to their marriage. The contribution of the primary income-earning spouse, usually the man, often grows over time, but the contribution of the spouse who works at home, usually the woman, can decline after their children have grown. Over the duration of a marriage, the potential contributions of both spouses created the incentive that was the basis for the mutually advantageous exchanges that resulted in the parties' decision to marry, but the asymmetry of their contributions can create incentives for men to dissolve their marriage.[10] After the children leave the home, the husbands may question why they continue to share their income with a woman who they may feel is not providing comparable value to the marriage.

The problems associated with this asymmetry have been recognized by economists in a business setting: When businesses specialize, they often make long-term arrangements to protect themselves from other firms taking advantage of them through opportunistic behavior.[11] For example, a company might build a plant to produce a good that has value to only one buyer. After the construction of the plant, the buyer might be tempted to offer a price for the output of the plant that is only slightly higher than the direct cost of producing the good, a price inadequate to cover all the costs of production. The owner of the plant would be unhappy with that situation, but he would still be better off producing the good and receiving a price greater than the direct cost of production than not producing at all. When producers recognize that opportunistic behavior can occur, they tend to require a long-term contract before the construction of the plant to guarantee a price that covers all its costs. In situations in which these long-term contracts are difficult to draft and enforce, companies have found it attractive to combine all activities within the same firm through vertical integration.

Similar opportunistic behavior can occur within a marriage.[12] Recognizing the potential asymmetry of the timing of the contributions of the parties during a marriage, the marriage laws in the United States historically attempted to create a long-term contract to protect the parties, usually women, who specialized in household production. Although the fault divorce laws did not define marriage as a long-term contract, the effect of the fault grounds for divorce was to turn marriage into a long-term arrangement in which a wife who specialized in household production could make that choice with the understanding that compensation would be required as an adjustment for the potential cost that she would incur if the marriage was dissolved.

Because the marriage agreement even under fault divorce was not easy to enforce, men and women have adapted to the problems associated with women specializing in household services in other ways. Lloyd Cohen argues that one way society has dealt with the value of the services provided by women being at an earlier phase of marriage than those provided by men is reflected in the relative ages of spouses.[13] Women tend to marry older men. The effect of this age gap is to make their contributions to marriage more contemporaneous. This increases the period during which women should expect to be widows, but it decreases the likelihood that their marriages will be dissolved. As the comparative advantages of men and women have been reduced and we find less specialization in marriage, the age gap between men and women at the time of their first marriage has fallen.[14]

Marriage and Children

Economics thus provides an alternate explanation for marriage being associated with children. Often people who are living together only decide to marry when the woman becomes pregnant. A common reason given for this decision is to make the child legitimate. Given the rise in the number of children born to unmarried mothers, legitimacy clearly is not a universal concern.[15] The economic explanation recognizes that the arrival of a child dramatically increases the incentives for one parent to specialize in household production if the parents plan to remain together. This specialization has a potential cost to at least one of the parents for which a long-term marriage contract provides some protection. If the parents do not plan to remain together or the woman will not incur a significant loss in future earnings due to her working at home, then the parents have a smaller incentive to marry even if there is a child.

Before the broad availability of contraceptives, social mores tended to require marriage as a prerequisite for sexual relations. In that environment, sexual relations were almost guaranteed to result in children. If the couple was not married and did not marry, the children could become a burden on the mother and given her limited employment opportunities, potentially, society. Society responded by placing a significant social stigma on premarital sex.

Less Specialization

If people find either fewer opportunities or fewer incentives to specialize, then men's and women's production possibility frontiers become more similar. A reduction in the opportunities to specialize occurs as the earnings of men and women converge.[16] The reduction in the incentive to specialize also could be a result of less protection for the person who would normally specialize in household production. Either of these trends reduces the motivation for people to marry. Figure 3.2 portrays a man and a woman who have identical production possibility frontiers. Both have similar income-earning capacities and neither wants children. Pooling their outputs results in essentially double what they could produce by themselves. Half that combined output is essentially the same amount that they could produce single. Such couples might choose to live together without specialization, but have fewer incentives to marry.[17]

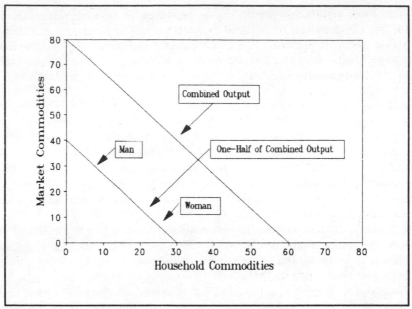

Figure 3.2 A Relationship Without Specialization

Despite gains to both men and women from marriage, some people choose to remain single; this is especially true if they had a strong preference for the type of commodities for which they have a comparative advantage. The large percentage of adults married in the United States reflects the large percentage of people who gain from the opportunities offered within marriage.

Incentives to Live Together

There are advantages for people living together besides love and physical attraction that do not necessarily make marriage attractive. First, there are economies of scale available to households. The size of a comfortable house does not normally increase as much as the increase in the number of occupants; thus the cost per occupant falls as the number of occupants increases up to some point. In addition, some commodities consumed in a household are public goods, which are a special case of commodities with economies of scale: A public good has the characteristics that additional people can consume it at little or no additional cost and people cannot easily be excluded from the enjoyment of the commodity. A private good, by way of contrast, is costly to provide to additional people and people can be excluded from enjoying it. A television set can be a public good; an apple exemplifies a private good.

The most significant public goods produced in many households are children. Children can be enjoyed by both parents at no more cost than if only one parent is present. It is often difficult to exclude one parent from that enjoyment. As discussed above, however, the presence of children in itself creates pressures for couples that are living together to marry.

Evidence of the Economic Explanation for Marriage

In a test of the economic analysis of marriage, Alan Freiden concluded that marriage is a rational choice based especially on the gains from the specialization of labor. He shows that three factors--the ratio of the sexes, the potential returns to marriage, and the cost of divorce--explain the variation in the percent of married women across different political divisions in the United States.[18]

Economic analysis concludes that the major reason people marry is the welfare gain that they expect from that state. Not all marriages are successful in fulfilling that expectation. Some end in divorce. As a large percent of people that divorce remarry, divorce cannot be seen as a rejection of marriage so much as a rejection of a particular mate.[19] In the next section, the search for the best mate will be used to analyze the decision to divorce.

The Economics of Divorce

A divorce occurs when at least one party after marriage decides that there is no distribution of the future output of that marriage that will make him or her better off compared with the opportunities outside that marriage. Two people marry when both anticipate they will be better off married than single, with the choice of a particular spouse the result of a search process. Sometimes the search that culminates in marriage does not produce the results that were anticipated. The change in the anticipated gains from marriage can be due to two situations: an unanticipated outcome or the asymmetry of the spouses' contributions.

The Search for a Spouse

The choice of an individual to marry is the result of a search that continues so long as the benefit exceeds the cost: The question is always whether the individual should accept a current candidate or look for a better one. The expected benefit from continuing to search equals the probability of finding a better mate times the expected increase in welfare from that better mate. The cost of continuing to search for a better mate is the sum of the money, time, and emotional effort of searching plus any welfare foregone by remaining single rather than marrying an available mate. The welfare gains from marriage may be available from several potential spouses. Even after marriage, there can remain a question whether the current spouse is the best mate. The decision to marry a particular person is made with some uncertainty.

Uncertain Outcomes

A divorce can be caused by the uncertain outcomes that can occur during marriage.[20] People usually marry with the expectation that their marriage is a lifelong commitment, but at least one party can decide later that he or she would be better off outside that marriage. In the seminal work on this topic, Gary Becker, Elizabeth Landes, and Robert Michael concluded that the probability of divorce depends on two factors: the expected gain from marriage and the distribution of the unexpected outcomes.[21] The probability of divorce is smaller the greater the expected gain from marriage and the smaller the variability in the outcomes during marriage. People who do not want to specialize and do not appreciate the commodities made available by their spouse do not gain very much from marriage. Even if they marry, the marriage is vulnerable. Alternatively, if a couple marries based on certain expectations such as continued good health, a major change in the health of one spouse can increase the likelihood of divorce.

Gains from Marriage. Certain factors have been identified as influencing the amount of the gains from marriage.[22] For example, the increase in specialization during marriage that often accompanies the production of young children reduces the probability of dissolution. The more people commit themselves to specialized roles, the more they gain from marriage and the more they lose from divorce. And, the more they find they are compatible with their present spouse, the more likely they are to choose to specialize. Less specialization during marriage increases the probability of divorce.

Variation in Outcomes. Other factors influence the success of the search process. A better search produces a more predictable outcome during marriage. The people who spend more time and energy on their search will be more likely to find the most desirable mate. For example, people who marry when they are younger than average have significantly higher probabilities of divorce. The amount of search also will vary with the cost of search. For example, the costs of search are higher in isolated areas than in urban areas.

A larger deviation between actual and expected outcomes during marriage, such as a significant change in the earnings or health of the spouses, will raise the probability of dissolution. This is less likely to occur when the spouses are better matched in attributes such as religion and education. A marriage is also less likely to be dissolved the longer it lasts because people tend to discover their mistakes fairly early. But people also tend to repeat their mistakes, so that the probability of dissolution is higher in subsequent marriages.[23]

Asymmetric Contributions

Another potential cause of divorce is the asymmetry of the timing of the contributions of the spouses during marriage that was discussed above. During marriage, it has been common for the man to place more emphasis on earning income and for the woman to shift her emphasis toward the production of household commodities. Initially, both the husband and the wife are better off. But when their children grow up and leave the home, the value to the man of the household commodities provided by this woman are reduced, even as the value of the market commodities that he brings to the marriage are likely to have increased. He may decide that he is better off dissolving this marriage. The goal of the man may not be to be single so much as to find a new and more desirable spouse at this point in his life. With a higher income, he may feel that the pool of potential mates is larger than when he married for the first time. Of course, this outcome is also the result of a flawed search. If the search for a spouse by a woman led her to expect this type of behavior from a man, she would have hesitated to marry him in the first place.

Although uncertain outcomes and asymmetrical contributions can lead to a desire for a divorce, the ultimate decision to seek a divorce is influenced by a comparison of the cost and benefit of dissolving the marriage. The demand for divorce will increase if the cost falls or the benefit rises. Some of the cost consists of the loss of the commodities produced by the ex-spouse. An additional cost is the emotional strain and financial transfer required to dissolve the marriage. When a spouse who does not want to dissolve the marriage has legal or social protection, part of the cost will be the incentives such as additional property or child custody necessary to convince that spouse not to exercise those rights. The cost shifts over time with changes in laws or social expectations. As discussed earlier, no-fault divorce significantly lowered the cost of divorce to divorcing spouses by reducing the legal protection of spouses who did not want to dissolve their marriage. The benefits of divorce--being single or marrying a different spouse--also change over time.

The Incentive for Women to Specialize in Household Production

The incentive for women, who are often more adversely affected by divorce, to marry and specialize in household production during marriage is in part based on the expected compensation if their marriage is dissolved. Elizabeth Landes found that in states that prohibit alimony there is a lower rate of marriage and a reduced marital fertility rate than in states that do not restrict alimony awards.[24] People marry with certain expectations. A change in the grounds for divorce has a different impact on people already married, under a presumption of the earlier laws, and those people who marry with the expectation that divorces will be governed by the new laws. Historically, women specialized in household production during marriage with the expectation that the fault grounds for divorce provided substantial protection against their marriage being dissolved against their will. A change in that contract through a change in the grounds for dissolution came as a surprise to those married women and they found themselves worse off after divorce than they would have been under fault divorce. Unmarried women contemplating marriage incorporate the new divorce laws in their decision making. They will be less likely to marry and certainly less likely to specialize in household production during marriage.

The Effect of Marriage on Wealth

Decisions during a marriage affect the wealth of the parties. This can be particularly important at divorce. The courts attempt to recognize these effects through the financial arrangements at the dissolution of a marriage including property settlements, alimony, and child support, but their decisions are limited by statutory restrictions.[25] The community property system provides an illustration of the factors involved.

The community property system has become increasingly attractive to legal reformers because it treats marriage as a partnership.[26] In an unequivocal community property system, at divorce each spouse recovers his or her separate property and their community property is divided equally. (As mentioned before, community property is all property that is not statutorily defined as either spouse's separate property; separate property is property that the parties brought into the marriage or that came to them during the marriage by will, bequest, or devise.)

A marriage affects the wealth of the parties in ways that go beyond the property commonly recognized by the courts in practically all jurisdictions. The courts have traditionally recognized physical items such as houses and financial items such as shares of common stock as property, but for a meaningful economic analysis this definition of property is too narrow.[27] The effect of marriage on the most important property possessed by most people--human capital--has not been recognized by the courts in a systematic way.[28]

The items courts have defined as property are what economists call assets.[29] An asset has value because it will provide a stream of future returns. No one would pay a positive price for an automobile that was going to be destroyed a moment later, nor would anyone pay a positive price for a share of common stock in a corporation that was never expected to produce any profits or pay any dividends. An individual's wealth consists of the claims that he or she has on future income flows. That wealth can consist of an automobile providing services that could be converted into a market value, stocks and bonds that will provide dividends and interest, and the earnings based on human capital that he or she can expect in the future. In contrast to a house, a share of common stock, or a bond, the future earnings from human capital cannot be sold. Conceptually, however, they are all the property.

How and When Do We Acquire Human Capital?

To understand the effect of marriage on human capital, it is important to have an understanding of how and when human capital is acquired. An individual's wealth can be increased through investment. Individuals have the innate ability to generate earnings based on natural intelligence and physical strength, but any increase in earnings beyond that level are a result of the investments that are made in the individuals. These investments occur in a formal educational environment or on the job, they result in either general or specific skills, and they are financed either by the recipients or by others. This process can be illustrated by formal education in which different investments that produce human capital are often interconnected. Learning college biology may not result in a substantial increase in an individual's future earnings, but the medical training that it may permit can substantially increase the individual's future earnings. The earnings of a medical doctor, therefore, should be attributed to both his or her medical education and the preceding investments in education that made admission to medical school possible. Investments that result in a professional obtaining, for example, above-average earnings are interrelated and extend over his or her life.

The funding of the investments in human capital can be made by the individual who is the beneficiary of the investments or by others. The cost of an investment in education is the direct expenditures such as tuition and books and the indirect costs due to the individual's sacrificing earnings. The individual will usually personally incur the cost of the sacrificed earnings, but the direct costs are often incurred by others--the direct cost of elementary and secondary education, for example, is usually provided by parents or taxpayers. When the individual reaches an age at which employment is available, the proportion of the cost of the investment incurred by the recipient as sacrificed earnings increases.

At some point, the individual may have to incur both the direct and indirect cost of the investment in education. This is commonly the case with graduate education and the question then becomes whether to fund the direct cost through employment or to shift it to the future through borrowing. The amount of borrowing will depend on the cost of the funds and the expected return: the lower the cost or the higher the return, the larger the amount of the loan.[30] The usual criterion for choosing the source of a loan is the one with the lowest cost. Funding by the family or the spouse of the student increases the student's standard of living during the educational period without a corresponding need to make payments later. Usually this form of funding is not essential to obtaining education, but simply reduces the future burden incurred during the educational process.[31] Except for a few high-cost private universities, the greatest impediment to obtaining access to high-quality professional education is probably not the direct cost of the education, but the difficulty of gaining admission. The ability to gain admission is the result of earlier investments, and after admission, the most substantial cost of graduate education is usually the earnings sacrificed by the student.

It is important to recognize that the amount of human capital acquired by an individual is determined by the investments that have been made in the individual. The value of the human capital is based on the future earnings that it will produce. Finally, human capital is accumulated over an extensive period.

The Affect of Marriage on Human Capital

Conceptually, human capital is similar to the assets that the courts traditionally have recognized as property in financial settlements in conjunction with divorce proceedings. At the dissolution of a marriage, the courts have tended to identify property as either separate or marital. Normally, all property acquired by either spouse before marriage or by will, bequest, or devise during marriage is his or her separate property. In contrast, the property acquired by the spouses during the marriage belongs to both of them. From an economic perspective, the critical distinction between separate and marital property is the timing of the investments that created the property. Separate property is created outside the marriage; marital property is created by the combined activities of the spouses during the marriage.

Human capital can be evaluated within that same framework. At any moment, an individual has a stream of expected future earnings based on the investments that have already taken place in him or her. These earnings are net of any future investments and the value of this net earnings stream is the individual's human capital. The human capital that individuals possess at their marriage is separate property just as much as any stocks they owned. If they had not acquired an education, but instead they and their families had taken the cost of the education and invested those funds in stocks and bonds, the courts would have no difficulty treating those financial assets as separate property.

The human capital possessed by an individual at marriage can be illustrated by the example of a medical student. A third-year medical student who marries already has human capital that is based on an anticipated net earnings stream. The value of the human capital has little relation to the medical student's current earnings. Admittedly, some additional investments, such as the completion of medical school, may be required to receive the future earnings. Usually, these additional investments will be small compared with the investments that have already occurred. For a medical doctor, the major increase in his or her anticipated earnings occurred when he or she entered medical school. Medical doctors obtain higher earnings than college graduates who majored in pre-med courses, but did not go to medical school. The essential investments had already occurred when the student entered medical school, and the probability is high that he or she will finish that education. There remains concern about class work and financing medical school expenses, but these are probably a lesser concern than getting admitted in the first place.

Under normal circumstances, the investments in human capital that occur before marriage will be so large and essential compared with the investments after marriage that an individual's human capital is best treated as separate property. When the investments after the marriage are substantial, it may be appropriate to treat the additional human capital as marital property. The courts have used the concept of "professional goodwill" to attempt to describe the increase in the earnings of professionals during marriage.[32] In addition, when the earnings from one spouse's human capital are used to fund an increase in the human capital of the other spouse through education, an adjustment is appropriate at divorce for that funding plus any accrued interest.

Marriage can permit income-earning spouses to increase their specialization in that role, enabling those spouses to acquire human capital that would not have been acquired without their marriage. That is probably not a common situation, because many jobs do not permit greater specialization due to their requiring a set work period such as forty hours per week. Even when a job is flexible, a single person can often specialize as much as a married person. In most cases, the gain from marriage for the income-earning spouses occurs because of reductions in the time needed to provide household commodities for themselves, rather than a higher income through job specialization. During marriage, income-earning spouses normally receive more household commodities than they provided themselves before marriage, such as meals and house cleaning. In addition, they can receive additional household commodities, such as children, that were not available to them as single individuals.[33]

The same analysis can be used to illustrate the situation in which individuals' human capital decreases in value during marriage. Each individual has an anticipated net earnings stream and, therefore, an amount of human capital when he or she marries. The value of this human capital is based partly on the expectation of future investments, such as those provided by on-the-job training, that complement the prior investments. The future investments may be small compared with the prior investments, but they can have a significant effect on the individual's future earnings and his or her human capital. If these investments are not made, a person's human capital will decline in value.

Thus human capital can decline in value due to decisions made during marriage. It is common for couples to decide that they will benefit from one of them reducing participation in the labor force to increase specialization in household production. Those individuals sacrifice opportunities for maintaining and increasing their future earnings stream, the loss of which reduces the value of those individuals' human capital.[34] For example, with normal additional training in a chosen field, a married woman might expect to have an annual income of $50,000 at age thirty-five. Instead, she leaves the labor force to work at home and does not receive the additional training. For various reasons, that opportunity may never exist again. If she returns to the labor force after a divorce at age thirty-five, she can then only earn $20,000. The specialization in the production of household commodities has reduced her human capital and her wealth. The reduction in the value of her wealth can be calculated by comparing the stream of net earnings that she can expect after the divorce in contrast to the earnings that she could have expected to earn if she had never left the labor force.[35]

In summary, marriage can affect the wealth of the parties in different ways. By saving, the couple can acquire physical and financial assets. The trend has been for the courts to divide these assets equally at the time of a divorce, but courts have tended to ignore the effect of marriage on the human capital of the spouses. Individuals possess human capital at the time of their marriage based on their anticipated earnings. If their anticipated earnings increased during the marriage, additional human capital has been created. Alternatively, if a spouse's anticipated earnings decreased during the marriage, the effect is a reduction in that person's human capital. Much of the injustice incurred by divorced women since the introduction of no-fault divorce is due to the courts' not recognizing the effect of marriage on the spouses' human capital.

Overall, no-fault divorce has had a detrimental effect on the financial condition of divorced women. How is it possible that laws were passed that are so adverse to the interests of spouses who work at home? In the next section, we will look at how economists analyze the political process that created those laws.

The Economics of the Political Process

Since 1970, there has been a radical change in the laws establishing the grounds for divorce. Between 1970 and 1985, all the states enacted statutes either making irretrievable breakdown or incompatibility the sole ground for divorce or adding one or both of them to the existing fault grounds. These laws were written and approved by the members of state legislatures.

We often hear elected officials called public servants implying that they base their decisions on a broad vision of the public interest. Economists argue that their assumption that people make decisions in markets based on their self interest is just as appropriate for analyzing the behavior of elected officials as that of consumers.

The contrast between the goals of self-interest and the public interest is important for understanding the reasons why no-fault divorce statutes were passed in the United States. The use of economic tools to investigate the issues usually investigated by political scientists, called Public Choice,[36] assumes that the primary goal of elected officials is to be elected and to remain in office. To obtain that goal requires votes, which candidates can attract in two ways: They can either vote for specific pieces of legislation voters favor or collect the funds necessary to obtain voter recognition through advertising. Economists have shown that voters do not bother to be very well informed about the votes that they cast,[37] so name recognition can be particularly important for candidates. The advertising required to generate name recognition costs money and necessitates obtaining financial contributions.

David Friedman used the Public Choice framework to make three predictions about the behavior of elected officials:[38] First, they will favor concentrated interest groups over dispersed interest groups. Second, they will prefer more efficient to less efficient transfers. Last, they prefer transfers disguised as something else. It is much easier for concentrated groups--such as cattle ranchers--to organize than for dispersed groups say, beef eaters. The concentrated groups are more likely to vote for candidates for public office based on the candidates' views or record on narrow issues. In addition, these concentrated groups can be more easily organized to provide financial support for the elected officials that support their views. These concentrated groups want to be the beneficiaries of the political process, but they do not want to cause the wealth transfers generated by the political process to elicit an adverse response that would occur if large costs were imposed on other members of society. Therefore, among the alternate ways that they could be benefited by the political process, they have incentives to choose the least expensive. For example, cattle ranchers might receive similar benefits from government programs that restrict the importation of beef or those that provide subsidized grazing on federal land. Public Choice predicts that they would choose the program that imposes the smaller cost on consumers and taxpayers. Last, although the politicians want the ranchers to know that they have benefited, neither group wants the consumers and taxpayers to recognize the costs. Often the program chosen to benefit a special interest group will be presented to the voters, who do not have incentives to make a thorough review of the facts, as a reaction to unfair trade practices. The beneficiaries of the program have incentives to understand it better, and they recognize that they have benefited.

In the next chapter, I will use the Public Choice approach to examine the rapid passage of no-fault divorce statutes that turned out to be detrimental to the welfare of divorced women. There is no easy answer to why these laws were passed by legislatures so quickly, but as would be predicted by economists, the role of special interest groups, especially divorced men and self-interested politicians was of particular importance. In addition, we will observe that no-fault was disguised as something different from what it actually was and sold as being fairer to married and divorced women.

Legislatures pass laws that dictate how people should act under different circumstances. When people have disagreements about the law, they can either negotiate a settlement or litigate their dispute before a court. Divorce is no exception: A divorce can be obtained through a negotiated settlement or litigation. The change in the grounds for divorce from fault to no-fault had a significant change in the incentive for people to settle or litigate, the most important result being a reduction in the negotiating power of married women at divorce. In the next section, I discuss these issues from an economic perspective.

The Economics of Negotiation and Litigation

Economists conclude that individuals decide to settle a dispute or litigate it based on the expected costs and benefits of the alternatives with the incentive to settle a dispute increasing as the outcome of litigation becomes more predictable.[39] The incentives to settle or litigate in divorce proceedings have some unique traits because of the role of the state: Because the state was the party to a marriage, it also has to be a party to a divorce. The courts will only grant a divorce when specific procedures and standards have been met. Negotiated settlements were particularly important during the period when the grounds for divorce were based on fault because the outcome of litigation was reasonably predictable. One of the spouses had to be at fault, but spouses opposed to divorce were unlikely to make it easy to prove that they were at fault. Therefore, it was difficult for individuals to dissolve a marriage when their spouse was unwilling to cooperate. Litigation was then not only expensive, but it was unlikely to be successful and a divorce was usually the result of a negotiated settlement with evidence being produced to conform to the legal standards.

A desire by both parties to negotiate a settlement is no guarantee that an agreement will be reached. A necessary condition for a settlement is that the result each spouse would receive is better than each expects to receive under any other circumstances. Settlement negotiations will fail when, for example, the minimum offer the wife is willing to accept to cooperate in dissolving the marriage is greater than the maximum offer the husband is willing to pay.

Under fault divorce, the negotiations that resulted in the divorce included the custodial and financial arrangements that were part of the divorce. The importance of these negotiations changed dramatically with the introduction of no-fault divorce, when the cooperation of the "innocent" party was no longer required. A divorce could be obtained in many jurisdictions by the unilateral action of one spouse. The emphasis in divorce proceedings then shifted from the grounds for the divorce to the custodial and financial arrangements. The range of issues subject to negotiation was reduced. With less negotiating power in the hands of the unwilling party, the minimum compensation acceptable to that party and the maximum compensation offered by the other would be expected to decrease.

The new environment increased the importance of the legal rules that controlled these arrangements. Because under fault divorce the custodial and financial arrangements were usually part of the negotiated settlements, the existing legal standards had not often been the subject of attack as conditions changed. Differences of opinion about how those newly important rules applied in a specific case increased the likelihood of litigation. Similarly, it is common for litigation to increase when the legal rules change, as there often is initially some uncertainty about the effect of the law on final outcomes. Thus, more litigation on financial issues could be anticipated after the introduction of no-fault divorce until the legal rules on the financial arrangements became less ambiguous.[40]

Gary Becker argues that the change in the legal grounds for divorce would be expected to change the financial settlements at divorce, but not the divorce rate.[41] If couples contemplating divorce can easily bargain with each other, they may be just as likely to divorce under no-fault divorce as under fault divorce. Becker also argues that although a change in the rules would not change the incentives to reach a negotiated settlement, it would change the bargaining power of the parties and thus he expected the introduction of no-fault divorce to reduce the financial settlements received by wives.[42]

Many proponents of the reform of the fault divorce laws felt that married women had too much negotiating power under fault divorce. They argued that the outcomes of the negotiations were unfair to men. The courts' ignoring of human capital and some of the other costs of divorce, especially for women, under no-fault divorce would not support those arguments. Because of this loss of negotiating power for divorced women under no-fault,

fault divorce may have been what economists call a second-best solution to the problems associated with dissolving a marriage.

The Economics of the Second Best

Economists are interested in the conditions necessary for efficient outcomes. If one condition necessary for a desirable outcome cannot be fulfilled, then the best attainable situation, that is the second best, can only be achieved by departing from all the other optimal conditions. This principle can be illustrated with competitive markets, which are held in high regard by economists for allocating society's scarce resources efficiently. Efficiency calls for goods to be produced so long as the incremental benefit exceeds the incremental cost. But not all market transactions are efficient. When a production process creates external effects, such as pollution, social welfare will be increased by reducing production below the level chosen by competitive producers. At the competitive level of output, the cost to society, including the cost of the pollution, exceeds the benefit, and social welfare would be improved by reducing output. Often this can be accomplished by forcing the producers to recognize the full cost of their actions--the reduction in output could be accomplished with a tax on pollution. A tax may not be possible, however, and there may be no other way to deal with the pollution. Then society may be better off with a monopolistic producer that reduces output--and pollution--below the level of the competitive producers. The best solution would be competition and a pollution tax; if that is not possible, the second-best solution is a decrease in both pollution and competition.

The divorce laws can be viewed similarly. The most desirable divorce laws might first make it easy to obtain a divorce when the marriage relationship has irretrievably broken down; second, make any necessary adjustments to divide the financial repercussions of the dissolution between the spouses; and last, recognize the full costs of divorce. If there is an inappropriate definition of property that interferes with the second and third results, we might be better off not enacting laws that permit the first: If the best outcome is unavailable, the second-best outcome might be to continue the fault grounds for a divorce with the understanding that divorce is available, but only after a negotiated settlement.

With the fault grounds, couples who wanted to dissolve their marriage negotiated an acceptable settlement or made other arrangements such as premarital or postmarital agreements. The preferred long-term solution, however, should still be to correct the failure of the other requirements and then enact the first so that the best outcome is produced.

Conclusion

In this chapter, I have introduced the economic principles that can be used to more clearly understand the introduction and effects of no-fault divorce. Marriage occurs when two people anticipate that they will benefit from the relationship. Part of the benefits of marriage flow from the parties assuming specialized roles during marriage. Specialization becomes particularly important if a couple decides to have children, but can result in an uncompensated cost to the party who specializes in household production if the marriage is dissolved. Therefore, incentives were created to make marriage a long-term arrangement. Divorce, which usually occurs when the parties' expectations about marriage are not realized, as well as marriage can have substantial effects on the wealth of the parties. The courts have traditionally used a narrow definition of the property that is affected by marriage and divorce, partly because under fault divorce most divorces with substantial property were negotiated and the courts were not often asked to address the issue of the appropriate definition of property. I have argued that the traditional narrow definition of property that has been applied under no-fault divorce has resulted in a deterioration in the welfare of women at divorce. In the next chapter, I review the development of no-fault divorce in California using the analysis of Public Choice and the second best to present new insights into that development.

Notes

1. Much of the initial work was done by Gary S. Becker. See *Human Capital,* 2d ed. (New York: Columbia University Press, 1975); *The Economic Approach to Human Behavior* (Chicago: University of Chicago Press, 1976); and *A Treatise of the Family* (Cambridge, MA: Harvard University Press, 1981). For a discussion of economics as applied to a broad variety of human actions, see Victor R. Fuchs, *How We Live: An Economic Perspective on Americans from Birth to Death* (Cambridge, MA: Harvard, 1983).

2. Fuchs, *How We Live,* p. 12.

3. Much of this work, especially as it applies to marriage and divorce, is contained in Becker, *Economic Approach,* and *Treatise.*

4. Becker, *Economic Approach,* p. 206.

5. An additional reason for marriage is insurance, if one accepts the element of the marriage vow in which the parties agree to fulfill their duty "for rich or for poor, in sickness and in health." See Lloyd Cohen, "Marriage, Divorce, and Quasi Rents; or 'I Gave Him the Best Years of My Life,'" *Journal of Legal Studies,* Vol. 16, June 1987, p. 270.

6. The idea that individuals do not receive welfare just from goods and services but also from commodities that result from the combining of goods and services with time was developed in Gary S. Becker, "A Theory of the Allocation of Time," *Economic Journal,* Vol. 75, September 1965, pp. 493-517; and Kevin Lancaster, "A New

Approach to Consumer Theory," *Journal of Political Economy*, Vol. 74, April 1966, pp. 132-157.

7. Between 1981 and 1989, the ratio of female wages to male wages increased from .59 to .68 annual full-time earnings. For women and men with similar characteristics, the gap is smaller. See June O'Neill, "Women and Wages," *American Enterprise*, Vol. 1, No. 6, November/December 1990, pp. 25-33.

8. This section benefits from the discussion in Francine D. Blau and Marianne A. Ferber, *The Economics of Women, Men, and Work* (Englewood Cliffs, NJ: Prentice-Hall, 1986), pp. 58-66.

9. The idea that marriage is based on the gains from specialization is often ignored. Individuals can usually find members of the opposite sex whom they find attractive and with whom they can acquire the additional commodities available through marriage. In that environment, the focus is usually on the individual mate rather than the gains from marriage. In other situations, for example on the American frontier, marriages were arranged without the parties knowing each other because of the gains that the parties expected from a marriage to essentially anyone. See Ray Allen Billington, *America's Frontier Heritage* (Albuquerque: University of New Mexico Press, 1974), p. 215.

10. An excellent discussion of this problem is contained in Cohen, "Marriage."

11. The seminal article on this subject is Benjamin Klein, Robert G. Crawford, and Armen A. Alchian, "Vertical Integration, Appropriable Rents, and the Competitive Contracting Process," *Journal of Law & Economics*, Vol. 21, No. 2, October 1978, pp. 297-326.

12. In their article on the incentives for businesses to vertically integrate to avoid opportunistic behavior, Klein, et al. discuss marriage as illustrating the same problems. Ibid., p. 323.

13. Cohen, "Marriage," p. 293.

14. The gap was 2.5 years in 1960 and it fell to 1.8 years in 1986. *Statistical Abstract of the United States, 1990* (Washington, DC: Government Printing Office, 1990), Table 129, p. 87.

15. The percent of children born to unmarried women rose from 10.7 in 1970 to 24.5 in 1987. *Statistical Abstract*, Table 90, p. 67.

16. The female to male hourly earnings ratio for white men and women in the twenty to forty-four age group increased from 65.6 percent in 1977 to 71.4 percent in 1987. Standardized for age, region, schooling, industry, occupational skill level, and labor force turnover, the female to male hourly earnings ratio for people without children rose to 90.7 percent. For people with children, the ratio was 72 percent. O'Neill, "Women and Wages," pp. 30-32.

17. The median age of women at their first marriage rose from 20.6 in 1970 to 23.3 in 1986, while for men the median age rose from 22.5 to 25.1. *Statistical Abstract*, Table 129, p. 87. Although there are a number of reasons why fewer women marry, it should be noted that between 1970 and 1988 the percent of women who were married in the United States fell from 68.5 to 60.4. Ibid., p. 43.

18. Alan Freiden, "The United States Marriage Market," *Journal of Political Economy*, Vol. 82, No. 2, Pt. II, March/April 1974, pp. s34-s53. Based on supply and demand, he found that the proportion of females married is positively related to the male/female ratio. Comparative advantage was likely to increase as the ratio of male

wages rose relative to female wages. He found that for persons over age twenty-five the percent of women married in a state was positively related to the male/female wage ratio. This relationship was not statistically significant for people under age twenty-four. In other words, young people are less likely to marry based on a decision to increase the commodities that will be available to them. But people who marry when they are young have higher divorce rates, indicating that they are less likely to make the best long-term decision when they marry. Marriages based on substantial long-term gains from the comparative advantage of the parties can be expected to last.

Last, Freiden found that the marriage rate increased as the difficulty of obtaining a divorce fell for people under age twenty-four, but not for older people. He argues that if the cost of correcting a bad marriage is high, young people will hesitate to marry in the first place. The discussion presented in this book suggests the reverse: I would expect to observe the marriage rate decreasing when the difficulty of divorce is low, but if it is easy to obtain a divorce, women should hesitate to specialize in household production, with the result that there is a smaller gain for her and a man to marry. The variable used in Freiden's study for the cost of divorce was highly subjective and may not have been sufficiently precise enough to pick up that effect. In addition, in 1960 no state had as easily obtainable divorce as became available with no-fault divorce a decade later.

19. Approximately one out of every three people who marry have been married at least once before, and almost half of all weddings involve at least one person who has been previously married. See Fuchs, *How We Live*, p. 151. If their first marriage is dissolved, most women remarry quickly. Nearly 50 percent of women whose first marriage ended in widowhood or divorce remarried within five years. As marriage has become less attractive, the probability of remarriage has declined. See Kathryn A. London, "Cohabitation, Marriage, Marital Dissolution, and Remarriage: United States, 1988," U. S. Department of Health and Human Services, Advanced Data No. 194, January 4, 1991, p. 5.

20. Gary S. Becker, Elizabeth M. Landes, and Robert Michael, "An Analysis of Marital Instability," *Journal of Political Economy,* Vol. 85, No. 6, 1977, pp. 1141-1187.

21. Ibid., p. 1143.

22. Ibid., p. 1156.

23. Ibid., pp. 1156-1157.

24. Elizabeth Landes, "Economics of Alimony," *Journal of Legal Studies,* Vol. 7, 1978, pp. 35-63.

25. Homer H. Clark, Jr., *The Law of Domestic Relations in the United States,* 2d ed. (St. Paul, MN: West, 1988), p. 589.

26. See Allen M. Parkman, "Dividing Human Capital With an Eye to Future Earnings," *Family Advocate,* Vol. 12, No. 2, Fall 1989, pp. 34-37.

27. *The MIT Dictionary of Modern Economics,* 3d ed. (Cambridge, MA: MIT Press, 1986), p. 452, defines wealth as anything that has a market value and can be exchanged for money or goods. It can include physical goods, financial assets, and person skills that can generate an income.

28. The concept of human capital is developed in Becker, *Human Capital.*

29. This section is adapted from Allen M. Parkman, "Human Capital as Property in Divorce Settlements," *Arkansas Law Review,* Vol. 40, No. 3, 1987, pp. 439-467. An "asset" is defined in Alan C. Shapiro, *Modern Corporate Finance* (New York:

Macmillan, 1989), p. G-2, as "property that has value, as measured by the asset's ability to generate future cash."

30. Most loans require some security from the borrower. Until the borrower puts some of his or her own effort and money into a project, he or she will find it very difficult to borrow additional funds. The borrower's own resources are called equity, the borrowed funds debt. The equity funds are essential and their sources are very limited, usually coming from the individual or from a close associate. The initial investment in human capital that occurred in elementary and secondary school was usually made by members of the individual's family or taxpayers. The sources of debt financing on the contrary can be numerous. Most colleges offer loan programs in addition to the government loans available through lending institutions. In general, someone with an equity interest has a claim to a share of the returns to an investment, those with a debt interest only have a claim to the contracted rate of return.

31. The best method for handling an investment made by a working spouse is for the student spouse to pay back the loan with interest if the marriage is dissolved before the working spouse has received a fair return on the investment.

32. Allen M. Parkman, "The Treatment of Professional Goodwill in Divorce Proceedings," *Family Law Quarterly*, Vol. 18, No. 2, Summer 1984, pp. 213-224.

33. In 1976, the average woman in a household spent 25 hours a week on meal preparation and cleanup, cleaning, laundry, and child care; while the average man in a household spent 6.9 hours on those activities. The average woman spent 33.6 hours per week on all household services, the average man only 15.1 hours. See Janice Peskin, "Measuring Household Production for the GNP," *Family Economics Review*, Vol. 1982, No. 3, pp. 20, 22.

34. The value of an individual's human capital depreciates by approximately 1.5 percent per year during the period that he or she is out of the work force. The depreciation rate increases as the education level of the individual increases. Jacob Mincer and Solomon Polachek, "Family Investments in Human Capital: Earnings of Women," *Journal of Political Economy*, Vol. 82, No. 2, Pt. II, March/April 1974, pp. s76-s108.

35. This loss of human capital due to a spouse specializing in the production of household commodities can be introduced into the traditional legal definition of property by the use of an implied contract of indemnification. The decision by a couple for one spouse, usually the wife, to specialize in household production is in the best interest of both spouses if the marriage lasts, but it can result in a substantial reduction in the wife's human capital if the marriage is dissolved. If the loss is recognized as the basis for indemnification, the loss is a debt of the couple and an asset of the person incurring the loss.

36. The renewed interest was created in this area by Duncan Black, *The Theory of Committees and Elections* (Cambridge, UK: Cambridge University Press, 1958). Dennis C. Mueller, *Public Choice II* (Cambridge, UK: Cambridge University Press, 1989) provides a recent survey.

37. Anthony Downs, *An Economic Analysis of Democracy* (New York: Harper and Row, 1957), pp. 207-278.

38. David Friedman, *Price Theory*, 2d ed. (Cincinnati, OH: Southwestern, 1990), pp. 548-549. Another discussion of the economic theory of legislation is contained in

Richard Posner, *The Economic Analysis of Law,* 3d ed. (Boston: Little, Brown, 1986), pp. 496-499.

39. This is discussed in Posner, *Economic Analysis,* pp. 522-528.

40. Substantial litigation has occurred over the appropriate legal definition of property as applied to such intangible items as degrees and licenses. Also, litigation has addressed the issues of separate and marital property. Annual summaries of this litigation are contained in a series of articles in the *Family Law Quarterly.* For example, see Doris J. Freed and Timothy B. Walker, "Family Law in the Fifty States: An Overview," *Family Law Quarterly,* Vol. 23, No. 4, Winter 1990, pp. 495-608.

41. Becker, *Treatise,* p. 226.

42. These conclusions were verified in H. Elizabeth Peters, "Marriage and Divorce: Informational Constraints and Private Contracting," *American Economic Review,* Vol. 76, No. 3, June 1986, pp. 437-454.

4

The Introduction of
No-Fault Divorce Statutes

Seldom in U.S. history have laws been enacted with higher hopes and poorer results than the no-fault divorce statutes. In this chapter, we will examine why the no-fault divorce laws were passed and why unexpected results occurred; we will focus on the California experience because of its central role.[1] The economic analysis of Public Choice will be used to help understand the specific laws that were passed in California and the notion of "second best" to analyze why the no-fault divorce laws have produced poorer results than anticipated.

Case Law Versus Statutory Law

The rules that control marriage and divorce are based on statutes. By way of contrast, large areas of U.S. law, such as contracts and torts, are still controlled by judicial decisions in the common law tradition. Economists have argued that the judge-made common law rules tend to produce more efficient outcomes than legislatively created statutory laws.[2] Efficiency is promoted when the benefits of decisions exceed their costs, and common law rules with those characteristics tend to evolve because inefficient rules--ones that result in more costs or fewer benefits than efficient rules--will be challenged until they are overturned. In addition, the common law is based on judicial decisions that evolve in a decentralized process: Judges are confronted not with abstract ideas, but with actual litigants. As changing conditions render existing rules inefficient, litigants press the common law to change to produce more efficient rules.

Statutory laws respond to different pressures. Statutes are introduced or changed in discrete steps based on the political process of majority rule strongly influenced by special interest groups. Legislators are thus confronted with abstract concepts rather than actual parties, and rules established by the political process are more inclined toward wealth distribution than efficiency.[3] These pressures acting on the divorce laws can be illustrated by the history of no-fault divorce in California.

No-Fault in California

The nations's first uneqivocal no-fault law became effective in California in 1970.[4] The earlier law in that state based divorce, property division, alimony, child support, and custody on fault grounds. The new law removed consideration of fault from the grounds for divorce, the award of spousal support, and the division of property. Fault was retained as a relevant factor for only two issues: to prove the existence of the no-fault grounds and to determine child custody. This legislation, the result of six years of deliberation, is especially important because the National Conference on Commissioners of Uniform State Laws based the standard for dissolution in the Uniform Marriage and Divorce Act on the California requirement of "irretrievable breakdown."[5]   The remainder of the states followed the California lead in enacting similar statutes over the following fifteen years.

An improvement in the welfare of spouses and their children was the initial goal of the new legislation in California. The numerous criticisms of the fault-based divorce statutes made by proponents of no-fault divorce included the charges that the fault system tended to aggravate and perpetuate bitterness between spouses and that the widespread practice of using perjured testimony in collusive divorce proceedings promoted disrespect of the legal system. The wide gulf existing between the divorce law on the books that declared that marriage was indissoluble except for fault and the legal system that in practice tolerated divorce by mutual consent made extreme mental cruelty the almost universal ground for divorce.[6]   In fact, most divorces were uncontested and granted on cursory testimony of marital fault.[7]

It is impossible to identify exactly when the reform movement began, but the California legislature took its first steps in that direction in 1963. A House Resolution was passed in that year initiating a study of the laws on divorce and an interim committee began the study apparently without contemplating any radical change. Four major themes emerged from the 1964 hearings in the California Assembly, which set the agenda for the legislative proposals that followed. There were widespread concerns about:

1.   the high divorce rate,
2.   the adversary process creating hostility, acrimony, and trauma,
3.   a need to recognize the inevitability of divorce for some couples and attempt to make the legal process less destructive for them and their children, and

4.   charges made by divorced men that the divorce law and its practitioners worked with divorced women to acquire an unfair advantage over former husbands.[8]

The hearings reached no conclusions, nor was any legislation proposed and the interim committee disbanded.   In 1966, Governor Edmund G. Brown, who was enthusiastic about divorce law reform, established a twenty-two member Commission on the Family.[9] This commission consisted of one minister, four legislators, six lawyers, four judges, three psychiatrists, two law professors, one medical doctor, and one member of the State Social Welfare Board.   Two assemblymen were appointed cochairmen.[10] Noteworthy for their absence were economists and other professionals with backgrounds in financial analysis.   Governor Brown gave the commission four primary tasks:

1.   to study and suggest revisions, where necessary, of the substantive laws of California relating to the family,
2.   to determine the feasibility of developing significant and meaningful courses in family life education to be offered in the public schools,
3.   to consider the possibility and desirability of developing uniform nationwide standards of marriage and divorce jurisdiction, and
4.   to examine the establishment of family courts on a statewide basis and recommend the procedures by which they might function most effectively.[11]

The commission reviewed the condition of the family and made recommendations in two areas. First, it suggested revisions in the substantive law of divorce, and second, it examined the feasibility of establishing a system of family courts.[12] The commission proposed legislation in the form of a model Family Court Act that would have created a family court, eliminated fault as a ground for divorce, and revised the community property distribution rules. The family court proposal included both the creation of a family court system and the establishment of procedures to encourage the parties to use the court's conciliation and counseling services.   The commission also recommended that dissolution of marriage should be granted whenever the court found that the legitimate objectives of the marriage had been destroyed and there was no reasonable likelihood that the marriage could be saved.[13]

The commission's standard derived from a 1952 case, *DeBurgh v. DeBurgh* in which the California Supreme Court overturned the long-standing rule that only an innocent party could obtain a divorce.[14] In that case, with both parties arguing that they had fault grounds for divorce, the court granted the divorce on the grounds that the legitimate objectives of the marriage had been destroyed. The commission recommended a shift from fault to need as a basis for financial settlements. Alimony and support were to be awarded based solely on the needs and circumstances of the parties, with no consideration of fault, and the community property was to be divided equally between the spouses.

Although the commission's recommendations were never enacted, they did serve as the main working model for bills introduced in the assembly and the senate during 1967.[15] The major objection raised to these bills was the potentially high cost of the counseling. No definitive action was taken on the bills in 1967, but they were reintroduced in 1968, when the California State Bar also became involved. It proposed alternate legislation with limited counseling and a family court system that was a division of the existing superior court's. The bar also recommended giving judges more discretion in property decisions. This proposal was rejected by the legislature.

James A. Hayes, a member of the Assembly Judiciary Committee, independently put together another proposal that eliminated the major cost-incurring features of a separate family court system and mandatory counseling structure, but kept the marriage breakdown theory of divorce, with an emphasis on voluntary counseling for the parties.[16] The Hayes bill, introduced in the 1968 session, also failed to pass.

In 1969, Hayes was appointed chairman of the Assembly Judiciary Committee, and he introduced AB 530, entitled the Domestic Relations Act of 1969, in which the only grounds for divorce were irreconcilable differences and incurable insanity. "Irreconcilable differences" were defined as those grounds that are determined by the court to be substantial reasons for not continuing the marriage and that have caused the irrevocable breakdown of the marriage. Essentially, the new Hayes bill would enact no-fault divorce without the protective setting of a specialized family court.[17] AB 530 did not pass, but a similar bill drafted by a conference committee made up of Assemblyman Hayes, the chairman of the Senate Judiciary Committee, and two additional members from the judiciary committee of each house was enacted as the Family Law Act of 1969.[18]

The new Family Law Act established two grounds for marital dissolution, "irreconcilable differences which have caused the irremediable breakdown of the marriage"[19] and incurable insanity.[20] Other changes emphasized a new orientation in divorce proceedings. The term "divorce" was replaced by "dissolution of marriage." A neutral petition form, "*In re the Marriage of Mrs. Smith and Mr. Smith*," replaced the adversarial "*Smith v. Smith*." The parties were called petitioner and respondent rather than plaintiff and defendant, and the pleadings were replaced by a standardized form that permitted the petitioner to select the type of proceeding--legal separation, dissolution, or nullity of marriage.

Under the prior law, the property division was unequal when the grounds for divorce were adultery, extreme cruelty, or incurable insanity, with the innocent party allocated a disproportionately large share of the community property. Under the new act, community property usually was to be divided equally, with no regard for fault, unless the division would impair the value of the property, such as a business, or when community funds had been deliberately squandered or misused by one spouse to the extent that an equal division of the remaining assets would no longer be equitable.[21]

Alimony was redefined as "support" and was to be determined by fairness rather than fault.[22] Fairness was based on three factors: (1) the duration of the marriage, (2) the ability of the supported spouse to engage in gainful employment, and (3) the economic condition of the parties. Child custody continued to be governed by the best interests of the child, but evidence could be presented on parental fault.

The act essentially pushed though the California legislature by Hayes was quite different from the 1966 proposals by the Governor's Commission on the Family. The major changes to the old rules were the elimination of the fault grounds for divorce and the requirement of an equal division of the community property; the new act had no provisions for a family court system or counseling. All the same, the legislation was viewed as path breaking. Lenore Weitzman identified six major innovations:

1. No grounds were needed to obtain a divorce.
2. Neither spouse had to prove fault or guilt to obtain a divorce.
3. One spouse could decide unilaterally to get a divorce without the consent or agreement of the other spouse.
4. Financial awards were no longer linked to fault.
5. New standards for alimony and property awards sought to treat men and women "equally," repudiating the traditional sex-based assumptions.[23]
6. The new procedures aimed at undermining the adversarial process and creating a social-psychological climate fostering amicable negotiations.[24]

The initial response was very favorable. Howard Krom wrote, "But above all, the legislators themselves, at least the members who worked toward and supported the development of the Act and it final adoption, deserve recognition for their courage in instituting a most necessary though highly controversial element of social reform."[25] He added, "It can be expected that the California reform will chart the path for the civilization of domestic relations law throughout the United States."[26] Stuart Brody asserted, "To their credit the California Legislature, by enacting the Family Law Act of 1969, has attempted to bring divorce laws more in line with reality and to reduce the hypocrisy of strict divorce laws administered by a lenient process."[27]

Problems developed when the courts attempted to interpret the new law, aided only by a legislative report drafted by Hayes after the act had been adopted.[28] This report suggested a connection between the act's financial provisions and the achievement of equality between women and men. Herma Hill Kay of the University of California, who had been a member of the Governor's Commission on the Family, argues that the theme of equality between men and women was introduced into the legislative history of the act for the first time after the act had been adopted.[29] Lenore Weitzman's research revealed that trial court judges were interpreting the Family Law Act based on Hayes's idea of equality developed in the legislative report.[30]

Throughout the deliberations, no-fault had broad support.[31] Because the governor's commission's goal was viewed as a reform, groups that would normally have been antagonistic, such as the Catholic church, were supportive: The efforts were viewed as being aimed at preserving the family and minimizing the opportunities for divorce. Throughout the legislative proceedings, the most vocal proponents of a shift to no-fault divorce were groups of divorced men.[32] Initially, no feminist groups existed to participate in the deliberations, but as women became aware of the movement for no-fault divorce, many supported the idea. The California Commission on the Status of Women supported the removal of fault from divorce as a desirable elimination of hypocrisy in the legal system.[33]

The no-fault divorce movement was not unique to California. The Commissioners on Uniform State Laws conducted a study of the fault divorce laws in 1968 and recommended a uniform divorce statute that contained irretrievable breakdown of the marriage as the sole ground for divorce.[34] Reformers both in California and the nation at large were preoccupied with the question of fault and its role in both obtaining a divorce and securing a financial settlement. Few thought about the consequences of the new system or foresaw how its fault-neutral rules could work to the disadvantage of divorced women, but as no-fault laws were enacted across the United States, people started to become aware that the idea had fundamental flaws.[35] Observers argued that new financial provisions were needed to accompany the no-fault laws in order to protect divorced women and children of divorced parents.[36]

There was a feeling that the reformers and the legislators had proceeded with the best intentions, but somehow the process had produced less than ideal results. An economic analysis of the introduction of no-fault suggests the parties had less innocent motives.

The Economic Perspective on the Introduction of No-Fault

The economic perspective on the introduction of no-fault divorce recognizes that there was a growing demand for easier procedures for obtaining a divorce in the period after World War II. The specific legislative response to those pressures reflects the self-interest of the elected officials, focused on the response that the legislators feel is most likely to ensure their reelection. Moreover, some legislators may find that they can initiate legislation that will produce direct benefits for themselves.

The Demand for Reform

Without a demand for reform, there would have been no incentive for the legislators to act. Divorce becomes more attractive for a married couple when either the gain from marriage decreases or the uncertainty of expected outcomes during marriage increases. Although the divorce rate has been increasing for most of this century, Victor Fuchs identified some unusual changes that occurred during the period between 1965 and 1975 and contributed to a rapid increase in the divorce rate.[37] These included economic changes such as the growth of real earnings and the increase in government entitlement programs; technological changes such as the expanded availability of contraception; and social and cultural changes, including feminist ideology and widespread criticism of traditional institutions and norms.

The growth in the wages available to women increased the divorce rate because it tended to reduce the gains from marriage. Higher wages are an inducement for married women to work outside the home, reducing specialization by both spouses. Evidence that the causality runs from wives' working to divorce is the fact that the rise in the labor force participation of married women with small children preceded the rise in the divorce rate by several years.[38] Enhanced social programs provided married women with still more flexibility: The large increase in Aid to Families with Dependent Children (AFDC) payments, the relaxation of eligibility requirements, and the growth of other economic subsidies during this period increased the options for women who found themselves in unsatisfactory marriages.

Improvements in contraception were identified by Robert Michael as an important source of the increase in the demand for divorce.[39] Contraceptives made it easier to reduce the number of children per couple, and children are both the cause and effect of a stable marriage. Children can cause a marriage not only for the traditional moral reasons, but also because their arrival increases the need for one of the parents to increase specialization in household production. As this specialization may not be in that party's best interest if the relationship is dissolved, it creates pressures for that party to seek the protection traditionally provided by marriage. Also, people who feel that they have desirable spouses are more likely to make the commitment reflected in children. A reduction in fertility would be expected to increase the divorce rate, and fertility did fall during this period, with its decline preceding the increase in divorce by several years. Contraceptives also reduced uncertainty about subsequent fertility, thus encouraging women to focus more on their careers and to increase their economic independence, again resulting in less specialization within marriage. Finally, contraceptives decreased inhibitions concerning extramarital sex, by reducing the risk of pregnancy; this reduced the cost of searching for a better spouse even during marriage.

Some authors have found that changes in the economic and social status of women during this period led to more female-headed households, with a resulting increase in both divorce and births to unmarried women.[40] Certainly, any rapid change in social values will tend to be disruptive for marriages and increase the divorce rate.

Trends during this period tended to reduce the gains from marriage as well as creating more uncertain outcomes during marriage. The result was an increase in the demand for easier procedures for dissolving marriages. The perjury and fabricated testimony observed in the courts were evidence of this shift. In the face of this increased demand for new procedures for divorce, the state of California considered a range of options when it revised its divorce laws. Some of the possibilities discussed were a family court system, counseling, equal division of property, and more relaxed grounds for divorce, but only the last two were enacted into law. Some observers might conclude that the others were lacking in merit--that elected officials considered the options and in their wisdom decided that a more limited divorce reform act would best serve the public interest.

Public Choice

Public Choice presents the alternate explanation of the elected officials operating in their self-interest rather than the public interest. One aspect of self-interest is a focus on the issues that an individual finds important. Although divorce reform was undoubtedly important to Governor Brown, many professionals concerned with the issue, and some legislators, most legislators probably had other issues that they considered much more important. The bill that passed the California legislature hardly reflected the collective wisdom of that body. A better explanation for the passage of that particular bill is that it contained the provisions for which there was a strong constituency. The family court system and counseling had great appeal for academics, but only the change in the grounds for divorce and the financial arrangements had a strongly motivated constituency: men. The histories of this legislation identify male groups, especially divorced men, as attacking the fault-based divorce law and its financial provisions. Although the fault-based divorce laws gave substantial negotiating power to women that would be lost if the grounds were removed, the histories do not suggest that this concern was expressed with much vigor during the deliberations. Some very critical issues were ignored. For example, no one appears to have questioned whether the legal definition of property subject to division at the dissolution of a marriage was accurate.

Every movement needs a leader. Often the question *ex post* is whether the leader made the revolution, or the revolution made the leader. Pressures existed for change. The individual who recognized those pressures and used them to create a revolution was Assemblyman James Hayes. Often ignored in the histories of the development of no-fault divorce in California was the special interest that Hayes brought to his advocacy of no-fault.

James A. Hayes was involved in a bitter divorce action during the evolution of no-fault in the California legislature. His divorce case was initially filed in 1966.[41] James and Janne Hayes had married in 1941 when they were nineteen-year-old college students. Except for a brief Christmas job during the first year of the marriage, Janne Hayes never worked outside the home. They had four children. After twenty-five years of marriage, the last few of which were reported to be stormy, Janne Hayes filed for divorce under the existing fault divorce laws.[42] A final decree, including a negotiated property settlement, was approved by the court in 1969. Janne Hayes was awarded the family home and custody of the two minor children. In addition, she was to receive $650 per month in alimony until her death or remarriage and $175 per month child support until the children became adults. James Hayes was awarded his law practice.

In 1972, Hayes filed a petition to end his financial obligations to his wife and children based on the argument that his financial condition had changed. His financial situation was complicated by his having remarried. Hayes's brief in support of his request included a quotation from the 1969 California Assembly Judiciary Committee Report on the new California Family Law Act, which he helped write. Part of the quotation included:

> When our divorce law was originally drawn, woman's role in society was almost totally that of mother and homemaker, She could not even vote. Today, increasing numbers of married women are employed, even in the professions. In addition, they have long been accorded full civil rights. Their approaching equality with the male should be reflected in the law governing marriage dissolution and in the decisions of courts with respect to matters incident to dissolution.[43]

When the judge's decision was handed down in March, 1973, James Hayes prevailed. Child support was ended and alimony gradually reduced to $300 per month. A year later, Hayes returned to court. His monthly expenses had increased because of the purchase of a new house. The mortgage on the house in conjunction with the payments on his country home came to over $2,000 per month. He again triumphed in court. The *Los Angeles Times* reported, "Los Angeles County Supervisor James A.

Hayes, 53, who earns $40,322 a year but complains that his expenses are nearly double his net income, was successful Tuesday in his bid to reduce the alimony he pays to his first wife, Mrs. Janne M. Hayes, 53. Superior Judge Julius A. Title lowered the payment from $300 to $200 monthly and told Mrs. Hayes, who complains of asthma and back pains, to get a job."[44]

On October 3, 1975, the Court of Appeals overruled the 1973 decision holding that the original agreement was not subject to modification. The court noted that even if the agreement had been modifiable, "The reduction in support made by the trial court appears to constitute an abuse of discretion."[45] Hayes then returned to court arguing that the original agreement was a "mutual mistake." In March, 1976, Janne Hayes's demurrer was sustained based on the prior court proceedings, but James Hayes continued to fight the financial obligations to his wife.

During the deliberations that resulted in the no-fault statute being enacted in California, Hayes was obviously not a casual observer. He was instrumental in enacting no-fault divorce in California; after its passage, in the report that rationalized its passage, he emphasized the equality between men and women. He then used the law and the report to attempt to reduce the financial arrangements that he had agreed to as a condition for his divorce. When Janne Hayes filed for divorce in 1966, she was forty-four years old. She had had one year of college twenty-five years earlier. Compared with the position that she would have been in if she had not specialized in being a housewife and mother, she was much worse off. The financial arrangements that they negotiated do not appear to be excessively generous to Janne Hayes.

In most histories of the passage of the law, James Hayes's role is given only passing notice. If anything, he is pictured as a very active public servant. But, the passage of no-fault in California bears witness to the process of legislative self-interest. This is not a well-intentioned law that innocent people permitted to go astray. This is a law that was passed by a male-dominated legislature in a process of benign neglect reenforced by the lobbying efforts of male interest groups and maneuvered through the California legislature by a man who personally had a great deal to gain from a reduction in the negotiating power of married women.

Public Choice predicts that special interest groups will attempt to sell their proposals as benefiting the groups that are eventually adversely affected. Many proponents of reform argued, and undoubtedly many believed, that "equality" would be beneficial for divorced women. The problem with the passage of no-fault was not so much the new grounds as the lack of recognition of the critical relationship between the grounds for divorce and the financial arrangements after divorce. James Hayes and the male advocates of no-fault were able to pass it because this link was not recognized. As is so often the case, the political process was oriented toward a vague notion of equity with little concern for efficiency.

The proponents of no-fault objected to the hypocrisy of the fault-based divorces without understanding that the fault grounds themselves were not particularly relevant: Their importance lay in their forcing the parties to negotiate a dissolution. Divorce in effect was based on mutual consent, and because most divorces involving substantial property under the fault grounds were negotiated, the legal definition of property had not been closely scrutinized.

The fault divorce laws were not perfect, but the no-fault divorce laws enacted in California and the other states have not been an obvious improvement. The problems with no-fault occur because the interrelationship among laws was not recognized. This is especially true of the connection between the grounds for divorce and the financial arrangements at divorce. Under fault divorce, the legally defined financial arrangements served a minor role compared with the agreements worked out by the parties privately; relaxing the grounds for divorce shifted the emphasis in dissolution cases in California to the financial arrangements based on the legal requirements of an equal division of community property. A second-best situation deteriorated into a third-best situation.

Second Best

The concept of second best states that if one of the conditions necessary for a perfect outcome cannot be fulfilled, then the best attainable outcome (the second best) can, in general, only be achieved by departing from all the other optimal conditions. Within the framework of efficiency, the best divorce law probably should have three components. First, the law would contain low-cost procedures for dissolving marriages that are no longer efficient. No-fault would be a reasonable standard for those procedures. Second, the law would allocate property based on the effect of marriage on the property. Property unaffected by marriage, separate property, should be returned to its owner, but property created by the joint efforts of the spouses, marital property, should be divided between the spouses. Last, a spouse desiring a divorce should be confronted with the true costs of the divorce. No-fault has produced less than desirable results because property is not properly defined and divorcing spouses are not confronted with the true costs of divorce.

With hypocritical grounds and inappropriate property awards, especially for the spouse who specialized in household production, fault divorce may have been a second-best solution to the increased demand for easier divorce procedures. The fault divorce laws essentially provided for specific performance of marital contracts. If those contracts had been strictly enforced, as in Great Britain before 1857, the outcomes would have been highly inefficient. But, the courts were willing to permit parties to reach negotiated settlements. If the party who wanted to dissolve the marriage wanted the dissolution more than the other party wanted to maintain the marriage, then an agreement was reached that dissolved the marriage. The fault grounds gave the party who did not want the divorce, often the wife, negotiating power. She usually was able to extract an acceptable agreement from her spouse. The upper limit on her ability to extract an acceptable agreement was the alternatives available to the husband for dissolving the marriage.

The fault grounds for divorce gave individuals who did not want to dissolve a marriage bargaining power, but this power was not absolute. At some cost, a divorce could be obtained in another state with more liberal laws. In Nevada, for example, one of the grounds for divorce was, "When the husband and wife have lived separate and apart for one year without cohabitation, the court may, in its discretion, grant an absolute decree of divorce at the suit of either party."[46] An uncooperative spouse could be harassed or even abandoned. Although the claims of the male advocacy groups were worthy of concern, it is not clear how many wives under fault divorce received compensation at divorce that exceeded the loss that they were about to experience due to the dissolution of their marriage.

Fault divorce may have been a second-best solution, but no-fault can only be described as third best. The shift from fault to no-fault essentially shifted the remedy in divorce cases from specific performance with the possibility of a negotiated settlement to damages based on reliance.[47] No-fault divorce has resulted in an equal division of marital property, spousal support based on fairness, and child custody based on the best interest of the child. If these rules accurately reflect the reliance costs incurred by the parties who do not want the dissolutions, then people will be encouraged to make welfare-increasing decisions. The parties can increase their specialization during marriage with the knowledge that any sacrifices will be compensated at divorce. In addition, the divorce will tend to occur only when the collective benefits exceed the costs; with an accurate measure of the reliance costs of marriage to the potentially divorced spouse, efficient outcomes are more likely. If the courts understate the reliance costs incurred by the parties, however, the outcomes will tend to be inefficient.

It is difficult to place a monetary value on these decisions, but monetary units can be used here for illustrative purposes. Let us say that the spouse who wants to dissolve the marriage values that alternative at $10,000, and the loss that will be incurred by the other spouse, who relied on the continuation of the marriage, is $20,000; under these circumstances, social welfare is improved by continuing the marriage. This is a situation that can occur later in a marriage because of the timing of the typical contributions of men and women to marriage. If the financial transfer required by law from the divorcing spouse to the divorced spouse is only $5,000, that divorcing spouse will make that payment and dissolve the marriage. The outcome will be inefficient in that the collective benefits do not exceed the collective costs. This may be a common situation, as the financial loss of the divorced spouse who has specialized in household production during the marriage has not been recognized in any systematic way by the courts under the no-fault divorce laws.

Not only is the outcome inefficient and unfair, it has undesirable long-term effects. Men and women marry because they anticipate that they will gain from that arrangement. Some of the benefits of that arrangement flow from their increasing their specialization during marriage. The responsibilities that follow from parenthood contribute to the trend toward additional specialization by spouses, for example, as it is usually difficult or financially unrealistic for the parents to assume equal responsibilities for child rearing. Therefore, one spouse has to increase his or her specialization in that role compared with other potential roles--an increase that leaves that spouse vulnerable later in the marriage.[48] That decision was made by married women during most of the history of the United States based on the assumption that the divorce laws protected them from the opportunistic behavior of their husbands.

No-fault divorce changed that situation. Spouses who committed themselves to specialized roles as housewives and mothers during marriage discovered that they had less protection. Women who married with the expectation of this protection were made worse off, incurring a cost in the form of a reduced future income-earning capacity for which there was little compensation if they were divorced. Many men who divorced under no-fault were made better off relative to the negotiated settlements they would have been forced to make under fault-based divorce.

The gains experienced by these men occurred because of the change in the law, not the law itself. Married women specialized in household production because they thought that the divorce laws would continue to protect them. When they discovered that the laws would not protect them, many of them changed their behavior. Women started to recognize that the losses that they incurred when they specialized in household production were not the basis of adequate compensation. They rationally reduced their specialization in that activity. More married women chose to work outside the home and maintain their marketable skills. In addition, more married women went back to school during marriage to increase or maintain their human capital. As women thus adapted to the new legal environment, opportunistic behavior by men became more difficult.

The decisions by married women to increase their labor market participation and education can result in an overall reduction in the welfare of their families as illustrated in the following example: A married woman recognizes that a decision to specialize in household production during marriage will reduce her human capital by $200,000 at age forty-five due to the lower earnings that she can expect after that age compared with the income that she could earn if she focused on her career. She does not expect to divorce, but she knows that it is a possibility and that the financial arrangements under no-fault divorce provide very little compensation for her sacrifice. The services that she would provide her family by working at home are worth $25,000 a year. The financial and psychic income from her best employment opportunity after adjustment for taxes and job-related expenses come to only $15,000, but she still has an incentive to work outside the home--employment outside the home will assist her in increasing or maintaining her human capital.[49]

Overall, the family would be better off if the wife's loss due to working in the home was protected by the law. Then both spouses could focus on their comparative advantages, which might still involve both working in the home and at a job, but the spouse with the lower earning capacity probably would tend to specialize more in household production.

Conclusion

The current no-fault laws can best be described as third-best laws. First-best laws would encourage efficient outcomes at divorce. Because the fault divorce laws were potentially costly and hypocritical, they were a second-best alternative. They did have the advantage of forcing the parties to recognize more of the costs incurred by older married women at divorce. No-fault divorce laws with inaccurate estimates of the costs of divorce are third-best laws. The change in the laws necessary to arrive at the best outcome will be discussed in the last chapter. In the meantime, no-fault has had numerous effects on individual decisions, which will be the subject of the next chapter.

Notes

1. A reform movement was occurring in other jurisdictions. In England, the Archbishop of Canterbury appointed a group in 1964 to investigate the divorce laws in England. It issued a report, *Putting Asunder: A Divorce Law for Contemporary Society* (London: SPCK, 1966), that recommended the replacement of fault with no-fault grounds for divorce. New York, which had one of the most restrictive divorce laws in the country, also moved toward reform: In 1966, New York enacted a divorce reform bill that added other fault grounds for divorce to the single existing ground of adultery. The reduction in the waiting period for a divorce based on separation in New York was reduced to one year by legislation enacted in 1968 and 1970. In effect, New York enacted no-fault divorce. See Lynn D. Wardle, "No-Fault Divorce and the Divorce Conundrum," *Brigham Young University Law Review*, Vol. 1991, No. 1, pp. 79-142.

2. Richard Posner, *The Economic Analysis of Law*, 3d ed. (Boston: Little, Brown, 1986), p. 495.

3. Ibid.

4. Some of the sources reviewing the development of California's no-fault divorce laws are contained in Herma Hill Kay, "Equality and Difference: A Perspective on No-Fault Divorce and Its Aftermath," *University of Cincinnati Law Review,* Vol. 56, No. 1, 1987, pp. 1-90; Herma Hill Kay, "An Appraisal of California's No-Fault Divorce Law," *California Law Review,* Vol. 75, 1987, pp. 291-319; Howard Krom, "California's Divorce Law Reform: An Historical Analysis," *Pacific Law Journal,* Vol. 1, No. 1, 1970, pp. 156-181; Lenore J. Weitzman, *The Divorce Revolution* (New York: Free Press, 1985); and Michael Wheeler, *No-Fault Divorce* (Boston: Beacon, 1974).

5. Uniform Marriage and Divorce Act § 305, 9A U.L.A. 91, 132-3 (1979). The reporter for the Uniform Marriage and Divorce Act presented his reflections on the intentions of the drafters of the uniform act in Robert J. Levy, "A Reminiscence About the Uniform Marriage and Divorce Act--And Some Reflections About Its Critics and Its Politics," *Brigham Young University Law Review,* Vol. 1991, No. 1, pp. 43-78.

6. Lynne Carol Halem, *Divorce Reform* (New York: Free Press, 1980), p. 250. Although all states now permit divorce on no-fault grounds, some states also permit dissolution by an affidavit procedure when there is mutual consent to the divorce. Mutual consent divorce is also available in some states when the marriage is of short duration and without children, there is no maintenance request, and there is an agreement concerning property division. See Doris Jonas Freed and Timothy B. Walker, "Family Law in the Fifty States: An Overview," *Family Law Quarterly,* Vol. 23, Winter 1990, p. 514. Also see Bureau of Vital Statistics, California Department of Public Health, *Divorce in California: Initial Complaints for Divorce, Annulment and Separate Maintenance 1966,* 1967, p. 14.

7. The "Report of the Governor's Commission on the Family," Sacramento, CA, December, 1966, pp. 30-31 found that 94 percent of divorce proceedings in California were uncontested.

8. Wheeler, *No-Fault,* p. 138.

9. Halem, *Divorce Reform,* p. 239.

10. "Report of the Governor's Commission," pp. 145-147.

11. Ibid., p. 1.

12. Ibid., p. 60. Herma Hill Kay provides the insights of one of the commission members in "A Family Court: The California Proposal," *California Law Review,* Vol. 56, No. 5, October 1968, pp. 1205-1248. In contrast to Kay's academic view, John Goddard, Commissioner of the Los Angeles County Superior Court, was concerned about the effect of the commission's proposals on the financial condition of divorced women. See John Leslie Goddard, "The Proposal for Divorce Upon Petition and Without Fault," *Journal of the State Bar of California,* Vol. 43, 1968, pp. 90-102.

13. "Report of the Governor's Commission," p. 91.

14. 39 Cal. 2d 858 (1952).

15. *Journal of the California Assembly,* pp. 8054-8055 (Reg. Sess., 1969).

16. Krom, "Divorce Law Reform," p. 173.

17. Kay, "Equality," p. 39.

18. Hayes defended the new California law in James A. Hayes, "California Divorcee Reform: Parting is Sweeter Sorrow," *American Bar Association Journal,* Vol. 56, July 1970, pp. 660-663. Hayes emphasized that equality between men and women was one of the goals of the legislature in enacting this legislation.

19. Cal. Civ. Code, § 4506(1).

20. Cal. Civ. Code, § 4506(2).

21. This was viewed as a substantial change from the existing law. See William E. MacFaden, "California's New Divorce Legislation," *Journal of the Beverly Hills Bar Association,* Vol. 3, No. 7, September 1969, pp. 31-36.

22. Commentators at the time of the passage of the act questioned whether the courts would be willing to award substantial support except in unusual situations. See Stuart A. Brody, "California's Divorce Reform: Its Sociological Implications," *Pacific Law Journal,* Vol. 1, No. 1, 1970, pp. 223-232.

23. Whether the act was intended to create equality between men and women has been hotly contested. Herma Hill Kay, who was active in the development of the divorce law reform, argues that Lenore Weitzman was ill informed and that the idea of equality was introduced in the assembly report by Assemblyman Hayes after the act had been passed. See Kay, "Equality," p. 3.

24. Weitzman, *Divorce Revolution,* p. 15.

25. Krom, "Divorce Law Reform," p. 181.

26. Ibid.

27. Brody, "California's Divorce Reform," p. 231.

28. Kay, "Equality," p. 42.

29. Ibid., p. 3.

30. Ibid., p. 44.

31. Krom, "Divorce Law Reform," p. 158.

32. Kay, "Equality," p. 56.

33. "Report of the Advisory Commission on the Status of Women," *California Woman,* 1969, pp. 79-80.

34. Robert Levy, *Uniform Marriage and Divorce Legislation: A Preliminary Analysis* (Chicago: American Bar Association, 1968).

35. Weitzman, *Divorce Revolution,* p. 19.

36. Kay, "Equality," p. 57.

37. Victor R. Fuchs, *How We Live* (Cambridge, MA: Harvard University Press, 1983), p. 150.

38. Ibid., p. 149.

39. Robert T. Michael, "The Rise in Divorce Rates, 1960-1974: Age-Specific Components," *Demography,* Vol. 15, No. 2, May 1978, pp. 345-347.

40. Heather L. Ross and Isabel V. Sawhill, *Time of Transition: The Growth of Families Headed by Women* (Washington, DC: Urban Institute, 1975).

41. Hayes v. Hayes, D700 518, Superior Court, Los Angeles, CA, November 6, 1969. For a discussion of the Hayes case, see Riane Tennenhaus Eisler, *Dissolution, No-Fault Divorce, Marriage, and the Future of Women* (New York: McGraw-Hill, 1977), pp. 24-31 and Weitzman, *Divorce Revolution,* pp. 211-212.

42. It was the common practice under fault divorce for the wife to file for divorce even when she was not the party who initially requested the divorce. Since the grounds for divorce required the defendant to be at fault, the normal outcome of the negotiations was for the wife to file the complaint.

43. "Assembly Committee Report on Assembly Bill No. 530 and Senate Bill 252 (The Family Law Act)," submitted by Committee on Judiciary, James A. Hayes, Chairman, on August 8, 1969, printed in *Assembly Daily Journal,* August 8, 1969, as

quoted in Respondent's Opening Points and Authorities, Order to Show Cause, Hayes v. Hayes, D700 518, filed December 13, 1972.

44. "Hayes' Ex-Wife Seeks Welfare, Food Stamps," *Los Angeles Times,* June 6, 1975.

45. Hayes v. Hayes, Court of Appeals of the State of California, Second Appellate District, Division Five, 2d Civil No. 45168, October 3, 1975 (unpublished opinion), pp. 27-28.

46. Doris J. Freed, "Grounds for Divorce in the American Jurisdictions," *Family Law Quarterly,* Vol. 6, No. 2, Summer 1972, p. 178.

47. For the argument that a central historical theme underlying marriage and divorce has been the protection of the reliance interest in marriage, see Margaret F. Brinig and June Carbone, "The Reliance Interest in Marriage and Divorce," *Tulane Law Review,* Vol 62, 1988, pp. 870-882. Damages in a breach of contract case can be based on expectations, reliance, restitution, or liquidated damages. The effects of these different standards on whether outcomes are efficient are discussed in A. Mitchell Polinsky, *An Introduction to Law and Economics,* 2d ed. (Boston: Little, Brown, 1989), pp. 27-38 and 59-65. An expectation standard for damages tends to produce more efficient breaches than a reliance standard, but a restitution standard is more likely than a reliance standard to induce an efficient amount of reliance under a contract. The concepts of efficient breach and efficient reliance will be discussed in more detail in Chapter 6.

48. Some authors have argued that employment is an important source of power during marriage. Male dominance is stronger in marriages in which the wife is exclusively a housewife than when she is employed outside the home. See Paula England and George Farkas, *Households, Employment, and Gender* (New York: Aldine De Gruyter, 1986), p. 54.

49. For some people, the psychic income from jobs can be important. But, it can also be overstated. The labor force participation rate of married men over sixty-five decreased from 37 percent to 18 percent during the period 1960 to 1988. *Statistical Abstract of the United States, 1990* (Washington, DC: Government Printing Office, 1990), Table 634, p. 384. Obviously, many married men were not receiving substantial psychic income from their jobs as more of them chose leisure over work as retirement benefits rose.

5

The Impact of
No-Fault Divorce

In the period since World War II, U.S. society has undergone dramatic changes. The introduction of no-fault grounds for divorce has played a central, and often unrecognized, role in those changes. Of particular importance has been the reduction in the stability of marriage. The rising divorce rate and pressure for simpler procedures for dissolving marriages led to no-fault divorce. The introduction of no-fault divorce, in turn, has had feedback effects that have made a major contribution to the changes.

The role of no-fault divorce in the changes that we have observed since World War II is the subject of this chapter. Individuals alter their prior decisions when their tastes and preferences shift or the costs or benefits associated with the activities change. Tastes and preferences tend to change only slowly, and the following discussion focuses on the more rapid effects of changes in the costs and benefits of activities. Many trends in U.S. society since 1970 can be linked to no-fault divorce. Because of no-fault, people have done things that they would not have done if the divorce laws had not changed. Many of these effects are subtle. The discussion will include changes in the divorce rate, the financial condition of divorced women and children of divorced parents, the definition of property subject to division at divorce, the incentive to marry, the incentive for married women to work outside the home and continue their education, and the quality of life for them and their families. We will see that not only did people change their behavior, but often they found themselves worse off than under fault divorce. An inescapable conclusion is that no-fault divorce has reduced the quality of family life for many people, both men and women.

The Divorce Rate

The stability of marriage in the United States has declined dramatically since World War II. The annual divorce rate for married women rose from 10.3 per 1,000 in 1950 to 20.8 per 1,000 in 1987 after peaking at 22.8 per 1,000 in 1979, as shown in Table 5.1.[1] The divorce rate doubled between 1965 and 1975. Whether the increase in the divorce rate caused no-fault divorce or whether the causation ran in the opposite direction has been the source of some debate. Certainly, new laws can alter human behavior, but the laws themselves often reflect legislators' attempts to respond to changes in basic socioeconomic forces. Both effects may have been present with no-fault divorce.[2] As the divorce rate was increasing before the introduction of no-fault divorce, it is difficult to escape the conclusion that some causation went from the increase in the divorce rate to the introduction of no-fault divorce laws.[3] That is not to say that the introduction of no-fault divorce laws had no feedback effect.

The increase in the demand for simpler divorce procedures was caused by marriage becoming a less attractive institution. People marry because they expect to be better off in that state than single. They divorce if this expectation turns out to be false. This can occur when there is either an unexpected reduction in the gains from marriage or an unexpected decline in the predictability of outcomes during marriage--both of which happened after World War II. The gains from marriage declined because of the reduction in the incentives for spouses to specialize during marriage and the predictability of outcomes decreased because of the rapid changes that were occurring in U.S. society. The effect of these changes on divorce was not broadly recognized at the time.

The Reduction in the Gains from Marriage

Marriage is an attractive institution for both spouses so long as both expect to be better off married than single. A significant share of the benefits of marriage, in contrast to dating or living together, flows from an increase in the specialization of labor during marriage. People become more efficient by focusing their energies on one or a limited range of activities. This specialization results in people having too much of some goods and too little of others and therefore becomes more attractive when there are opportunities for trade. During marriage, the husband traditionally increased his specialization in the production of earnings, while the wife increased her specialization in activities in the home. Through an exchange of their outputs during marriage, both spouses were better off.

When women were confronted with low wages and limited employment opportunities, marriage with specialization in household production was a rational choice for essentially all adult women. Conditions changed when

TABLE 5.1 Divorce Rates and Related Data

Year	Divorce Rate for Married Women[a]	Average Hourly Earnings[b]	Ratio Male/ Female Earnings[c]	Births[e]
1950	10.3	$5.34		24.1
1955	9.3	6.15	.639	25.0
1960	9.2	6.79	.603[d]	23.7
1965	10.6	7.52	.599	19.4
1970	14.9	8.03	.600[d]	18.4
1975	20.3	8.12	.588	14.6
1980	22.6	7.78	.594[d]	15.9
1985	21.7	7.77	.646	15.8
1987	20.8	7.73		15.7
1990		7.54		

[a]Per thousand.
[b]1982 dollars.
[c]Median year round.
[d]Average of adjacent years.
[e]Rate per thousand population.

Sources: Divorce rate, average earnings and births from *Statistical Abstract of the United States* (Washington, DC: Government Printing Office, various years). Male and female earnings from Claudia Goldin, *Understanding the Gender Gap*, (New York: Oxford University Press, 1990), pp. 60-61.

wages and opportunities available to women increased. After adjustment for inflation, in 1982 dollars the average hourly real wage rose from $5.34 in 1950 to $7.78 in 1980 and then fell slightly through most of the 1980s.[4] (See Table 5.1.) The real wage can be used to convert the time spent working at home into purchasing power--the ability to buy a larger house, for example, or more restaurant meals. Higher wages therefore create an incentive for families to decide that the value of the goods that the people who would otherwise work at home can generate through outside employment exceeds the value of at least some commodities that these people can produce in the home. In fact, the labor force participation rate of married women rose from 24 percent in 1950 to 58 percent in 1989.[5]

When both spouses increase the amount of time they work outside the home, the specialization of labor during marriage is reduced. Based on data from 1975-1976, Janice Peskin reported that women not otherwise employed provided 42.6 hours per week of household services; women who were employed full-time outside the home provided 20.1 hours.[6] Women working full-time outside the home worked less in the home than women not otherwise employed, but the hours worked outside the home by these women did not result in a corresponding reduction in their work at home. Victor Fuchs observed the work habits of women in 1960 and 1986 and noted a similar pattern over time. He found that women worked less at home as they increased the hours they worked outside the home,[7] but overall they ended up working 7 percent more hours in 1986 than in 1960. Although the specialization between men and women during marriage has decreased, there has been an increase in the specialization among women. Between 1960 and 1986, married women reduced their annual hours of housework by 200 hours, but men only increased their annual hours of housework by 3 hours. Some responsibility for household services shifted to other women, who provided, for example, day care or cleaning services.[8]

An unexpected result of this decrease in the specialization between husbands and wives can be a decline in the gains from marriage. This is especially true because higher wages for women reduce the incentive for couples to have children. A rise in the wages available to women increases the cost of children because the mother has to leave the labor force to deliver the child. In addition, at least one parent usually has to limit his or her employment to help in the raising of the child. This has traditionally been the mother because the wages available to women tend to be less than those available to men.   For example, during the period before the introduction of no-fault divorce laws, the average wage of females was approximately 60 percent of the average wage of males.[9] Table 5.1 shows that as females' wages rose, the fertility rate fell. Between 1950 and 1970, the number of births per thousand population fell from 24.1 to 18.4,[10] and continued to fall to 14.6 in 1975, when the maturation of the baby boom generation started to reverse the trend. The desire for children historically has been a primary reason that people marry; as the demand for children fell, so did the gains from marriage.

The higher wages and broader employment opportunities available to women had both a direct and an indirect effect on gains from marriage. The direct effect came from higher wages raising the opportunity cost of either spouse working at home. The upshot was an increase in the percentage of married women working outside the home and a corresponding decrease in their specialization in domestic activities. There is also an indirect effect on the incentive to specialize in domestic production from higher wages decreasing the demand for children. With fewer children, there is less to be gained from either spouse working in the home.

A reduction in the gains from marriage should not necessarily affect the divorce rate. If the reduction is anticipated it should lead to fewer but equally stable marriages. The divorce rate increases when the change in the gains from marriage is unexpected. Marriage traditionally has been a long-term arrangement and the higher wages and broader range of employment opportunities that became available to women after World War II were not contemplated at the time of many marriages. As married women entered the labor force in response to the unexpected employment opportunities, they reduced their specialization in household production. As many couples had not anticipated this change when they married, their marriages became vulnerable with a resulting increase in the number of married people who wanted a divorce.

The Predictability of Outcomes During Marriage

Rapid changes in society in the postwar period also affected the predictability of the outcomes that people experienced during marriage. Higher wages and the growth of the service sector after World War II led to more females being employed and wives becoming less financially dependant on their husbands. The increased availability of contraceptives changed sexual habits. At the same time, the fertility rate continued to fall. Few of these changes were anticipated.

People enter marriage with a set of expectations that are the basis of the decision to marry. If the expectations are realized, the marriage is likely to continue, but when actual events during marriage differ from the expectations, the marriage becomes vulnerable. For example, a woman may marry because she feels that her employment possibilities are limited and a marriage proposal has come from an acceptable man. If she later discovers that attractive jobs arc available for women, she may decide that she is better off divorced and employed than married to this person. This is especially likely to occur if her husband married with the expectation that his wife would be a housewife and mother.

The reduction in the gains from marriage and the predictability of outcomes during marriage made marriage a less attractive institution for many people--some of whom were already married. In some cases, the reaction to these changes was a desire for a divorce. The fault grounds for divorce made divorce difficult, though not impossible; the increased desire for divorce was accompanied by an increase in the demand for simpler procedures for dissolving marriages.

The Affect of No-Fault Divorce

No-fault divorce appears thus to have been partly a response to the demand for simpler procedures for dissolving marriages, but it also may have had a feedback effect on the divorce rate by reducing the transaction costs incurred by the parties to a divorce. These costs consist of the expenses incurred in acquiring a divorce that reduce one party's welfare without necessarily increasing the other's welfare and can consist of the social stigma associated with divorce as well as the negotiation and litigation expenses.

If one believes that the legal grounds for divorce under fault divorce controlled whether a marriage was dissolved, then one probably would conclude that simpler grounds such as no-fault divorce would lead to a higher divorce rate. There is evidence, however, that the legal grounds for divorce under fault were not a major impediment to the dissolution of marriages. Mary Ann Glendon found that negotiation was the primary mechanism under fault divorce for settling disputes about property, spousal and child support, and child custody.[11] Settlements were reached when the party wanting a divorce could offer the other party compensation adequate to induce him or her to participate in the dissolution of the marriage. Thus a divorce tended to occur only when both parties expected to be better off divorced than in their current marriage. The divorced spouse might have preferred the continuation of a "happy marriage," but that situation was probably no longer an option. Thus even the spouse unwilling to divorce, if sufficiently compensated, could be better off divorced than continuing with the situation in the current marriage.

No-fault divorce reduced the bargaining power of spouses who did not want to divorce, with the potential of shifting some costs of divorce from the divorcing spouses to the divorced spouses. It is not clear, however, if this affected the divorce rate. Observers have argued that when transaction costs are low, the same divorces might occur under no-fault divorce as would have occurred under fault.[12] With low transaction costs, the major difference between the legal environments would be the financial settlement: It would be expected to be smaller under no-fault divorce for the spouse who preferred to continue the marriage.

This process can be illustrated with a numerical example. Although physical attraction is an important factor in people's choice of a particular person for dating, as I have noted earlier, the decision for two people to marry rather than continue to date or live together tends to be based on an expected increase in the welfare of both due to marriage. This increase has been presented in the context of the commodities that would be available during marriage, including a house, home-cooked meals, and children. Divorce often occurs when the parties later reject their initial expectations. New information causes them to reevaluate their marriages. For simplicity, let us assume that the commodities produced during marriage are divisible.[13] First, consider a situation in which the husband expects 50 units if he remains in his current marriage sharing his income with his family, and 100 units if he divorces and gains sole control over most if not all of his income. The wife expects 50 units if she remains married and 25 units if she divorces. If a divorce requires mutual consent, as was the situation under fault, the husband might offer the wife 30 units if she will consent to the divorce. The husband will then have 70 units if he divorces, which is better than the 50 he expects from marriage, and the wife will have 55 units, which is more than the 50 units that she receives from staying married. They divorce. Alternatively, if divorce is unilateral--which is essentially the situation in many no-fault divorce states--a divorce also will occur. There is no transfer that the wife can make that will make her husband better off in the current marriage than divorced. There is no longer the need for the husband to make a payment to the wife to induce her cooperation. The husband will not have to give up the 30 units to obtain the divorce. He will be better off, and the wife will be worse off. But they divorce under either legal system.

A contrasting situation exists with a couple that does not divorce. A husband might expect 25 units during marriage and 50 units after divorce; his wife expects 50 units during marriage and 10 units after divorce. In a situation requiring mutual consent, as the husband's 25-unit gain fails to cover the wife's 40-unit loss the marriage continues. With unilateral divorce, the husband might contemplate a divorce. If the output of the marriage is divisible, however, the wife could offer the husband 30 units from her share of the output of the marriage, which would make him better off married.[14] After the transfer, both the husband with 55 units and the wife with 20 units are better off married than divorced and they stay married under both legal systems.

In these scenarios in which the output of the marriage is divisible and there are no transaction costs, the different laws do not change the divorce rate, but only the distribution of the gains and loses. Unilateral divorce, in both cases, increased the resources available to the persons who preferred a divorce. This situation can change if there are significant transaction costs associated with divorce. These costs include, first, transfers of property, support, and custody rights to the divorced spouse either by law or due to a negotiated settlement and, second, costs to the divorcing spouses that are not necessarily gains for the divorced spouse. Under fault divorce, divorce placed a social stigma on the "guilty" spouses that was potentially a cost to those parties, especially in small communities. The negotiations and the construction of the evidence required by fault could be costly. The benefits to the parties who wanted to dissolve their marriage are net of these transaction costs as well as the transfers to the other spouse.

No-fault divorce might reduce the transaction costs of divorce. There no longer is a "guilty" party, so fabricating fault as adultery or mental cruelty is no longer necessary. The range of issues to be negotiated also has been reduced. Some marriages might have continued under fault divorce that are dissolved under no-fault divorce. This would occur if the parties who wanted to dissolve the marriages realized that after allowance for the transaction costs of the divorce, they would be unwilling to compensate their spouse enough to cover the spouse's costs. The reduction in transaction costs that came with no-fault divorce might make the divorces more attractive.

Consider the example above in which the couple divorced under both legal systems. If the transaction costs were 30 units under fault divorce and 10 units under no-fault divorce, the couple would stay married under fault but divorce under no-fault divorce. If no-fault divorce reduced the transaction costs, it could induce some divorces that would not have occurred under fault. This shift would only apply to existing marriages, however, so the change in the grounds for divorce would only be expected to cause a short-term increase in the divorce rate.

The longer-term effect of no-fault divorce can differ from the short-term effect. No-fault divorce changed the assumptions that people make before marriage. Knowing that it is easier to dissolve a marriage might lead people to enter marriages that they would not have considered when dissolution was more difficult, resulting in an additional number of fragile marriages and eventually an increase in the divorce rate.[15] Alternatively, people might recognize that marriage under no-fault divorce provides less protection for the parties who otherwise would have specialized in household production. Without that protection, the spouses who normally would have assumed that role would be reluctant to specialize and the incentive to marriage would be reduced. Couples might live together, but not find it attractive to marry. If the couples who do not have much to gain from marriage under these new circumstances did not marry, the divorce rate might fall.

In addition, no-fault divorce can influence the decisions of people who are already married. Women who committed themselves to roles as housewives and mothers during marriage now find themselves unexpectedly vulnerable at divorce under no-fault divorce. They can be expected to respond by reducing their commitment to those domestic roles and taking steps to protect themselves through employment or additional education. This would reduce their specialization during marriage and increase the likelihood of divorce. Because these women and their spouses often entered marriage with different expectations about their marriage, the divorce rate might increase for this group after no-fault divorce was introduced.

Although no-fault divorce thus would be expected to have a short-term effect on the divorce rate, the long-term effects are ambiguous. Gary Becker found that the change in the grounds for divorce in California in 1970 led only to a short-term increase in the divorce rate in that state, with the rate quickly returned to its old trend.[16] Elizabeth Peters found in a study of no-fault divorce states with statutes in place for a range of years that residence in a no-fault divorce state in 1979 did not increase the probability that a woman would divorce.[17] Most other studies conclude that the divorce rate under no-fault divorce has not increased substantially above the earlier trend.[18]

It appears that no-fault divorce was a response to rather than a cause of the forces that caused an increase in the divorce rate. People wanted simpler procedures for divorce. No-fault divorce did have a feedback effect that led to an increase in the divorce rate for a period shortly after its introduction, but the divorce rate then returned to its earlier trend.

The Financial Condition of Divorced Women

Perhaps the most striking consequence of the introduction of no-fault divorce has been the deterioration in the financial condition of divorced women and the children of divorced parents. The dissolution of a marriage can include financial arrangements to cover the property settlement, spousal support, and child support, but after the introduction of no-fault divorce, the financial settlements received by divorced women declined substantially. This was especially the case for women in marriages of long duration. The smaller settlements are due to no-fault divorce reducing the negotiating power of spouses who do not want to dissolve their marriage. The surprising thing is that it took so long for this effect to be recognized.[19] Lenore Weitzman was the first author to present this effect to a large audience with her 1985 book, *The Divorce Revolution.*[20] As she summarized the problem in California, "The reformers were so preoccupied with the question of fault and its role in both obtaining a divorce and securing a financial settlement, that few of them thought sufficiently about the consequences of the new system to foresee how its fault-neutral rules might come to disadvantage the economically weaker party."[21]

When Weitzman initiated her research in the 1970s, she reported that she had "assumed, in the optimistic spirit of the reformers, the 'California experiment' with no-fault divorce could only have positive results,"[22] but her research led her to the conclusion that no-fault divorce eliminated the leverage possessed by the "innocent" parties.[23] This leverage had given those parties power, with the outcome of the parties' negotiations being reasonably successful private agreements. Weitzman, however, emphasized that those financial awards were linked by the courts to fault.[24] Without the fault grounds, she attributed most of the deterioration in the financial condition of divorced women to the courts' decisions. She implies that the courts established the awards under both fault and no-fault divorce, but it appears that it was not common for the courts to decide the actual amounts under fault divorce. The initially unwilling plaintiffs usually would have been unlikely to agree to filing the suit if they did not already know the financial outcome. The negotiations and the settlements were essential for inducing their cooperation. The fault grounds for divorce were important for providing leverage for the initially nonconsenting spouses, not for determining the details of financial arrangements. The courts' role was generally only to certify the parties' agreements.

No-fault divorce reversed the roles of the parties and the courts. With no-fault divorce, the parties who did not want their marriage to be dissolved had significantly less negotiating power, and in many states a divorce could be obtained unilaterally. That often placed the courts in the position of having to make the financial settlements, and they based these settlements on the existing laws that dictated how property was to be divided and alimony and child support awarded. These laws had not been critically analyzed during the fault divorce era because they had seldom been applied in controversial cases. Most couples with substantial assets or unusual problems reached agreements outside the court system.

The change in the financial settlements in no-fault divorce states can be illustrated by reviewing the situation in California. As the leader in this movement, that state has been subjected to the most scrutiny. Although the divorce statutes vary slightly in other states, the effects should be similar with their being more pronounced the easier it is for just one spouse to obtain a divorce.

For some couples, the financial arrangements at divorce in California changed dramatically after the introduction of no-fault divorce in 1970. The California Family Law Act[25] specified that courts must divide the marital property equally,[26] a rule touted as fair and "protective" of wives, being based on the idea that marriage was an equal partnership in which the financial and nonfinancial contributions of the two spouses were of equal value. Weitzman found that the idea of an equal division of the community property had met with widespread approval by both men and women, including lawyers and judges, that she interviewed.[27] No one appears to have questioned whether the legal definition of property was accurate or appropriate.

In practice, the average couple had few assets at divorce. This is not surprising because many divorces occur in the early years of marriage.[28] The women who are the most adversely affected by a reduction in negotiating power at divorce, however, are women who have been married for a long time. These women are more likely to be in marriages in which some property has accumulated, and no-fault divorce had a particularly adverse effect on them. Under fault, the wife usually received most of the couple's property at divorce,[29] but the percentage of cases in which the community property was divided equally rose dramatically after the introduction of no-fault divorce.[30] Between 1968 and 1972, that percentage rose in San Francisco from 12 percent to 59 percent and from 26 percent to 64 percent in Los Angeles.[31] Over the same period, the percent of women receiving most of the property fell in San Francisco from 86 percent to 34 percent and from 58 percent to 35 percent in Los Angeles. By 1977, equal division of the property was typical.[32]

The percentage of divorced women receiving property settlements has declined during the period after the introduction of the no-fault divorce laws. Between 1979 and 1990, the percentage of divorced women receiving property settlements fell from 44.5 to 32.3.[33] This trend was similar for old as well as young women.

Under fault divorce, negotiating wives had incentives to place a special emphasis on the property component of the settlement. The law treated the property settlement, alimony, and child support as serving different purposes and subject to different criteria; but the wives were concerned primarily with the size and predictability of the overall amount. They would have been expected to trade smaller amounts of alimony and child support for larger property settlements because property settlements usually occur in a lump payment, but alimony and child support come in smaller, periodic payments that can be difficult to collect. Furthermore, property settlements, in contrast to alimony and child support, are not subject to modification. As the unequal distribution of property under fault tended to benefit unwilling plaintiffs, usually women, the shift toward equal divisions of property under no-fault divorce appears to confirm that divorced women were worse off under no-fault divorce.

Weitzman found a similar pattern for spousal support after 1970,[34] although the evidence is weaker than for property settlements. First, there was a shift away from permanent awards, based on the idea that the wife was able to become self-sufficient after the marriage. Second, the courts looked at the wife's skills and experience in calculating support rather than at the issue of fault. Between 1968 and 1972, the percentage of divorced women awarded support fell from 20 percent to 15 percent in both Los Angeles and San Francisco.[35] In 1977, only 17 percent of divorced women in California were awarded support. Among those women receiving support, the median and average awards were about $2,500 and $4,000, respectively, per year.[36] Even women with custody of young children, women in need of transitional support, and older homemakers incapable of self-sufficiency were seldom awarded support.[37]

Weitzman found no direct evidence of the effect of no-fault divorce on child support. In the period after the introduction of no-fault divorce, the amount of child support received was low, reflecting both the low awards and the low probability of collection.[38] Her discussion of child support includes a valuable insight on the process that has been emphasized in this book. She notes that a third of divorced women reported that their husbands had threatened to ask for custody as a ploy in negotiations to reduce the amount of child support.[39] This situation further illustrates the change in position of spouses under no-fault divorce. Under fault divorce, the husband who wanted a divorce had to negotiate with the wife; under no-fault the wife who wants the children has to negotiate with the husband. In both cases, the party with negotiating power is likely to receive a settlement more in line with his or her preferences.

Overall, husbands have rarely been ordered to part with more than a third of their income to support their ex-wife and children.[40] Based on interviews with divorced men and women in Los Angeles County, California, in 1978, Weitzman concluded that divorced men experienced an average 42 percent increase in their standard of living in the first year after divorce and divorced women and their children experienced a 73 percent decline.[41]

Saul Hoffman and Greg Duncan also found that the financial condition of divorced women deteriorated after the introduction of no-fault divorce,[42] although they argue that Weitzman's 73 percent decline in economic status for divorced women is probably too large. Using longitudinal data from the *Panel Study of Income Dynamics* collected by the University of Michigan, they found the economic status of divorced women fell an average of approximately 30 percent in the first year after divorce.[43] Both studies provide estimates of the reduction in the financial condition of women after divorce under no-fault divorce, but neither provides evidence of the amount by which divorced women were worse off under no-fault divorce in comparison with fault divorce.

Elizabeth Peters made a direct test of the effect of no-fault divorce on the financial arrangements at divorce arguing that the introduction of no-fault divorce should reduce the bargaining power of married women at dissolution so that their financial settlements would be reduced. As the components of the financial settlements are fungible, she investigated the effects of a divorced woman residing in a no-fault divorce state on all the components of the financial arrangements at divorce including alimony, child support, and property.[44] Using data from the March-April 1979 *Current Population Survey* collected by the U.S. Bureau of Labor Statistics, she found that divorced women in no-fault divorce states received $185 less alimony and $462 less child support per year than women in fault divorce states. These average figures are small, but the impact on some women must have been substantial. As many marriages are of a short duration and only limited alimony and child support would have been appropriate under fault or no-fault divorce, women from marriages of longer duration probably experienced substantial reductions.

Peters found that divorced women in no-fault divorce states received property settlements that were $137 smaller than in fault divorce states, a difference that is not statistically significant. Peters could not conclude that the property settlements were affected by the grounds for divorce in the states, but the evidence could in part reflect the fact that many divorces involved couples who owned little property. If they owned little property, there was little room for the awards to vary across states. For divorced women from marriages of longer duration, the effect of no-fault divorce on their property settlements may again have been significant.

Mary Ann Glendon confirmed that the courts were not generous to divorced women after no-fault divorce. She contended that part of the problem is the limited amount of child support awarded by courts.[45] She cited a former welfare commissioner of New York City, who observed that judges are reluctant to impose any significant burden on the absent father or to reduce the burden on society of Aid to Families with Dependent Children(AFDC) payments. Carol Bruch found judges unaware of or greatly underestimating the actual cost of raising a child.[46] Under fault divorce, the courts' influence on the level of child support would have been much smaller, with divorced women negotiating the child support as part of the financial settlement.

Criticism of Weitzman and Peters

All scholars do not agree that divorced women became worse off after the introduction of no-fault divorce. The Weitzman and Peters studies were attacked by some authors including Herbert Jacob.[47] Without acknowledging the change in the negotiating power of divorced women that occurred with the introduction of no-fault divorce, Jacob objected to Weitzman and Peters's focus on asset division, alimony, and child support. Jacob argued that any changes in property division and child support may be the result of changes in other statutes as much as the impact of no-fault divorce. He did not recognize that laws controlling the financial arrangements at divorce were generally not applied under fault divorce. It is true that the laws that controlled financial arrangements changed slightly with the introduction of no-fault divorce, but their importance has changed far more dramatically. It seems clear to me that the outcomes changed not because the laws changed, but because the laws rather than negotiated settlements began determining the awards in situations in which substantial assets or children existed. These laws were very detrimental to divorced women.

Jacob used data from the *National Longitudinal Surveys of Labor Market Experience* collected by Ohio State University to make three tests of the effects of no-fault divorce on divorced women to attempt to show that women were not worse off under no-fault divorce. His sample consisted of women who were considerably younger than those in the samples used by Weitzman and Peters. He looked first at the change in the salary and wage income of divorced women who had not remarried at the first contact by the survey after their divorce during the period 1968 to 1983. In all legal environments, fault and no-fault, he found that women's income at divorce and after divorce was substantially lower than before divorce,[48] and the effect of no-fault divorce laws on postdivorce salary and wage income either weak or nonexistent.[49] His test is ambiguous, however, as salary and wage income at and after divorce reflects the market conditions in the divorced women's state of residence rather than their financial settlements at divorce.

The critics of no-fault divorce argue that the deterioration in the financial condition of divorced women and their children is due to the reduction in their negotiating power, not to labor market conditions in no-fault divorce states. The key distinction is whether the financial settlements received by divorced women differed under the two legal systems and Jacob's test did not address that question.

Using data from 1983, Jacob further concluded that no-fault divorce did not affect whether a woman would receive child support. Again, the relevance of his test is not clear, as the awarding of child support was common under both fault and no-fault divorce. The real issues would seem to be how much was awarded and whether it was collected. Most critics of no-fault divorce have concluded that the amount of child support received decreased under no-fault and Jacob found no evidence to refute that conclusion. His conclusion that the probability of receiving any child support was not affected by no-fault divorce should not be a surprise, as receipt is a result of the enforcement laws unrelated to the amount of the award or the grounds for divorce.

Last, Jacob concluded, based on a limited sample, that no-fault divorce lacked a substantial effect on which party received the family house at divorce. Again, this should be no surprise. As Weitzman pointed out, few divorcing couples have substantial property, and Peters determined that the property settlement was not sensitive to the grounds for divorce. For most couples, the property settlements were not important. The property settlement was very important for some couples, especially those who had been married for a long time, but Jacob did not discuss the effect of no-fault divorce on the property settlements received by those women.

Marygold S. Melli is another critic of the conclusions of the Weitzman study. Pointing to the psychological aspects of divorce, she questioned Weitzman's conclusion that the financial condition of divorced women deteriorated after no-fault divorce.[50] Melli is particularly sensitive to divorced women feeling helpless, frustrated, and angry at the power that no-fault divorce gave to rejecting spouses. However, she notes that "by emphasizing the bargaining power of innocent spouses under fault divorce, Weitzman ignores the fate of mothers who decide to end a marriage and who therefore would suffer the economic hardship of a guilty spouse."[51]

Certainly many married women initiated divorce proceedings under both fault and no-fault divorce, but they usually had more to lose from divorce than men. They often made financial sacrifices by specializing in domestic production during the marriage for which there would be very little compensation at divorce. Under fault divorce, if they could not prove fault grounds, they also would be required to provide compensation to their spouses as an inducement to participate in the divorce. This compensation would have to come from the financial settlement that they would otherwise have received.

Older men often have more to gain from divorce. These men have maintained or increased their earning capacity during marriage. Usually, their income rose over time. They would lose the services provided by their wife if they divorced, but these services often decline in value later in marriage when the children leave the home. As noted earlier, the contributions of women to their marriage, especially raising children, tends to be front-end loaded compared to the contributions of earnings by their husband. Without a strong emotional attachment to their wife or a legal requirement for substantial compensation, older men might decide that they are no longer receiving sufficient household services to warrant the continuation of their marriage. Obviously, some women initiated divorces under both fault and no-fault divorce, but it would appear that men generally had more to gain from divorce. Even under fault divorce, most divorces probably were initiated by husbands, although filed by women. The fault grounds for divorce required the "innocent" party to be the plaintiff and filings did not reflect what party actually asked for the divorce. With the introduction of no-fault divorce, the party who actually wanted the divorce was more likely to file, and there has been a shift toward more filings by men.[52]

Some family law scholars, as was observed during the California no-fault deliberations, were concerned about the hypocrisy of the fault grounds for divorce. These same people tended to ignore the pragmatic side of fault divorce in providing negotiating power to spouses who did not want a divorce. Given the difficulty for a spouse who wanted a divorce to obtain one under fault divorce, if a husband, for example, wanted a divorce, he was usually forced to reach an agreement with his wife that would induce her to file for divorce naming him as the guilty party. One can only assume that this is not something that the wives did casually. As Melli emphasized, a request by a spouse for a divorce is humiliating. Some women may have been so humiliated by the request that they agreed to a divorce without asking for adequate concessions from their spouse. Others undoubtedly asked for substantial compensation. Whether they exercised the power that fault divorce gave them or not, married women who did not want their marriage to be dissolved had to be worse off under no-fault divorce.

Melli also expressed concern that, "Weitzman's preoccupation with the contemporary no-fault divorce structure and gender-neutral rules as major causes of straitened economic circumstances of many women and children following divorce leads her to inaccurately credit fault divorce with economic protection for women and children that it in fact never provided."[53] It is not clear how Melli explains how men under fault divorce were able to obtain the agreement of their wives to be plaintiffs in divorce cases. We have to be careful when accepting arguments that have been made before legislatures, but the divorced men who advocated no-fault divorce in

California certainly felt that fault was providing protection to married women. In fact, they felt that it was providing too much.

Finally, Melli states that "By assuming that the disastrous economic consequences of divorce were caused by a change in the law, *The Divorce Revolution* makes the problem appear to be a simple one: a few more changes in the law and the problems will be rectified."[54] When a social concern is not the result of incorrect laws, a change in the laws is probably not the solution to the problem. The difference between the wages of men and women is an example of this situation. But when the problem exists because of the laws, the appropriate solution *is* to change the laws. The problems created by no-fault divorce are clearly due to the existing laws that inaccurately define the property affected by marriage and the costs of divorce to the divorced spouses and their children. This situation can only be corrected by changing these laws. Reform of the current divorce laws will be discussed in Chapter 6.

Additional objections to Weitzman's conclusions have come from Jana Singer,[55] who attempted to prove that divorced women were not better off under fault divorce. Failing to acknowledge the critical role of the wives' negotiating power and private settlements in determining outcomes under fault divorce, she argued that married women were vulnerable under fault. She found evidence that fault-based divorces were awarded husbands on such weak grounds of marital misconduct as failure to prepare meals. As a large percentage of divorce cases were filed by women under fault, it is difficult to believe that many men succeeded in obtaining a divorce using those arguments.

The only aspect of the financial arrangements analyzed by Singer is alimony. She reviewed Weitzman's data on alimony and found no significant change between the two legal environments. As discussed above, of the elements of the divorce settlement, the least attractive component for the wife would be alimony, which was difficult to collect and subject to modification in case of changed circumstances of either the husband or the wife. Thus the wife would rationally prefer a large property settlement if the resources were available. Singer made no mention of the decrease in the property settlements of older divorced women documented by Weitzman-- the decrease that is probably the strongest evidence of the decline in the welfare of the divorced women who were most worthy of concern: those who were married for a long duration.

Alimony was also the subject of an attack by Marsha Garrison,[56] advertised as "an assessment of the currently available evidence on the responsibility of the no-fault divorce revolution for divorcing women's declining fortunes."[57] Her original research analyzed the effect of the introduction of equitable distribution in New York in 1980. Although New York permits no-fault divorce, the no-fault grounds have to be based on mutual consent. Garrison demonstrated that the likelihood and duration of alimony fell during the period from two years before to four years after the equitable distribution law was enacted.[58] This is not, however, a test of the impact of no-fault divorce, as the grounds for divorce did not change during this period. More important, she acknowledged that she had comprehensive financial data only for contested divorces and these were probably based on fault grounds. For mutually consensual no-fault divorces and default divorces, the information was more limited and it was typically impossible to determine the "spousal income or the value of assets owned and transferred."[59]

Stephen Sugarman, who also reviewed Weitzman's data, was unconvinced that "California women as a group fare importantly worse under no-fault as compared with how they fared under the fault system."[60] The *average* figures provided by Weitzman were not dramatic; Weitzman deliberately focused on the cases where there was some property to divide and some spousal support was awarded to demonstrate the effect of no-fault divorce. Looking at all divorced women, Sugarman concluded that "overall things are pretty much the same as always."[61] This argument misses the point. No-fault divorce probably had very little impact on many couples who decided after a few years of marriage and no children to divorce. They had made few changes to accommodate their marriage and acquired little property. The women who were adversely affected by no-fault divorce were the ones identified by Weitzman and ignored by Sugarman: those in marriages of long duration. Divorce was potentially very costly to these women, and no-fault divorce deprived them of leverage to obtain compensation at divorce. Sugarman offered nothing to contradict that conclusion.

Women's Earnings

Before concluding this section, I must make a distinction between the adverse effects on women's earnings due to their working at home and the adverse effects on the earnings of workers because they are women. Most women marry and have children. The decision by married couples for the wife to take primary responsibility for child rearing traditionally has made women less attractive employees than men, with the result that businesses have tended to pay them less and promote them more slowly.[62] The problem is circular. Women earn less than men, so it is rational for families to decide that the mothers will be the parents with the primary responsibility for rearing the children, but at the same time, one of the reasons why women tend to have lower wages is because they assume that role. Career-oriented women find it difficult to convince employers that they are not the typical woman and as a result, they often are adversely affected.

The loss in human capital experienced by women due to divorce is based on what they can earn after divorce being less than the wages they would be earning if they had pursued more continuous employment; it is *not* based on the average wage or the wages of men. The wage differential between the average man and the average woman has little directly to do with no-fault divorce.

No-fault divorce probably has had an indirect effect on the female/male wage differential. With less security during marriage, married women have increased their labor force participation. With an increase in women's attachment to the labor force, the ratio of women's wages to those of men has increased (see Table 5.1).[63] This is due to a number of forces. With more attachment to the labor force, women have been willing to invest in the skills necessary to enter higher-paying fields such as management where on-the-job training is important. Because of their stronger attachment to the labor force, women are more likely to be chosen for important in-house training programs. When their employment was more intermittent, women tended to specialize in jobs such as nursing and teaching where certificates were more important than on-the-job training.

In summary, there remains disagreement about the effect of no-fault divorce on the financial condition of divorced women. But the fact is that fault divorce required innocent spouses to be the plaintiffs in the divorce actions and in a majority of the cases, the wives were those parties. It is difficult to believe that it was common that these wives were the parties who truly initiated the divorces, and if they were not the initiating parties, their cooperation had to be induced. The primary inducements were financial settlements. No-fault divorce destroyed this process to the financial detriment of divorced women.

Property

As the deterioration in the financial condition of many divorced women was recognized, an attempt was made to use property settlements as a vehicle for reducing this effect. As we have seen, the introduction of no-fault divorce caused a new emphasis to be placed on the laws controlling the financial arrangements at divorce and the courts' role in divorce proceedings increased. Although couples could still negotiate, the laws placed a constraint on what the parties could demand. With the grounds for divorce less subject to negotiation, the spouses who did not want to dissolve their marriage had less to trade for more generous financial arrangements.

Without a negotiated settlement or a guilty party, many courts moved toward property settlements in which the parties shared the net assets of the marriage equally.[64] Traditionally, the laws in the community property states and the common law states took different approaches to the distribution of property at divorce.[65] In most community property states, each spouse had a one-half interest in all property acquired during the marriage. The common law states had often treated property rights as based on title with the spouses accumulating their separate property during marriage and, if they divorced, each receiving his or her property. Gradually, all the common law states abandoned the title system and adopted some form of equitable distribution, based on the concept that marriage is a partnership or shared enterprise.[66] The introduction of equitable distribution in the common law states has resulted in the differences between the systems tending to disappear for divorce.[67] Because the community property system has a longer history, the common law states have been inclined to use community property precedents to interpret equitable distribution. Some common law courts have stated explicitly that they will attempt to construe their statutes consistently with community property principles.[68]

Accompanying the movement toward an equal division of marital property has been an expansion of the definition of the property subject to distribution. An equal division of marital property, along with limited spousal and child support, often resulted in a poor financial situation for divorced women. Some of the critics of no-fault divorce, such as Lenore Weitzman, have argued that the courts should consider "career assets" as property. She defines these assets as "the benefits of employment, such as pensions and health insurance coverage, as well as the capacity to earn future income."[69] Legislatures and courts also have attempted to expand the definition of property subject to division at divorce to include wage-continuation schemes such as pension, disability, and worker's compensation payments; the goodwill of individuals; and professional degrees and licenses. The recognition of these less tangible assets has been an appropriate expansion of the definition of property, but the new laws are flawed by a lack of any clear understanding of how financial analysts identify assets and determine their value.

Wage-Continuation Schemes

Wage-continuation schemes include pension, disability, and worker's compensation payments, but most of the concern about these schemes has been directed to pensions.[70] With a reduction in the importance of the extended family and self-employment, the pensions provided by employers have become increasingly important assets for most families. Some pensions were recognized as marital property in community property states before no-fault divorce. In the common law states, pensions historically were treated as the separate property of the wage earner and were ignored at divorce, but a majority of both common law and community property states now accept the view that pension rights created during marriage may be divided at divorce.[71]

As states started to recognize pensions as marital property, a distinction continued to be maintained between vested and nonvested pensions. For example, when no-fault divorce was introduced in California, nonvested pensions were not property in that state because they were "mere expectancies."[72] This is a good example of the difference between the legal and financial concepts of property. From a financial perspective, pensions, both vested and nonvested, should be treated as property. A vested pension can generate a future income stream and therefore it is just as much property as a bond. If funds were contributed to the pension during the marriage, the pension should be treated as marital property. As a nonvested pension also has the potential to generate a stream of payments, it is just as much property as a vested pension. The payments from the nonvested pension are less certain than those for a vested pension, so the nonvested pension has a lower value than a vested pension. The lower value follows from applying a higher discount rate to the less certain future payments that the nonvested pension may provide.[73] The appropriate discount rate for a nonvested pension can be speculative.

Recognizing the injustice to divorced women of not treating nonvested pension plans as marital property, the California courts in *In re Marriage of Brown*[74] expanded the definition of community property to include nonvested pension rights. In this case, the court retained jurisdiction until the pension vested to avoid the problem of valuation. In other jurisdictions, the courts have attempted to value nonvested pension plans at divorce so that the courts and the parties can have a clean break.

The valuation and allocation of a nonvested pension at divorce can result in consequences that may be socially unacceptable. For example, a wage earner may receive a highly discounted nonvested pension as part of the settlement at the dissolution of a marriage. If the employee leaves the current position, the pension never vests, and the employee receives nothing. But if the employee stays in the position and the pension vests, there may be a substantial increase in its value. It is appropriate to apply a lower discount rate to the payments from a vested pension than those from a nonvested pension because they are more predictable. The lower discount rate increases the value of the pension and the result might be viewed as an unfair windfall for the wage earner. Therefore, the approach taken by the court in the Brown case is attractive: The pension can be allocated when it vests or the wage earner retires. The courts have developed a number of approaches for determining the appropriate shares of the pension payments for the spouses.[75]

Federal pensions have a unique history. The U.S. Supreme Court in recent years has been active in protecting federal rights and entitlements from division by state divorce courts. It held in 1979 that railroad retirement pensions were the property of the wage earner[76] and extended this interpretation to military pensions in 1981.[77] Congress then overturned both cases so that federal statutes now provide divorced spouses an interest in certain federal pensions.[78] Civil service pensions have been divisible by statute since 1978.[79] Based on the provisions in the social security statute that provide benefits for nonemployee spouses, most courts have determined that federal social security benefits cannot be divided at divorce.

Despite general recognition of pension rights as marital property, confusion remains about disability and worker's compensation payments.[80] Fewer courts have addressed the issue of whether these funds should be treated as separate or marital property. In most jurisdictions that have considered the issue, the conclusion has been that disability payments received after divorce are separate property. Worker's compensation payments are usually treated similarly. Both are insurance payments for which the premiums came from the worker's productivity irrespective of whether the insurance was purchased by the worker or employer. The worker's productivity is based on the worker's human capital, most of which was acquired before marriage and therefore is separate property. This is especially true for workers who are not the beneficiaries of extensive education. Consequently, it is usually reasonable to treat these payments as a return to separate property.

Goodwill of an Individual

The concept of property also has been expanded to include intangible assets, such as the goodwill of an individual. An obvious injustice often occurs in divorces in which one spouse is a professional who continues to have a high income after divorce while the other spouse's financial condition plummets. A housewife whose children have left home might not qualify for child support. Depending on the family's life-style, there might be little marital property and the contemporary standards for spousal support might not justify substantial or long-term payments.

Searching for a way to expand the definition of property to allow a larger property award for these wives, the courts created a concept called "professional goodwill."[81] The courts expanded marital property to include not only the goodwill of businesses, but the goodwill of professionals themselves. A business can be marital property, and courts have long recognized that a part of the value of a business can be goodwill: The goodwill of a business is an asset that reflects the higher profits that can be produced by an established business in contrast to a new business. The higher profits are based on the established relationships of the older business with both its workers and its customers. These relationships produce additional profits and the additional profits can be converted to a present value that is an asset, goodwill. This goodwill is an asset of the business, not of any individual.

In steps that seemed logical to judges, but not to financial analysts, the concept of goodwill has been extended to individuals. Most courts agree that professional goodwill created during a marriage is marital property, but the future earning capacity of a spouse at divorce is not marital property.[82]

Thus the courts have held that an asset can exist for which the future returns are not relevant in determining its value--a holding that from a financial perspective is deeply flawed. An asset is worthless if it does not have the capacity to generate future returns. An immobile house that is about to be destroyed and therefore will provide no future services is worthless even though it is solid and attractive today. Goodwill, either business or professional, has value based on its ability to produce future income.

The goodwill of an accounting practice and of the accountant as an individual, for example, are often viewed as synonymous in these cases,[83] but they are very different concepts. Although there are established methods for placing a value on the goodwill of a business, even an accounting practice, problems develop when the concept is expanded to individuals. First, there is no systematic way to value professional goodwill. By contrast, there is a standard approach for determining the goodwill of an ongoing business that is not being sold. The excess profits that the firm is expected to generate are converted to a present value based on a comparison of the profits of the firm to those of a similar business, usually new, without goodwill. The difference in their profits can be attributed to goodwill. This can be a difficult calculation under ordinary circumstances, but almost impossible when applied to individuals. With professionals, no two are alike because each is unique in his or her willingness to accept risk, qualifications, ambition, and so forth. Physicians in private practice cannot be compared with salaried physicians because of the inconveniences and risks inherent in private practice. What the courts have treated as professional goodwill is just the return to reputation. If that is the case, everyone has a reputation.

Second, a critical issue in determining whether property is separate or marital property is the date it was acquired. The education, training, and experience that result in older workers, including professionals, having higher incomes have occurred over many years of life, but most of the investments in human capital probably occurred in their earlier years as full-time students. In the professional goodwill cases, the timing of the acquisition of the professional goodwill is usually ignored, with the courts tending to assume that it was acquired during marriage.

Goodwill was expanded to professionals to attempt to correct for the financial problems faced by older divorced women under the existing divorce and property laws. The courts used professional goodwill to generate funds to cover the deficiencies that they found in the marital property allocation system. Weitzman found that in California the goodwill value is often set to equal the equity in the family home.[84] It is unfortunate that an ad hoc system was developed for dealing with the deficiencies in the marital property laws rather than a fundamental reform of the laws.

Professional Degrees and Licenses

Traditionally, human capital created by education during marriage was not recognized as property subject to division at divorce.[85] Human capital can be acquired with the support of a spouse who pays some of a student spouse's expenses and provides household services. One of the injustices associated with divorce that is often noted is the case of wives who finance their husband's professional education. Seldom are these sacrifices made with the intent that they are a gift: The supporting spouses are making an investment in the other spouse's human capital for the benefit of their family. There is an expectation that the supporting spouses will share in the increased income that the investments will produce. Often an analogy is made to business investments.

The courts started to recognize that an injustice was occurring when one spouse worked so that the other spouse could receive an education, but the marriage was dissolved before the supporting spouse received a fair return on the investment. A few states recognize the professional degree or license of a spouse as marital property. But the issue has not been addressed systematically. Some states have passed legislation, with others relying on case law.[86] There has been dispute whether the education or license should be the basis for reimbursement to the supporting spouse or should be treated as marital property subject to division. A few states have divided the present value of the increased earnings attributable to the education.

Most states that recognize a degree or a license as property require reimbursement, with the amount of the reimbursement depending on the duration of the marriage. After a long marriage, the courts often have concluded that the supporting spouse has received an adequate return on the investment. In California, this is established by statute.[87] Some states also provide equitable remedies such as alimony or spousal support for the supporting spouse.

The issue of whether education is a marital property is often presented as one in which women are the victims,[88] and historically that was often the case. The number of women, married and unmarried, pursuing education has increased dramatically, however. By 1984, undergraduate women outnumbered men (5,612,000 vs. 5,007,000) and graduate women outnumbered graduate men (674,000 vs. 672,000). Only in professional education were there more men than women (185,000 vs. 94,000), and those numbers were converging.[89] Married women have been spending more time in school during marriage,[90] and the problem of compensation for education during marriage is taking on unisex characteristics.

No-fault divorce has caused the courts and legislatures to reconsider the definition of property subject to division at divorce. They have expanded the definition in a number of areas, but have given very little consideration to the financial analysis of property. Therefore, the expanded definition of property has not been systematic.

The Incentive to Marry

So far, we have observed that no-fault divorce often has had a detrimental effect on the financial condition of divorced women and children of divorced parents. Women should not be expected to remain passive in this changing environment and one change could be a new skepticism about marriage. Two people marry because they believe the arrangement will make both better off. It has already been noted that the increase in the labor force participation rate of women due to higher wages and better employment opportunities reduced the gains from marriage, decreasing the incentive for some women to marry.

No-fault divorce laws also contributed to this trend. The willingness to specialize in household production depends on the protection provided that spouse if the marriage is dissolved. No-fault divorce removed the requirement of mutual consent for divorce and replaced it with a financial settlement that underestimated the loss experienced by many divorced women. The reduced protection caused a corresponding decline in the willingness of people to specialize in household production during marriage.

Without this specialization, both men and women might find marriage less attractive. Under no-fault divorce, women have more to lose from making a premature decision, and they can be expected to require stronger assurances of the durability of a relationship before they are willing to marry. The marriage rate for unmarried women has fallen steadily since World War II. Above 80 per thousand in the 1950s, the rate fell below 60 per thousand after 1980 (see Table 5.2).[91]

With less to gain from marriage, the number of couples living together can be expected to increase and did increase from approximately a half million in 1970 to over 2.5 million in 1989. Paul Glick and Graham Spanier report that between 1960 and 1975 the number of unmarried couples in households with children present had not varied--the increase in nonmarital cohabitation was accounted for primarily by young couples without children.[92] After 1975, the number and proportion of cohabitating households with children increased. Part of this trend can be explained by the increase in the number of persons who live together who already have been married, as the children in the household are often from prior marriages. The lack of children was still a characteristic of most unmarried couples in the 1980s; in 1984, no children were present in approximately 70 percent of unmarried cohabitating couples.

We would expect cohabitation without marriage in the period after no-fault divorce among couples in which the women had the most to lose from

TABLE 5.2 Marriage Rates and Related Data

Year	Marriage Rate[a]	Unmarried Couples[b]	Median Age at First Marriage: Women
1950	90.2		20.3
1955	80.9		20.2
1960	73.5	439	20.3
1965	75.0		20.6
1970	76.7	523	20.8
1975	66.9		21.1
1980	61.4	1,589	22.0
1985	57.0	1,983	23.0
1987	55.7		23.7
1989		2,764	

[a]Per thousand unmarried women.
[b]In thousands.

Source: Statistical Abstract of the United States (Washington, DC: Government Printing Office, various years).

leaving the work force and working at home. These women would tend to be those with an above-average education who are employed--women who are more likely to receive on-the-job training that would enhance their future productivity and earnings. In both 1975 and 1980, the women in unmarried cohabitating couples tended to be better educated than average with a high employment rate.[93] Probably the central characteristic of cohabitation without marriage is the limited sacrifices of employment or education that the individuals make to the relationship.

Not only are marriage rates decreasing and cohabitation rates increasing, but people are delaying marriage. The median age of women when they married for the first time rose from 20.3 in 1950 to 23.7 in 1987 (see Table 5.2).[94] Most of the increase occurred after 1970, as the median age at first marriage was 20.8 in that year. If the cost of a poor choice by a woman has gone up, there is an incentive for her to spend more time searching for an acceptable spouse. A similar pattern occurred for men whose median age at first marriage rose from 22.8 in 1950 to 25.1 in 1986. The median age for men did not increase as rapidly as for women, with the result that the gap between the median ages of men and women fell from 2.5 years in 1950 to 1.8 in 1986. No-fault divorce has made marriage a less attractive institution for many people. Fewer people are marrying, more are living together, and they are waiting longer before marriage.

The Labor Force Participation Rate of Married Women

Not only did no-fault divorce cause women to approach marriage more carefully, it caused them to take steps during marriage to protect themselves from the adverse consequences of divorce. One response to no-fault divorce has been an increase in women working outside the home during marriage. The labor force participation rate (LFPR) of women has increased dramatically since World War II, with the rate of married women rising from 23.8 percent in 1950 to 57.8 percent in 1989 (see Table 5.3).[95] This increase was particularly evident for the women who traditionally had the strongest attachment to the home, mothers with young children. The labor force participation rate of married women with children under six years of age rose from 11.9 percent in 1950 to 30 percent in 1970, the year in which no-fault divorce was introduced in California. It continued to rise to 58.4 percent in 1989 having accelerated after 1970.

James Smith and Michael Ward found that the growth in real wages explains a majority of the increase in the LFPR of women between 1950 and 1980.[96] In the period after the introduction of no-fault divorce, however, the growth rate of the LFPR of women rose while the growth rate of real wages slowed. The introduction of no-fault divorce has been identified as contributing to the change from the earlier pattern. Without the protection of fault divorce, married women have had to take steps to protect themselves. Employment that increased, or at least maintained, the women's human capital during marriage was one of those steps. With the introduction of no-fault divorce, married women would be expected to maintain a stronger attachment to the labor force.

Elizabeth Peters showed that living in a no-fault divorce state in 1979 increased the probability that a married woman would be in the labor force.[97] She argued that the increase was due to the married women's response to the lack of compensation for marriage-specific investment in being better housewives and mothers. I agree that no-fault divorce increases the LFPR of married women, but argue that the increase is due instead to a lack of compensation for the loss in the value of housewives' human capital.[98]

A lack of compensation for marriage-specific investment implies women are not being compensated for being good housewives and mothers, a situation that would not be expected to vary across the demographic characteristics of women. But marriage could affect the human capital of women based on their demographic characteristics. For example, younger married women have more to lose from foregoing opportunities for

TABLE 5.3 Labor Force Participation Rates for Married Women

Year	All Married Women[a]	With Children Under 6[a]
1950	23.8	11.9
1955	27.7	16.2
1960	30.5	18.2
1965	34.7	23.3
1970	40.8	30.0
1975	45.4	36.6
1980	50.1	45.0
1985	54.2	53.4
1989	57.8	58.4

[a]Percent.

Source: Statistical Abstract of the United States (Washington, DC: Government Printing Office, various years).

enhancing or maintaining their human capital through working outside the home and they have a longer period over which to receive the benefit of that investment. As a consequence, younger women should be more likely to be in the labor force in a no-fault divorce state than in a fault state. The empirical results from my study suggest that married women are sensitive to the effect of no-fault divorce on their human capital and the married women who are most adversely affected by no-fault divorce have reacted by increasing their labor force attachment.

Rather than seeking employment, married women could use either pre- or postmarital agreements to deal with the lack of protection for sacrificed human capital during marriage. Traditionally, courts refused to enforce marital agreements that attempted to define the financial consequences of divorce on the grounds that these agreements encouraged divorce.[99] Some courts have become more willing to accept marital agreements that define the financial arrangements at divorce, a movement that has come through the courts themselves rather than by legislation, and disagreement remains over enforcing agreements that limit alimony. An additional difficulty with using marital agreements to resolve the problems discussed in this book is the lack of recognition of the effects of no-fault divorce by many people: As most couples fail to recognize the impact of no-fault divorce, they are incapable of providing for it in a contract. For this reason, as well as problems of legal ambiguity, these agreements are not currently a reliable means for protecting married women. They are more common and appropriate for second marriages, when the parties have a greater amount of tangible separate property.

No-fault divorce imposed costs on many married women who had committed themselves to being housewives and mothers. With knowledge of that effect, married women have an incentive to change their behavior. One reaction has been to place a higher emphasis on working outside the home during marriage. Another reaction has been to increase their human capital by pursuing additional education during marriage.

Education

Before the introduction of no-fault divorce, married women often specialized in work at home, ignoring employment outside the home and further education. Marriage was often the reason that women concluded their education.[100]   Because of this choice, women's income-earning capacity later in life was significantly less than it would have been if they had furthered their education during marriage. Often additional education would have been a small investment compared to prior investments, but the joint decision of the spouses during marriage was that the family was better off not making that investment. Although these decisions reduced the human capital of married women, women made those decisions in an environment in which marriage was a fairly stable institution. Even if their marriage was dissolved, they anticipated being in a position to receive some compensation from their spouse as part of the negotiations necessary for any divorce.

This all changed with no-fault divorce. One reaction by married women has been to increase their employment outside the home to maintain their marketable skills in the event that their marriage is dissolved. An alternate method for maintaining or enhancing their marketable skills is to continue their education during marriage. No-fault divorce also would influence unmarried women who recognize that marriage is no longer the stable institution it was in their mothers' time.

There has been a dramatic increase in the number of women attending postsecondary educational institutions. A majority of both undergraduate and graduate students are now females. The proportion of bachelor's and first professional degrees being conferred on women increased from 23.9 percent in 1950 to 50.3 percent in 1987 with much of the increase occurring between 1970 and 1980, when the percentage went from 41 percent to 48 percent.[101]   This trend was particularly evident among married women. Married women are spending more time in school.[102]   Over the same period, married women between the ages of eighteen and twenty-nine increased the number of years that they were in school by .30 years if they were childless and .14 years if they had children. This trend was most pronounced for married women with more than twelve years of education. Because they could qualify for higher-paying jobs, these were the women who had the most to lose from sacrificing employment or educational opportunities. They increased the proportion of their time enrolled in school from 16 percent to 22 percent while childless and from 6 percent to 13 percent when they had children.

As has been the case with other factors, there are links that go both ways between educational attainment and no-fault divorce. Better employment opportunities gave women incentives to invest more in education. The additional education in turn increased their potential income and their incentives to seek employment during marriage. If these changes are expected, they can contribute to making marriage a less attractive institution. If these changes are unexpected, they can contribute to making marriage a less stable institution. Thus, the increase in educational attainment of women itself could lead to fewer and less stable marriages.

No-fault divorce created incentives for women who wanted to marry to reject the earlier pattern of married women who ended their education. As the loss that they might experience if they specialized in working at home was not recognized by the courts at divorce, they had an incentive to maintain or increase their human capital during marriage by furthering their education. With marriage being less predictable, unmarried women also had an incentive to seek more education.

The Quality of Life for Married Women

The deterioration in the financial condition and therefore the quality of life of many divorced women due to no-fault divorce has already been discussed. There also is evidence that no-fault divorce may have reduced the quality of life for married women. There are many potential criteria for judging quality of life, and some might argue that by accelerating a transition toward women becoming more self-reliant, no-fault divorce improved the quality of life of married women. Here quality of life will be analyzed within the framework of hours worked. Victor Fuchs found that married women are working more hours per year under no-fault divorce than they had worked under fault,[103] and when they work outside the home, their responsibilities at home are not absorbed by the other members of their families. Between 1960 and 1986, women increased the annual hours that they worked in the house and at a job by 7 percent, even as the hours spent by men in those two activities fell by the same percent. From working 90 percent of the hours of men in 1960, women increased their hours of work to 105 percent of those of men in 1986. The difference was particularly noticeable for married couples: Wives increased their total work by four hours per week, but husbands decreased theirs by two and a half hours.

Much of this shift was due to women continuing to assume most of the responsibility for child care. Fuchs attributed this role to women's stronger demand for children and their stronger concern for their children after they are born: "In short, there is a difference on the side of preferences, and this difference is a major source of women's economic disadvantage."[104]

The no-fault divorce laws provide an additional explanation for this process, which otherwise would border on the irrational: Married women may feel compelled under no-fault divorce to work harder to maintain their marriage. The decision by married women to work outside their homes should not necessarily result in their working more total hours. They might work outside their homes as part of a plan to increase the overall welfare of the family and could expect the other members of the family to assume responsibility for providing some commodities the women had been providing in the home. The specialization of labor during marriage is a joint decision of the spouses. The arrangement is in the best interests of the spouses and the children, so they usually agree to it voluntarily. Labor market conditions may change to make it attractive for wives and mothers to shift some of their time to employment. These women only would volunteer to make the shift if the benefits to them exceeded the costs. Family members may agree that the shift is also in their best interest and some of the benefits to the wives should be other family members assuming responsibility for some commodities that had been provided by the women in the home. The husband or children might assume some of the responsibility for cooking or cleaning. If married women were working outside the home as part of family plans, we would not necessarily assume that their total hours of work would increase.

Alternatively, married women can pursue employment to protect themselves from the adverse effects of no-fault divorce rather than to improve the welfare of their family. As these decisions are not part of family plans, the family members would be less likely to assume the responsibility for providing the commodities that had been provided by the wives and mothers. The evidence provided by Fuchs supports the second hypothesis: Although the hours worked outside the home by married women rose dramatically between 1960 and 1986, the hours worked at home by husbands remained essentially unchanged. Married women were working harder to maintain the protection that they had under fault divorce--and still receiving less protection.

An additional effect of no-fault divorce may be on the distribution of the output of marriage. People marry because they expect collectively to be better off married than single. That statement alone does not tell us how the gains from marriage are divided.[105] No-fault divorce reduced the cost of divorce for husbands who feel they are better off divorced than married. Wives may have reacted by attempting to make marriage more attractive to their husband by providing him with more commodities by working longer hours. The maintenance of their marriage under no-fault divorce costs them more effort.

Thus no-fault divorce not only made many divorced women worse off, it also may have made many married women worse off. Women's working outside their home to protect themselves from the adverse effects of no-fault divorce has not provided commensurate support at home, and in addition, they may have had to work longer hours to make marriage attractive to their husband. Either way, their quality of life may have deteriorated.

The Quality of Family Life

So far we have observed the adverse effects of no-fault divorce on divorced and married women and the ways that the courts and women have reacted to that situation. In this section we will look at the impact of no-fault divorce on families. Although not as obvious as the trends discussed above, an important effect of no-fault divorce is probably a reduction in the overall quality of family life in the United States. Marriage can be an efficiency-enhancing arrangement that increases the welfare of all participants, with efficiency occurring when activities only continue so long as the incremental benefits exceed the incremental costs. In a family setting, the benefits and the costs are those of the members of the family. Often some costs or benefits of activities within families are external to the persons making decisions. The income earned by one spouse can benefit all members of the family. The meal cooked by the other spouse can benefit that person and the other members of the family. If these external effects are not considered by individuals, less than efficient outcomes will occur.

External effects can be important for the decisions made by individuals within families. As a consequence, altruism is very important within families.[106] People tend to make decisions in market situations based on narrowly defined self-interest, but the same people might base their decisions within the family on altruism. That is not to say that they are rational in one setting, but not in the other. Relationships in markets are often temporary. If a decision in a market confers uncompensated benefits on a stranger, the actor is not likely to receive anything in return.

Relationships within families can continue for a longer term. Actions within families that benefit the other members often result in the other members acting similarly at another time. Consideration of these external effects is more likely when the persons bestowing benefits on others anticipate that the other family members will reciprocate. This is more likely to occur when marriage is a long-term arrangement, or at least if the persons making the decisions know that they will be compensated for any costs that they incur. Under those circumstances, the parties recognize that there is a quid pro quo: They act with the knowledge that their actions will benefit others and they in turn will benefit from the acts of the other members of the family. The incentive for these activities is often the external benefits received from the other parties' activities.

If marriage can be dissolved unilaterally without adequate compensation, the incentive structure changes. This is especially true if the external benefits generated by the parties' actions are not concurrent as with the services provided by wives during marriage, which often occur before those of husbands. For example, the child-rearing services provided by wives tend to occur before husbands' peak earnings period. Both child rearing and income earning confer benefits on the other family members, but wives may question whether their marriage will continue long enough for them to receive the external benefits produced by their husband's future income. If the wives do not have faith that their marriage will continue into that period, they do not have as much incentive to specialize in child rearing.

Husbands may want children and may expect their marriage to continue, but it may be difficult for them to provide creditable assurances to their wife. Marital contracts can make the spouses uncomfortable and are often difficult to enforce. If wives then reduce their specialization in domestic production and increase their employment or education, everyone may be worse off. This can be illustrated by reviewing the gains from specialization. In Chapter 3, it was assumed that husbands and wives specialized completely in either income earning or household production during marriage. There are many cases in which families would benefit from the spouses specializing, but not completely. The criterion for choosing how much time each party should devote to working at home and working at a job is the value of the output in each setting. Efficiency occurs when an individual works at home so long as the value of the output in that activity exceeds the value of what can be bought with the income generated by being employed for the same period. The increase in the wages available to women during this century has created an incentive for married women to shift some of their time to jobs outside the home. Efficiency may not require a complete shift--the members of a family might find that their collective welfare is maximized if the wife shifts twenty hours of labor from the home to a part-time job. The value of the goods and services that can be purchased with the earnings exceed the value of the goods and services that she can produce at home. The next twenty hours of labor, required to move to a full-time job, may not produce goods that are as valuable as the household production sacrificed. Overall, the family may be better off with her working outside the home only part time.

If the marriage is not viewed as a long-term arrangement, conflicts arise between preferences of the family and of individuals who worry about their fate if the marriage is dissolved. Some individuals who limit their employment opportunities may fear that they will not be compensated for any reduction in their human capital that occurs if they work only part time, since full-time jobs provide opportunities for on-the-job training that are not available in the part-time jobs. Wives have incentives to evaluate the trade-off between working at home or at a job by their welfare rather than that of their family. Increasing their work outside the home from twenty to forty hours per week might impose more costs than benefits on the family--the net benefits for the family are negative. Conceptually, the benefits include the psychic income of the wives from the jobs,[107] but from the wives' perspective, the extra hours of employment provide them with skills that would be beneficial if their marriage is dissolved. Therefore, the benefits of the jobs to the wives exceed the costs and they decide to work full time.

These wives might act differently if they felt that their reduced human capital due to working at home was protected. They would have a stronger incentive to choose the combination of working at home and at a job that was more likely to maximize family welfare. The protection could come either from negotiating power due to the grounds for divorce or by financial arrangements at divorce provided by law.

The deterioration in the financial condition of divorced women that has occurred since the introduction of no-fault divorce often has been viewed as benefiting men. When no-fault divorce was introduced, there were some men who obviously benefited from the new legal environment--the men who wanted to dissolve their marriage and found the cost of divorce had been reduced benefited from the reduced negotiating power of their spouse. Most married men, just like married women, then and now, marry because they feel that marriage will increase the quality of their life. They marry with the expectation that their marriage will be a long-term relationship. Within that relationship, the parties benefit from increased specialization and their welfare is reduced when the law distorts their incentives to specialize. Although the discussion here centered on the spouses, the quality of life for many children has probably decreased. As parents spend more time at jobs, they have less time to devote to their children. One result could very well be the deterioration in the performance of children in school as the amount of parental involvement in their children's education has fallen.

The effects of no-fault divorce have often been viewed as a zero sum game with the losses experienced by the divorced spouses, often women, balanced by gains to divorcing spouses, often men. It may be more appropriate to describe the effects of no-fault divorce as a negative sum game, as the sum of the effects is probably negative. Without adequate protection for the spouses who traditionally limited careers to work at home during marriage, these spouses have become less willing to devote their energies to those roles. The result has been a lower quality of life for all members of the affected families.

Conclusion

No-fault divorce has contributed to many changes since 1970. It had a short-term effect on the divorce rate, but the divorce rate appears to have returned to its long-term trend. It contributed to the deterioration in the financial condition of many divorced women and the children of divorced parents. In response to the deteriorating conditions of divorced women, married women increased their labor market participation and education and unmarried women delayed marriage. It might appear that no-fault divorce only made women worse off, but no-fault also reduced the incentive for married women to specialize in domestic production and thus may have reduced the quality of life for their entire family. No-fault divorce has caused this reaction because the compensation provided divorced women is inadequate. It is inadequate because the effect of marriage on human capital and some of the costs of divorce are not being recognized. Reforms necessary to correct for that omission and make marriage a more efficient institution are the subject of the following chapter.

Notes

1. *Statistical Abstract of the United States* (Washington, DC: Government Printing Office, various years).

2. See for example, Victor R. Fuchs, *Women's Quest for Economic Equality* (Cambridge, MA: Harvard University Press, 1988).

3. Robert T. Michael, "Why Did the U.S. Divorce Rate Double Within a Decade," in T. Paul Schultz, ed., *Research in Population Economics*, Vol. 6, 1988, pp. 367-400.

4. *Statistical Abstract.*

5. Ibid.

6. See Janice Peskin, "Measuring Household Production for the GNP," *Family Economics Review,* Vol. 1982, No. 3, pp. 16-25.

7. Fuchs, *Women's Quest,* p. 78.

8. See Margaret F. Brinig and June Carbone, "The Reliance Interest in Marriage and Divorce," *Tulane Law Review,* Vol. 62, No. 5, May 1988, p. 866.

9. The ratio of female to male wages for median year-round earnings remained in the range from .57 to .61 during the 1960s and 1970s, but this ratio has had a steady increase in the 1980s, rising to .66 in 1987. See Claudia Goldin, *Understanding the Gender Gap* (Oxford, UK: Oxford University Press, 1990), pp. 60-61.

10. *Statistical Abstract.*

11. Mary Ann Glendon, *Abortion and Divorce in Western Law* (Cambridge, MA: Harvard University Press, 1987), p. 81.

12. See Gary Becker, *A Treatise of the Family* (Cambridge, MA: Harvard University Press, 1981), pp. 226-229. This argument is tested in H. Elizabeth Peters, "Marriage and Divorce: Informational Constraints and Private Contracting," *American Economic Review,* Vol. 76, No. 3, June 1986, pp. 437-454.

13. Many of the commodities produced during marriage are joint or public goods. One of the reasons that people are collectively worse off after divorce is the reduction in these joint or public goods. For example, both parents enjoy the children at the same time when they are together, but when they divorce, the children can only be enjoyed by each parent separately.

14. Victor Fuchs notes that when women work outside the home they do not reduce their work at home by a corresponding amount. See Victor R. Fuchs, *How We Live* (Cambridge, MA: Harvard University Press, 1983), p. 77-78. By working harder, married women can make marriage more attractive to their husband.

15. Richard Posner, *The Economic Analysis of Law*, 3d ed. (Boston: Little, Brown, 1986), p. 132. Robert T. Michael observed that between 1960 and 1970 the largest increases in the divorce rate were among younger women. See Robert T. Michael, "The Rise in Divorce Rates, 1960-1974: Age-Specific Components," *Demography*, Vol. 15, No. 2, May 1978, pp. 345-347.

16. Becker, *Treatise*, p. 229. He found that the actual rates for California were higher than the "trend" in 1970-1972, but they returned to the long-term trend by 1973.

17. Peters, "Marriage and Divorce," p. 446.

18. Steven J. Bahr, "Marital Dissolution Laws: Impact of Recent Changes for Women," *Journal of Family Issues*, Vol. 4, September 1983, pp. 455-466; Gerald C. Wright, and Dorothy M. Stetson, "The Impact of No-Fault Divorce Law Reform on Divorce in American States," *Journal of Marriage and the Family*, Vol. 40, August 1978, pp. 575-580 and Robert Schoen, Harry N. Greenblatt, and Robert B. Mielke, "California's Experience with Non-Adversary Divorce," *Demography*, Vol. 12, May 1975, pp. 223-244. Other economists have cautioned against broad economic conclusions about the effects of no-fault on the divorce rate as influences such as religion also influence the divorce rate. See Marianne A. Ferber and William Sander, "Of Women, Men, and Divorce: Not by Economics Alone," *Review of Social Economics*, Vol. 47, Spring, 1989, pp. 15-24. They found that religion as well as economic variables such as male and female wages and the legal cost of divorce explained the percent of 15 to 54-year olds who were divorced in a state in 1980.

19. For example, authors wrote about the deterioration in the income of divorced women long after the introduction of no-fault divorce without ever mentioning no-fault as contributing to that situation. See Thomas J. Espensade, "The Economic Consequences of Divorce," *Journal of Marriage and the Family*, Vol. 41, August 1979, pp. 615-625.

20. Lenore J. Weitzman, *The Divorce Revolution* (New York: The Free Press, 1985). She published some of her results earlier in Lenore J. Weitzman, "The Economics of Divorce: Social and Economic Consequences of Property, Alimony and Child Support Awards," *UCLA Law Review*, Vol. 28, 1981, pp. 1181-1268.

21. Weitzman, *Divorce Revolution*, p. 19.

22. Ibid., p. xi.

23. Ibid., p. 8.

24. Ibid., p. 12.

25. Cal. Civ. Code, §§ 4000-5174 (West 1970 and Supp. 1981).

26. Ibid., § 4800 (West Supp. 1981).

27. Weitzman, *Divorce Revolution*, p. 30.

28. The median duration of a marriage in 1970 was 6.7 years. *Statistical Abstract of the United States, 1990* (Washington, DC: Government Printing Office, 1990), Table 124, p. 79.

29. Weitzman, *Divorce Revolution,* p. 73.

30. Ibid., p. 30. Weitzman notes that under the old law, the "innocent" plaintiff, usually the wife, was typically awarded a significantly larger share of the marital assets. Most of these awards allowed the wife to keep the family home and its furnishings, which often were the most valuable family assets.

31. Ibid., p. 74.

32. Ibid.

33. Gordon H. Lester, "Child Support and Alimony: 1989," *Current Population Reports*, U. S. Department of Commerce, Series P-60, No. 173, September 1991, p. 14.

34. Ibid., pp. 143-183.

35. Ibid., p. 167.

36. Ibid., p. 171.

37. Ibid., p. 34. In 1977, 54 percent of women married more than fifteen years were not awarded support. Weitzman, "Economics of Divorce," p. 1222.

38. Weitzman, *Divorce Revolution,* p. 265.

39. Ibid., p. 310.

40. Weitzman, "Economics of Divorce," p. 1234.

41. Weitzman, *Divorce Revolution,* p. 323.

42. Saul D. Hoffman and Greg J. Duncan, "What Are the Economic Consequences of Divorce?" *Demography,* Vol. 25, No. 4, November 1988, pp. 641-645.

43. Greg J. Duncan and Saul D. Hoffman, "A Reconsideration of the Economic Consequences of Divorce," *Demography,* Vol. 22, No. 4, November 1985, pp. 485-497.

44. Peters, "Marriage and Divorce", p. 449.

45. Mary Ann Glendon, *Abortion and Divorce,* p. 87.

46. Carol S. Bruch, "Developing Standards for Child Support Payments: A Critique of Current Practice," *UC-Davis Law Review,* Vol. 16, No. 1, Fall 1982, pp. 49-64.

47. Herbert Jacob, "Another Look at No-Fault Divorce and the Post-Divorce Finances of Women," *Law and Society Review,* Vol. 23, No. 1, 1989, pp. 95-115. The same arguments are generalized in Herbert Jacob, "Faulting No-Fault," in Howard S. Erlanger, ed., "Review Symposium on Weitzman's *Divorce Revolution,*" *American Bar Foundation Research Journal,* Vol. 1986, Fall 1986, No. 4, pp. 773-780 and Herbert Jacob, *Silent Revolution: The Transformation of Divorce Law in the United States* (Chicago: University of Chicago Press, 1988), pp. 159-164.

48. Jacob, "No-Fault Divorce," p. 105.

49. Ibid., p. 107.

50. Marygold S. Melli, "Constructing a Social Problem: The Post-Divorce Plight of Women and Children," in Erlanger, "Review Symposium," pp. 759-772.

51. Ibid., p. 770.

52. Between 1974 and 1987, the proportion of divorces and annulments filed by husbands increased from 30 percent to 32.7 percent; filings by wives decreased from 70 percent to 60.7 percent. Joint filings rose from zero to 6.5 percent over the same period. *Vital Statistics of the United States* (Hyattsville, MD: National Center for Health Statistics, various years). In a Florida county, the percentage of divorces filed by men went from 29 percent in 1962-1963 under fault to 68 percent just after the

introduction of no-fault in 1972. See B. G. Gunter and Doyle Johnson, "Divorce Filing as Role Behavior: Effect of No-Fault Law on Divorce Filing Patterns," *Journal of Marriage and the Family,* Vol. 40, August 1978, pp. 571-574. Dixon and Weitzman also found a smaller increase in the percentage of filings by husbands after the introduction of no-fault divorce in California in 1970. In Los Angeles County, for example, the proportion of divorces filed by men rose from 22 percent in 1968 to 34 percent in 1972 and then to 36 percent in 1977. Under both fault and no-fault, they found that the husband was more likely to file when the marriage was longer or the wife was older. See Ruth B. Dixon and Lenore J. Weitzman, "When Husbands File for Divorce," *Journal of Marriage and the Family,* Vol. 44, February 1982, pp. 103-115 and especially p. 106.

53. Gunter and Johnson, "Divorce Filing," p. 771.

54. Ibid., p. 772.

55. Jana B. Singer, "Divorce Reform and Gender Justice," *North Carolina Law Review,* Vol. 67, 1989, pp. 1103-1121.

56. Marsha Garrison, "The Economics of Divorce: Changing Rules, Changing Results," in Stephen D. Sugarman and Herma Hill Kay, eds., *Divorce Reform at the Crossroads* (New Haven: Yale University Press, 1990), pp. 75-101.

57. Ibid., p. 75.

58. Ibid., p. 83.

59. Ibid., p. 82.

60. Stephen D. Sugarman, "Dividing Financial Interests in Divorce," in Sugarman and Kay, *Divorce Reform,* pp. 130-165.

61. Ibid., p. 135.

62. Fuchs, *Women's Quest.*

63. Between 1981 and 1989, the ratio of female wages to male wages increased from .59 to .68 measured by annual full-time earnings. See June O'Neill, "Women and Wages," *American Enterprise,* Vol. 1, No. 6, November/December 1990, pp. 25-33.

64. Joan M. Krauskopf, "Theories of Property Division/Spousal Support: Searching for Solutions to the Mystery," *Family Law Quarterly,* Vol. 23, No. 2, Summer 1989, pp. 253-278 and especially p. 258.

65. J. Thomas Oldham, *Divorce, Separation and the Distribution of Property* (New York: Law Journal Seminars-Press, 1989).

66. Lawrence J. Golden, *Equitable Distribution of Property* (Colorado Springs, CO: Shepard's/McGraw-Hill, 1983).

67. Oldham, *Property,* p. 3-11.

68. Ibid., p. 3-15.

69. Weitzman, *Divorce Revolution,* p. 61.

70. For a more detailed discussion of this topic, see Grace Ganz Blumberg, "Marital Property Treatment of Pensions, Disability Pay, Workers' Compensation, and Other Wage Substitutes: An Insurance, or Replacement, Analysis," *UCLA Law Review,* Vol. 33, 1986, pp. 1250-1308, and especially p. 1260.

71. See Harry D. Krause, *Family Law,* 2d ed. (St. Paul, MN: West, 1986), p. 384; Oldham, *Property,* p. 7-48.

72. French v. French, 17 Cal.2d 775, 112 P.2d 235 (1941).

73. Using a 10 percent discount rate, a $1,000 payment that is anticipated a year from now is worth $909 now; using a 20 percent discount rate, the $1,000 payment a year from now is worth $833 now.

74. In re Marriage of Brown, 15 Cal.3d 838, 844, 544 P.2d 561, 564, 126 Cal.Rptr. 633, 636(1976).

75. The different approaches taken to the valuation of pensions is discussed in Oldham, *Property,* pp. 7-50 - 7-74.

76. Hisquierdo v. Hisquierdo, 439 U.S. 572, 99 S.Ct. 802, 59 L.Ed.2d 1 (1979).

77. McCarty v. McCarty, 453 U.S. 210, 101 S.Ct. 2728, 69 L.Ed.2d 589 (1981).

78. The Railroad Retirement Act was amended to clarify that certain retirement benefits are divisible at divorce. 45 U.S.C. 231(b)(2). Military pensions not based on disability were made divisible by the Uniformed Services Former Spouses' Protection Act, 10 U.S.C. 1408.

79. 5 U.S.C. 8345(j)(l).

80. Blumberg, "Marital Property."

81. Allen M. Parkman, "The Treatment of Professional Goodwill in Divorce Proceedings," *Family Law Quarterly,* Vol. 18, No. 2, Summer 1984, pp. 213-224.

82. Oldham, *Property,* p. 10-23.

83. Weitzman found that the Los Angeles judges had found goodwill in the professional practices of an accountant, architect, banker, consultant, dentist, doctor, engineer, insurance agent, lawyer, pharmacist, professor, sales representative, and social worker, as well as a wide range of small and large businesses, including a barber shop, hardware store, restaurant, indoor sign business, and beauty salon chain. Weitzman, "Economics of Divorce," p. 1214.

84. Ibid., p. 1216, n. 124. She reported that one judge said that he was personally in favor of goodwill because it allowed him to give the wife the home.

85. Allen M. Parkman, "Human Capital as Property in Divorce Settlements," *Arkansas Law Review,* Vol. 40, No. 3, 1987, pp. 439-467.

86. For a discussion of the treatment of professional education by the courts, see Oldham, *Property,* pp. 9-1 - 9-24.

87. Cal. Civ. Code, § 4800.3 (West Supp. 1987).

88. Weitzman perpetuates this stereotype by identifying the problem as being the situation when the wife typically supports the husband through graduate school. Weitzman, *Divorce Revolution,* p. 1216. A number of recent cases have involved wives who acquired medical degrees during marriage. See Korman v. Korman, 12 *Family Law Reporter* (BNA) 1611 (N.Y. Supp. 1986), and Freyer v. Freyer, 524 N.Y.S.2d 147 (N.Y. Supp. 1987).

89. *Statistical Abstract, 1990,* Table 256, p. 153.

90. Between 1960 and 1980 married women between the ages of eighteen and twenty-nine increased the number of years in school on average from .12 year to .33 year. See James A. Sweet and Ruy Teixeira, "Breaking Tradition: Schooling, Marriage, Work, and Childrearing in the Lives of Young Women, 1960-1980," Center For Demography and Ecology, University of Wisconsin-Madison, CDE Working Paper 84-13, 1984.

91. *Statistical Abstract.*

92. Paul C. Glick and Graham B. Spanier, "Married and Unmarried Cohabitation in the United States," *Journal of Marriage and the Family,* Vol. 42, 1980, pp. 19-30.

93. Graham B. Spanier, "Cohabitation in the 1980s: Recent Changes in the United States," in Kingsley Davis, ed., *Contemporary Marriage* (New York: Russell Sage, 1985), pp. 91-112 and especially p. 96.

94. *Statistical Abstract.*

95. Ibid.

96. The labor force participation rate (LFPR) of women has been increasing for most of this century because of the increase in real wages. James P. Smith and Michael P. Ward, "Time-Series Growth in the Female Labor Force," *Journal of Labor Economics,* Vol. 3, No. 1, January 1985 Supplement, pp. s59-s90.

97. Peters, "Marriage and Divorce." Using data from 1972, Johnson and Skinner found that the probability of divorce increases the LFPR of married women, but they found that living in a no-fault divorce state had a negative effect on a married woman's labor supply. See William R. Johnson and Jonathan Skinner, "Labor Supply and Marital Separation," *American Economic Review,* Vol. 76, No. 3, June 1986, pp. 455-469; 1972 was probably too early in the no-fault divorce era to provide a reasonable test of its effect.

98. Allen M. Parkman, "Unilateral Divorce and the Labor-Force Participation Rate of Married Women, Revisited," *American Economic Review,* Vol. 82, No. 3, June 1992, pp. 671-678.

99. Oldham, *Property.*

100. A. E. Bayer, "Marriage Plans and Educational Aspirations," *American Journal of Sociology,* Vol. 75, 1969, pp. 239-244.

101. *Statistical Abstract, 1990,* Table 213, p. 131.

102. Sweet and Teixeira, "Breaking Tradition."

103. Fuchs, *Women's Quest,* p. 77.

104. Ibid., p. 68.

105. Becker, *Treatise,* p. 226.

106. Ibid., pp. 172-201.

107. Often the psychic income of employment is overestimated. As retirement benefits increase, many workers elect to take early retirement that indicates that they prefer leisure to their jobs. Better-educated workers are more likely to find interesting jobs and, therefore, work longer. See Fuchs, *How We Live,* p. 160.

6

The Reform of
No-Fault Divorce

No-fault divorce has had an impact on society that extends far beyond the changes foreseen by its initial proponents. It was expected to improve the welfare of divorced couples and their children by eliminating the hypocrisy and ill feelings produced by the fault grounds for divorce, but many who argued that an improvement in welfare would follow from removing the hypocritical fault grounds for divorce gave little consideration to the other laws affecting divorce. Others proposed additional changes to the divorce laws, such as conciliation procedures, but these were rejected by most states. The rejection of these other laws, however, has not been the primary source of the problems with no-fault.

The primary problem with no-fault divorce is that it ignores some costs of divorce. The most obvious examples of these omissions are the inadequate financial awards received at divorce by many women and children. These financial awards are often meager because of the limited definition of property used in divorce proceedings. The original no-fault divorce debate included no significant discussion of the definition of property subject to division at divorce, but there has subsequently been a recognition that there is a need to reform the financial arrangement at divorce. Some of this reform movement has focused on expanding the definition of property, but expansion so far has been unsystematic. The impact of no-fault divorce would be significantly improved by an expansion of the definition of the property to include human capital. The financial awards at divorce have been the most obvious problem with no-fault, but other costs have also been ignored, including the loss of companionship and the additional search costs incurred by the divorced spouse along with the costs to the children.

The reform of no-fault divorce is the subject of this chapter. This reform can occur at two levels: A limited reform of the no-fault divorce laws would retain the no-fault grounds for divorce with a change in the financial arrangements at divorce to recognize the effects of marriage and divorce on human capital. A more fundamental reform may require the recognition that no-fault divorce is fundamentally flawed. Mutual consent may offer a more desirable standard for the dissolution of marriage.

The Recognition of the Problem

The initial no-fault divorce law enacted in California in 1969 was broadly accepted as an improvement over the existing fault-based statutes. This broad support continued as no-fault was passed in the other states. Eventually, however, it was recognized that its proponents had been too optimistic, and no-fault divorce has been subjected to increasing criticism as its adverse effects on divorced women and the children of divorced parents have become more apparent. The reformers became aware that it was easier to condemn the fault divorce system than it has been to find an adequate replacement.[1]

The hypocrisy of the fault divorce era is gone, but the ill feelings associated with divorce remain. The ill feelings are particularly acute among divorced women who find that their financial condition has deteriorated. This deterioration goes beyond the fact that two households cannot live as cheaply as one. Part of the deterioration in women's financial condition is due to the shift from negotiated settlements under fault divorce to settlements that reflect the legal standards under no-fault. Most divorce cases continue to be settled rather than litigated,[2] but the negotiated settlements under no-fault divorce are radically different from those that occurred under fault divorce. Neither spouse has the veto power that often existed under fault divorce, and therefore the negotiated outcomes under no-fault divorce are strongly influenced by the outcomes that the parties expect if they litigate. Without the veto power that existed under fault divorce, it is difficult for a party to obtain a negotiated settlement that is a substantial deviation from the outcome expected from a trial.

Current legal standards provide divorced women with smaller financial settlements than they usually would receive from the negotiations that were common under fault divorce. The veto power under fault divorce was critical. In addition, the legal standards themselves have changed to the detriment of divorced women. With no-fault, the criteria for spousal support and property division emphasize need rather than fault divorce, with an attempt to achieve as clean a break between the spouses as possible at divorce. Property settlements rather than support awards have been encouraged as the preferred method for dealing with the parties' needs after dissolution.[3] The criteria for child support have not changed dramatically, but the amount of child support is now more likely to reflect the legal standards than the outcome of private negotiations.

The Emphasis on Property Settlements

No-fault divorce emphasizes the legally mandated property settlements. In both the community property and common law states, the property settlements now tend to return the parties' separate properties and then divide their marital property equally. With this emphasis on an equal distribution of marital property at divorce, the advantages of the community property system have been recognized.[4] From the perspective of the community property system, marriage is a partnership to which the parties bring different but equal contributions. Because both parties make essentially equal contributions to the creation of marital property, they should share equally in its distribution at divorce. For example, the California Family Law Act requires the court to divide the community assets and liabilities equally.[5]

Traditionally under the common law system, the ownership of property was determined by the name or names on the title to the property. Even though substantial property had been acquired during a long marriage, a marriage could end with little or no official marital property, and the courts of many common law states lacked the power to order transfers or divisions of property at dissolution. Although these common law rules often produced unfair results, they were not subjected to a concerted challenge during the fault divorce era because most actual property divisions at divorce in those states under fault divorce were based on negotiations rather than the law. With no-fault, as we have seen, the emphasis in property settlements shifted to the legal standards.

With the introduction of no-fault divorce and a reduction in the financial settlements received by many wives, unjust outcomes became more frequent in some common law states. If the property acquired by the family during the marriage was held only in the name of the husband, he received that property at divorce. Recognizing the injustice of that outcome, the common law states enacted statutes that required an equitable distribution of property at dissolution. The property division was to assume part of the role that alimony had played in addressing the needs of the divorced individuals, but it has been argued that property settlements seldom have been adequately adjusted to reflect the needs of divorced women.[6] The usual result has been an equal division of the marital property,[7] which has been touted as a victory for divorced women.

That victory was an illusion. Soon it was recognized that equal was not necessarily just and some obvious injustices were not covered by existing laws. Marriages were being dissolved in which working spouses had financed the education of student spouses. Long-term marriages were being dissolved in which there was little officially designated marital property, no right to child support, and only limited provision for spousal support. Yet professional spouses were leaving those marriages with their high income essentially intact. The prevailing rules for the financial arrangements at divorce did not fairly handle these situations.

Concern about these situations was less when the parties negotiated a settlement under fault divorce. In negotiations, the parties were free to use any method that they chose to identify and value the property, but the flexibility of that situation changed under no-fault divorce when the legal rules for identifying and valuing marital property came to control the proceedings. These rules could not be easily adapted to new situations. If wives have a property interest in the businesses that are operated by their husband, should they also have an interest in the profession of their husband? What is the appropriate method for valuing a profession? These were difficult questions that had not been addressed under fault divorce.

Reform in the Courts and Legislatures

Most reform efforts in the courts and the legislatures have focused on the definition of property, expanding the list of items that are treated as property to include those that are clearly assets from a financial perspective, such as pensions. The limited relevance of the legal definition of property under fault divorce is reflected in these decisions. All pensions had not been recognized as property under fault divorce, even though they had become increasingly important components of families' wealth. This omission had not been subjected to a systematic challenge because of the private financial arrangements at divorce. The new emphasis on the legal definition of property under no-fault divorce quickly exposed its limitations with these obvious financial assets.

The reform did not stop with these financial assets. A major focus of the ensuing reform movement in the courts and legislatures consisted of expanding the financial arrangements at divorce to include consideration of earning capacity.[8] The injustice of no-fault divorce often was associated with the higher income of the spouse who had focused on income earning during marriage. To capture part of the value of this income-earning capacity, the definition of marital property was expanded in some states to include educational degrees, licenses, and professional goodwill. When a spouse's earnings increased during marriage, it was often concluded that property was created at that time, and the issue of whether the underlying property was separate or marital was often ignored. Although most of these deliberations occurred in the courts, some legislatures addressed these issues. In California, legislation was passed that required compensation for the contribution made by working spouses to the education of a student spouse.[9]

Procedures already existed for valuing businesses, but they were often ignored when legal rules were established for valuing earning capacity. Principles have been borrowed from the fields of taxation, wrongful death, antitrust, and business litigation,[10] but there has been little uniformity or certainty in the valuation methods utilized by the courts. Although financial theory provides standard methods for valuing assets, some courts have turned to rules of thumb, such as one times gross revenues for valuing professional businesses. These rule-of-thumb techniques often have no analytical foundation.

The difficulties the courts have with earning capacity can be illustrated by the manner of their recognition of professional goodwill as marital property.[11] Professional goodwill is the excess earnings of a professional business, usually represented by an individual or individuals, that parallels the goodwill concept for other businesses. Business goodwill is a commonly recognized intangible asset of an established business. The recognition of professional goodwill as property was often a reaction to the financial situation of some older married women. At divorce, professional husbands left their marriage with an expectation of a high future income, but the income of their wife might decline dramatically. Under the existing legal rules, there might be no substantial marital property, and no right to child support or ample spousal support. To supplement the meager financial awards that the wives would otherwise receive at divorce, the courts started to recognize the intangible asset, professional goodwill, as marital property.

Professional goodwill created problems because the courts had difficulty conceptualizing intangible assets. Physical evidence accompanies the tangible marital property traditionally recognized at divorce. The family has a title to the house. There are stock and bond certificates. At divorce, these items can be documented and readily dated as to when they were acquired. Attempting to maintain a parallel, the courts required that the value of the professional goodwill should be determined at divorce by evidence that was already in existence and with no regard for the potential or continuing income of the professional spouse.[12]

In making this determination, the courts had no clear idea of the process that creates value. From a financial perspective, which is the only appropriate framework for valuing assets or property, property has no value if there will be no future income or services provided by the property. A solid, but unmovable, house that is about to be destroyed has no value. Its price, as a house, is zero. Similarly, professional goodwill has no value if the analyst is required to ignore the future. Commenting on a California professional goodwill case, Joan Krauskopf noted, "A certain amount of fictionalization is involved in arriving at a present value of the expectation of future patronage while at the same time forbidding consideration of future efforts."[13]

Among the states that recognize professional goodwill in a law practice, for example, there is no agreement on the appropriate method for valuing the goodwill.[14] Because law practices cannot be sold, the courts have reverted either to partnership agreements or to an accounting formula approach. Partnership agreements are created for a number of reasons, including potential divorce of the partners, and the value that is placed on goodwill in those agreements may be an unreliable measure of its true value. Large law firms, for example, can expect repeat business that is the essence of goodwill. In one of the most frequently cited cases on professional goodwill, a court held that if the shareholders' agreement in a large law firm stated that goodwill and other intangible assets were worth one dollar, that was their value for purposes of a divorce proceeding.[15] The accounting formula approach is more in line with normal business valuation in which goodwill is estimated by capitalizing the excess earnings of an established business compared with a similar, but new, business. The problem with applying this technique to a law firm is finding a similar business. Often the courts compare the income of partners to salaries of lawyers in the public sector to determine the excess earnings. That is like comparing apples to oranges because these practices are so different from each other.

Licenses and academic degrees were recognized in some states as a basis for an adjustment in the financial arrangements at divorce, but the parties found themselves with a variety of outcomes depending on the state in which their divorce was occurring.[16] Only a limited number of states recognized these items as property, in some cases including them in the property settlement, in others making them the basis for additional spousal support. Where recognized as property, the value of these items was based on reimbursement of the supporting spouse in some states and a share of the discounted value of increased earnings in others. Seldom was there an attempt to place the items into a systematic financial framework.

Expanding the definition of marital property to include professional goodwill, licenses, and academic degrees seldom included any objective analysis. Some commentators viewed this movement as an attempt to restore alimony through the property division.[17] The issue of what was property often arose when there was little traditional marital property and the wife's attorney was looking for a method for increasing the financial award.[18] The expanded legal definition of property was driven by the lack of other assets for division rather than any determination that the current definition was too restrictive.[19]

Academic Contributions to the Reform Movement

Along with the efforts of the courts and legislatures, suggestions for reforming no-fault divorce were presented by academics. The academic reformers tended to deal directly with the financial problems facing divorced women and children of divorced parents, but the resulting programs again were not systematic. The deterioration in the financial condition of divorced women and children of divorced parents caused Lenore Weitzman, for example, to direct her concerns to four groups: children, the long-married older housewife with little or no experience in the paid labor force, the mother with primary responsibility for the care of minor children, and the transitional generation of middle-aged women.[20] Concern for these groups suggests a variety of reforms. One reform would give the custodial parent a special preference in the family home. This may not be unreasonable, but it is no substitute for an accurate calculation of the true costs of acting as custodial parent. The primary problems with child support have been an inadequate recognition of the costs incurred by the custodial parent and a lack of satisfactory enforcement.

Weitzman's second reform would expand the definition of marital property to include career assets and divide those assets as part of the property settlement. Career assets are defined as "the tangible and intangible assets that are acquired in the course of a marriage as part of either spouse's career or career potential--pensions and retirement benefits, a professional education, license to practice a profession or trade, enhanced earning capacity, the goodwill value of a business or professional, medical and hospital insurance, and other benefits and entitlement."[21] The fact that Weitzman has to argue that pensions and business goodwill should be added to the list of items considered as property illustrates the limited challenges that were made to the definition of property during the fault divorce era. A couple can save for retirement by acquiring a portfolio of stocks and bonds. Alternatively, a pension right can be created by the employment of the spouses. Both are clearly assets from a financial perspective, but the courts seldom treated the pension as marital property.

Weitzman's concerns are less valid with human capital. She implied that the creation of a career is associated with when income flows occurred: A career established before marriage would be recognized as separate property, but a career partially or wholly built during the marriage should be viewed as a product of the marital partnership.[22] If only part of a career is developed during marriage, Weitzman argued, the courts should acknowledge that there are separate and community property interests in the career. A review of the process by which human capital is created shows, however, that the skills that result in individuals having the ability to generate high incomes are usually acquired over their lifetime. Any skills that were acquired during marriage built upon others that had been acquired earlier. To recognize every increase in income during marriage as being a direct result of the marriage partnership would overcompensate the couple at the expense of the individual. Without further guidance, I do not believe this reform would be an improvement over the current conditions.

Weitzman's third reform attempts to correct the injustices experienced by older women by using spousal support to equalize the standard of living of the two parties after divorce.[23] Although this suggestion has an aura of fairness, it is unrealistic and potentially extremely unfair. It would produce a perverse set of incentives, reducing the incentive for income earners to work and leaving the persons who had worked at home with little incentive to seek paid employment.

Weitzman's last reform deals with child support, essentially basing it on income sharing. Weitzman assumed that children are entitled to maintain the standard of living of the higher-income parent to the extent possible. It is difficult to object to this reform, but I believe reform of child support would benefit more from a recognition of the true costs of custody. The current rules do not recognize the human capital costs of custody incurred by the custodial parent. The costs of custody should include not only the support of the child but also the reduced social and employment opportunities of the custodial parent. The psychological costs of divorce to the children are not recognized as a cost of the divorce. Moreover, a cost is not a cost unless it is incurred by the person making the decision. In many cases, child support is not a cost because it is not paid. The lack of enforcement for court-ordered child support obligations is a critical problem.

Weitzman's policy recommendations focus on legislative reforms. She does recognize the need for education of both judges and lawyers,[24] but part of the problem in educating judges and lawyers is the lack of a clear program. Other than identifying the financial problems faced by divorced women and the children of divorced parents, Weitzman does not provide a systematic program for reform. Because of her adverse experiences with the judicial system, she concludes, "The route to divorce law reform must have a strong legislative focus."[25] Her concern is shared by many feminists; judges tend to be older males, and feminists fear that permitting these men discretion will work to the detriment of women.

Other academics have addressed reforms to specific problems faced by divorced women. One area of potential injustice occurs when education is acquired during marriage. Joan Krauskopf calculated a formula for determining the value of education acquired during marriage, subtracting the present value of the preeducation earning capacity and the present value of the cost of the education from the present value of the posteducation earning capacity.[26] The difference is the return on the investment, which Krauskopf argues is marital property.[27] This process would give each spouse an equal interest in the income produced by the education.

This approach conflicts with methods normally used to determine the value of investments in businesses. First, it ignores whether the investors acquired a debt or an equity interest in the education.[28] A debt interest would require reimbursement, while an equity interest creates a claim on a share of the profits. Second, this approach overestimates the return to the education because it underestimates the value of the individual's human capital before the additional education. A person who is admitted to a highly competitive program, such as medical school, is clearly an above-average college graduate. Therefore, it is inaccurate to estimate the gain from medical school by comparing the average doctor to the average person with a bachelor's degree.

Mary Ann Glendon, an authority on comparative legal systems, has also contributed to the debate about the reform of no-fault. She reports that the reformers soon realized that the shift to no-fault divorce required more consideration of the financial aspects of divorce.[29] The financial problems experienced by divorced women in the United States under no-fault divorce have not been unique. European women experienced similar problems when many European countries introduced no-fault divorce laws at the same time as the United States. To European reformers, it was intolerable that one spouse could obtain a divorce if either the other spouse or the children of the marriage were not fully protected from adverse financial consequences,[30] and in Europe as in the United States, a reexamination of the legal regulation of the financial aspects of divorce occurred. Glendon identified three responses. Most European countries retained considerations of fault and emphasized the financial obligations of the former income earner, supplemented with assistance by the state. In the Scandinavian countries, the idea of fault was minimized, with the emphasis instead on the spouses becoming self-sufficient; parents retain child support obligations, but there also are major programs of public benefits for families with children. Both of these European models include relatively rigid and predictable formulas for child support and an equal property division, but in the United States and Great Britain, both the parties and the courts have much broader discretion. The courts have broader discretion over both property distribution and child support and the spouses often are permitted to determine the amount of child support. Glendon included no discussion of whether the different environments have considered whether the definition of property is accurate.

Glendon identified most of the problem in the United States as centered on child support, with the awards being too small, not adjusted for inflation, and generally unenforced.[31] She advocated that the state become much more involved in establishing rules for child support that cannot be altered by the agreement of the spouses. She also called for special consideration for short, childless marriages, advocating a fixed rule for marital property. She was less concerned with the particulars of the rule than with reducing judicial discretion.

Glendon summarized her criticism of the current situation, "In sum, the idea of effecting a clean break by dividing property between the spouses and excluding maintenance after divorce does not come to grips with the fact that no legal system has been able to achieve this result on a widespread basis because, in most divorce cases, children are present and there is insufficient property."[32] She advocates an approach that she calls the "children-first principle": Having children imposes "a lien upon all of the parents' income and property to the extent necessary to provide for the children's decent subsistence at least until those children reach the age of majority."[33]   She argues that this principle has the twin virtues of being relatively noncontroversial and easily applicable to most cases, but admits that she does not provide detailed specifications for its implementation.

Marriage contracts also have been advocated to remedy the outcomes dictated by the no-fault divorce statutes.[34]   Glendon noted that marriage contracts are an established institution in the civil law European countries although they have been discouraged in the United States.   Weitzman argued that women would benefit from premarital agreements that address the property division and support obligations in case of divorce.   Subject to government regulation to protect the interests of the children, the expanded use of marriage contracts is very appealing.   They are not an ideal solution because people are often unaware at the time of marriage of the issues that they will need to address later in life.   Just as the Uniform Commercial Code provides rules to cover outcomes that often were not contemplated when commercial agreements were initiated, statutes are probably still necessary to cover similar outcomes of a marriage agreement.[35]

In summary, there has been substantial discussion about reforming no-fault divorce to improve the dire financial conditions of many divorced women and children of divorced parents.   Numerous programs have been advocated in the courts or by academics, generally emphasizing a shift of financial resources to the women and children who have been viewed as the victims of no-fault.   These programs suffer from not being systematic and not recognizing all the costs of divorce.

The Goal of Reform

Systematic reform of the divorce laws requires a more clearly defined goal.   Economists champion efficiency as the goal of human action, but given the common image of a smoothly functioning factory as the model of efficiency, people may reasonably question the relevance of efficiency as a goal for the divorce laws.   The concept of efficiency has broad applications, however.   Efficiency is important because we live in a world in which resources--time as well as money--are limited relative to wants, and therefore we have to make choices.   Marriage and divorce are the result of these choices.   At the same time, any action for which the benefit exceeds the cost increases efficiency--efficient decisions therefore increase social welfare.   Often efficiency is viewed as conflicting with other goals, such as fairness and equality, but for divorce reform, that may not be a problem.   A reform that is more efficient also may be fairer and produce more equal results.

Applying the concept of efficiency to marriage and divorce requires people to marry when they collectively will be better off and divorce when that is no longer true.   In both cases, the outcomes are efficient.   During marriage, efficiency is enhanced when the parties have incentives to make choices for which the benefits to the members of the family exceed the costs.

Fairness--defined as outcomes conforming to established rules--and efficiency are very closely related ideas. Efficient outcomes usually are fair. Both benefit from predictability. Receiving what one reasonably expects from an exchange is the essence of fairness. Efficiency also is enhanced by predictability, saving people from wasting valuable resources preparing for alternate outcomes. When two people participate in a mutually advantageous exchange, the outcome will tend to be both efficient and fair: The benefits will exceed the costs and the people receive the exchange for which they bargained. In longer-term contracts, conflicts may arise between efficiency and fairness. Conditions can change, and the outcomes that are required for efficiency can conflict with fairness. This conflict can be limited if changes in the rules only affect future agreements or the new rules provide compensation for the parties adversely affected by the changes.

Efficient rules also tend to promote equality. The characteristics of the participants in a transaction usually are not relevant in efficient decisions. There is much popular support in the United States for individuals to be treated equally, but in actual practice, equality can be a vague term. There is often confusion between equality of opportunity versus equality of outcome. Our present goal is narrower: Equality would occur if all spouses were treated similarly during marriage and at divorce.

The financial arrangements under no-fault divorce are inefficient, unfair, and unequal. They are inefficient in that divorces occur in which the collective benefits do not exceed the costs, primarily because divorcing spouses are not confronted with the complete costs, both financial and psychological, of divorce. If these situations are not recognized, the costs of divorce for the divorcing spouses are not fully accounted for, and without the negotiating power provided by the fault grounds for divorce, divorced spouses have often been unable to confront their spouse with the true cost of divorce.

No-fault divorce is also inefficient because resources are often wasted by married people trying to protect themselves from the potentially adverse effects of divorce. Married women pursue employment or education when the benefits to the family may not exceed the costs out of their concern about their situation if their marriage is dissolved. Improved legislation could provide financial protection to spouses who specialize in household production at a lower cost.[36]

No-fault divorce is unfair to many spouses who assumed that their commitment to household production was protected by the de facto requirement of mutual consent under fault divorce. Because no-fault divorce did not adequately address these conditions, it has not been fair. It changed the rules under which these persons married without providing adequate compensation.

Last, no-fault divorce produces unequal results. In the area of property settlements, equal results can be accomplished by returning separate properties to the owner of record and dividing equally the marital property. Because the current laws do not systematically recognize human capital as property, the financial arrangements at divorce often do not treat the spouses equally. When spouses provide funds that are separate property for the down payment on a house during marriage, those funds generally will be returned at divorce. Similarly, individuals can have income-earning capacities--human capital--at marriage. This human capital is conceptually separate property, just like the money used as a down payment on the house. Individuals can effectively sacrifice part of their human capital to the marriage by limiting their employment outside the home. In other words, their human capital is worth less at divorce than if they had maintained a more active role in the labor force during marriage, but these people usually do not receive adequate compensation for that contribution at divorce. The rules under no-fault divorce produce unequal results because contributions of financial property to marriages are treated differently from contributions of human capital property. Although either spouse can provide financial property, women are more likely to contribute separate property in the form of human capital to their marriage. The result has been a different treatment at divorce for wage earners in contrast to people who work at home.

To produce efficient, fair, and equal outcomes, any reform of the divorce laws has to attempt to recognize all the costs of divorce. In the next section, the costs of divorce are discussed.

The Costs of Divorce

The costs of divorce are much broader than those currently recognized under the no-fault divorce statutes. Currently, divorcing spouses may be required to pay child and spousal support as well as participate in a property settlement. Some additional costs that should be recognized can also be estimated with reasonable accuracy; these costs include the reduction in the value of the divorced spouse's human capital due to investments made in the other spouse or due to the decision to work at home during marriage.

Other financial and psychological costs of divorce are more difficult to estimate, such as the costs of lost companionship, searching for an alternative spouse or companion, and disrupting the lives of the children. The fact that the divorcing spouse no longer wants to be married to the divorced spouse tends to reduce the value the divorced spouse places on the companionship of the divorcing spouse, but that companionship may retain substantial value to the divorced spouse that is lost if the marriage is dissolved.

Divorce also imposes a search cost on the divorced spouse. The marriage was the result of a search process by the spouses, who searched as long as they individually believed that the benefit of additional search exceeded the cost. At divorce, the divorcing spouses have decided that they want out of their current marriage. This choice might mean that they are no longer interested in being married to anyone, but it is common for divorced people to remarry.[37] The divorcing spouses may have decided that their costs of searching for a new spouse will be low or zero. Some middle-aged men feel that their experience and higher income make them more attractive mates than when they were younger. They believe that with limited searches they can find a better mate than their current spouse. Of course, in some cases, they have already located their alternative spouse and their search costs are zero. Whether or not the divorcing spouses incur new search costs, they impose costs of a new search on the divorced spouses. For some divorced spouses seeking a new mate, the costs of these new searches are so high that they never remarry. These search costs recognize that one of the main costs of marriage and divorce is the sacrificed opportunity to have married someone else at an earlier date. Even if the divorced spouse has no desire to remarry, there are costs in establishing a social life that compares favorably to the marriage.

A major cost of divorce is imposed on the children.[38] The courts attempt to recognize the financial costs of divorce on the children, but other costs to the children are often ignored. Clearly, it is not in the best interest of the children to force parents to live together, but there are situations in which the parents do not hate each other, but only are no longer as strongly attracted to each other as they once were. The children would be much better off in this environment than being shuffled between the parents. The cost of the divorce to the children is often underestimated by the divorcing spouse, who tends to see the children as relatively well adjusted to the new situation.[39] This is especially a problem if the new households have only one parent.

All of these costs should be recognized at divorce. If these costs are underestimated, as is common under no-fault, divorces can occur when the collective costs exceed the benefits.

A Program for the Reform of Divorce

Any reform of no-fault divorce should attempt to increase efficiency, fairness, and equality by recognizing all the costs of divorce. For some valuable insights about how to improve the divorce laws, we can look to the incentives contract law provides for people to make efficient decisions. A contract is a voluntary exchange that all parties anticipate will make them better off. When the agreed exchanges occur simultaneously, the need for long-term protection of contractual rights is slight. But when the obligations under an agreement are not simultaneous, the danger arises of opportunistic behavior and unforeseen contingencies.[40] Opportunistic behavior occurs when, for example, one party to a contract attempts to take advantage of a party who has already performed part of a contractual obligation. After a house is painted, the homeowner may be attempted to renegotiate the price. The painter is in a weaker negotiating position than before he or she painted the house because the work is complete and cannot be withheld. Only if unfair behavior like the homeowner's is restricted can the parties to contracts have faith that future obligations will be fulfilled and refrain from wasting resources providing themselves with self-protection.

As no agreement can contemplate all the potential alternate outcomes, contract law also provides guidance for the effects of unforeseen contingencies on the parties' obligations.[41] The longer the duration of the obligations, the greater is the importance of contract law. As conditions change, contract rules also can change. Predictability is important, but adjustments to the common law can make for compensating improvements. For example, it has been argued that the evolution of the idea of mutual mistake as a ground for voiding contracts creates desirable incentives for contracting parties to generate the efficient level of information.[42]

The contractual outcomes that are efficient for the parties may not necessarily be efficient for society as the actions of the parties may impose costs or benefits on third parties. The government has established additional guidelines to recognize these third-party effects such as pollution regulations that require correction or compensation for the costs that producers and consumers can impose on third parties.

The Attractive Characteristics of Contract Law

Contract law serves an important role in encouraging both efficient breaches and efficient reliance. Under the common law, contractual obligations normally are not absolute. It has not been the policy of contract law to require adherence to an agreement, but only to require the parties to choose between performing in accordance with the contract or compensating the other party for any injury from a failure to perform. Participants are encouraged to breach contracts when the performance is no longer efficient and the benefits fail to exceed the costs. When a breach of a contract occurs, the issue becomes one of the proper remedy--either damages or specific performance. Damages can be based on the expected gain of the victim, the costs incurred by the victim in reliance on the contract, restitution that returns any money paid by the victim, or liquidated damages specified in the agreement. Alternatively, specific performance gives both parties a right to the performance that they expected. The subject of the contract rather than the preferences of the parties determines the applicable remedy, and the usual remedy for the breach of a contract is damages.

Contract law also can encourage an optimal reliance under a contract. The parties to a contract often change their position in reliance on the contract. These changes should occur as long as the benefits exceed the costs. Often the costs of reliance are current and predictable, but the benefits are in the future and speculative. Optimal decisions require that the assessment of the benefits be adjusted for these factors. Because distant, speculative outcomes are less attractive than current, certain outcomes, the value of the distant, speculative outcomes has to be reduced when making decisions.

Mitchell Polinsky has argued that an expectation remedy is most likely to produce efficient breaches when risk assignment is not a major factor in a contract, but restitution is the preferred remedy when substantial costs can be incurred in reliance to a contract.[43] When a contract involves a significant allocation of risk, the most efficient allocation will occur when the damages are specified in the contract through a liquidated damage provision.

An Efficient Breach

The process by which damages based on the parties' expectations induces parties to make efficient decisions can be illustrated with an example. A grocer promises to sell a customer five pounds of fish at $10 per pound for delivery tomorrow. The grocer has an expectation that a particular delivery will occur that will cost her $8 per pound. The customer wants to buy the fish because he values it at $15 per pound. For simplicity, we also assume that the customer can buy the fish today for $15 somewhere else. Both parties expect to gain from this transaction. The expected gain to the customer is ($15 − $10) x 5 = $25; the expected gain for the seller is ($10 − $8) x 5 = $10.

If the delivery does not occur, the fish may only be acquired by the grocer for $25 per pound. Social welfare is increased by permitting the grocer to breach the contract: The fish would cost the grocer more than it is worth to the buyer. The customer expects a gain of $25 from the transaction. The grocer will incur a loss of ($25 − $10) x 5 = $75, if she completes the transaction. Therefore, social welfare is increased by permitting the grocer to reimburse the customer for his loss--$25--rather than forcing her to comply with the contract and incur a loss of $75. An award of damages to the customer, rather than requiring completion of the contract, leaves the customer just as well off as if he had the fish. Meanwhile, the grocer is better off because she does not have to comply with the contract.

A breach of a contract is efficient when the benefit to the breaching party exceeds the cost to the injured party. This efficient outcome occurs in an impersonal manner if the damages accurately reflect the loss experienced by the injured party. If the damages awarded nonbreaching parties under the law are either too high or too low, the outcomes may not be efficient.[44] Under the initial assumptions made by the contracting parties in our example, they are both better off if the transaction takes place. If the cost to the seller rose to $13 per pound, they are collectively still better off if the transaction takes place: The gain to the customer, $25, is greater than the loss to the seller, ($13 − $10) x 5 = $15. If the measure of damages is accurate, the seller is confronted with the choice of incurring a $15 loss on the transaction or paying damages of $25. Given these options, the seller should complete the sale and collectively the parties are better off. Alternatively, the damages could be based on the fish being worth only $12 per pound to the consumer. The seller then has an incentive to breach the contract and pay damages of ($12 − $10) x 5 = $10 when compliance with the contract would produce a more socially desirable result, that is, a gain for the customer of $25.

The underestimation of damages also affects the individual welfare of the parties: The seller is better off, but the customer is worse off. With knowledge of these imperfections in the law, the parties can fashion provisions around them to produce efficient results. For example, many contracts specify the damages that will be awarded if there is a breach but in a complicated world, it is impossible to write a contract that covers every potential outcome. Therefore, legal rules that inaccurately estimate damages due to the breach of a contract will tend to produce inefficient outcomes.

Damages are the normal remedy for the breach of a contract, but the courts can require specific performance as an alternative remedy. Specific performance is a preferred remedy when there is no accurate external measure of the loss to the injured party, as can occur when the subject of the contract is unique. In that case, specific performance is more likely to produce efficient results than damages.[45] An individual agrees to buy a house with a unique view. Before the closing on the transaction, the seller finds a second buyer who is willing to pay a higher price. The seller attempts to renege on the first agreement. The difference between the selling price of this house and the price of a comparable house could be used to calculate money damages, but if this house is unique in the eyes of the first buyer, no amount of money will enable its replacement. In addition, the buyer will incur additional costs locating another house.

The usual method used to estimate damages is probably not an accurate gauge of this buyer's loss. That is not to say that the first buyer will always want to take possession of the house. Even with specific performance, if offered a higher price for the house, the first buyer may decide not to exercise his or her right under the agreement. This price could be paid by the seller or the second buyer. One of the major attractions of specific performance is its ability to force the parties to estimate their costs--

psychological as well as financial--due to the breach. The house is eventually acquired by the party who places the highest value on it.

Specific performance is a right rather than an outcome. Under specific performance, the nonbreaching party has a right to the exchange contained in the contract. This right can be waived by mutual agreement, however. The usual reason for waiver is compensation. One party may want to avoid the conditions of the contract more than the other party wants the contract completed. A financial transfer rather than performance will leave them both better off.

Specific performance might be appropriate in our fish example if there was no accurate way to estimate the customer's loss. The grocer can buy her way out of the contract if her gain from that action exceeds the cost incurred by the injured party. Both specific performance and damages, when accurately estimated, tend to force the contracting parties to reach efficient outcomes.

In actual practice, neither damages nor specific performance are perfect remedies.[46] Since actual damages are legally constrained, they will often underestimate the loss of the victim. As a result, damages as a remedy tend to result in excessive breaches. Specific performance gives the party wanting performance substantial power. If that party is motivated by spite, for example, specific performance can result in excessive performance. It has been argued that damages are the normal remedy for a breach because they can usually be administered at a lower cost.[47] Specific performance requires mutual consent to terminate a contract. This can cause substantial negotiating. Say that the seller of a house is willing to cancel a sales contract for $100,000, and the buyer who has a right to specific performance would surrender the right to buy the house for $50,000. The contract will be canceled if the seller pays the buyer between $50,000 and $100,000, with the actual outcome depending on the parties' negotiations. These negotiations can be long and involved and often are wasteful, merely shifting wealth rather than creating it. In contrast, the calculation of damages often can be much more straightforward.

In addition to the negotiating costs, there can be higher enforcement costs with specific performance. When damages are paid, the court's involvement in the dispute is over. With specific performance, the court's oversight obligation can go on for an extended period. Considering these trade-offs, U.S. courts have decided that damages will usually be preferred as a remedy in contract cases.[48] The preferred remedy in a situation in which the expectations of the contracting parties are not realized is a breachable contract and accurate estimates of the injured party's loss. Without accurate estimates of damages, the second-best outcome would require specific performance with the option for the parties to negotiate a settlement.

Contract law not only encourages efficient outcomes, it also tends to produce fair and equal results. Contract law promotes predictability, so it tends to be fair. Contract law is impersonal and therefore tends to produce similar results for all types of people. It generates equality. Therefore, contract law remedies tend to produce results that are efficient, fair, and equal.[49]

Marital Law and Contract Law

The parallels between marital law and contract law should be obvious.[50] A marriage agreement has all the elements of a common law contract: offer, acceptance, and consideration. Generally, the principles of contract law that deal with capacity, for example, apply to marriage laws.[51] When a marriage is based on fraud, annulment provides the contractual remedy of rescission. During marriage, the parties experience concerns similar to those addressed by contract law, such as opportunistic behavior and unexpected contingencies. The timing of the contributions of spouses to marriage, with the women's contribution often preceding the men's, can create incentives for opportunistic behavior by men. The fault divorce laws acted to protect women from this opportunistic behavior. When people say "I do" and thereby enter into an agreement, there are likely to be many issues that can affect that agreement that the parties never contemplated or discussed. Marital law attempts to provide for these unforeseen contingencies.

As with contracts, individuals do not have complete freedom to draft their marriage agreement. Governments have long had an interest in those contracts, not only defining many of the terms in the contract, but also acting to protect third parties. For example, governments establish guidelines to protect the children who are third-party beneficiaries of the marriage agreement.

Contract remedies have a parallel in divorce law. Our normal expectation in contractual disputes is that permitting dissolution of the contract accompanied by payment of damages is preferable to specific performance, but for most of the history of the United States, marriage agreements were subject to specific performance. Each spouse who complied with the marriage agreement had a right to the continuation of the marriage. This right could be waived, usually based on compensation. Historically, specific performance of marital agreements was a logical policy. First, each marriage was unique. Second, the costs of divorce were very high for society. The specialization of labor during marriage was much more extensive than it is today, with very few married women working outside the home. Married women's commitments to household production were evidenced by the much larger number of children per family. Under these circumstances, divorces could impose large, but indeterminate, costs on women and children. Also, in that less affluent society, men were less likely to be able to establish new households while adequately compensating the old households for their damages. In that environment, the fault grounds for divorce had the effect of making specific performance the normal remedy in a divorce case. The requirement of specific performance made divorce difficult, but not impossible. With the tacit approval of the courts, the parties gradually were permitted to reach negotiated settlements that permitted them to dissolve their marriage. These agreements could only be reached if the injured parties received compensation to cover their losses. If the gains to the parties who wanted to dissolve the marriage did not exceed the losses to the injured party due to the dissolution, no agreement could be reached and no divorce would normally occur. The outcomes tended to coincide with the best interests of society.

Conditions changed. As women's wages increased, the labor force participation rate of women rose, with the result that the specialization of activities during marriage decreased. The number of children per family decreased. The demand for children fell as the opportunity cost of children rose, due in part to higher wages available to women. Overall, society became more affluent. Some of the logic behind specific performance of marriage contracts started to erode. There were pressures for procedures that would permit marriages to be dissolved more easily. The product of these pressures was no-fault divorce, replacing specific performance with damages as the remedy in dissolution cases. This situation is similar to contract remedies that permit parties to breach most contracts subject to the payment of compensation to the nonbreaching party.

No-fault divorce can produce efficient outcomes if it forces the parties to recognize the costs of divorce through the arrangements at divorce. Because marriage is best viewed as a partnership, these arrangements at divorce that consist of completed transactions in the form of property and the ongoing obligations in the form of child support should be based on community property principles.[52] Property should be divided into separate and marital property based on when and how it was acquired. The separate property should be returned to its owner, but the partnership concept would require that the marital property be divided equally between the spouses. The cost of supporting the children includes both the direct expenses of raising children and the associated costs of the custodial parents. These costs should be shared between the parents.

This outcome does not arise under no-fault because the property laws do not provide compensation that adequately reflects the loss experienced by certain parties due to the dissolution of a marriage. One of the main reasons that this occurs is because property itself is not appropriately defined.[53]

What Is Property?

The community property principles leave open the issue of what items should be treated as property. Lawyers and economists would agree on most items that are property such as physical and financial assets. They would both agree that automobiles and bonds are property. But, economists also recognize individuals' income-earning capacity as their property--their human capital. Human capital is the major asset possessed by most individuals, but it has not been recognized as property by the law in an orderly manner. Human capital is property just like a house or a portfolio of stocks and bonds and therefore the tools of financial analysis can be applied to its identification and valuation.

Human capital exists when individuals have an income-earning capacity. It is normally created by a process that is not dissimilar from the investment process that results in the creation of a portfolio of stocks and bonds. For example, parents can buy shares of common stock that they give to their child or they can pay for the child's education. The student is wealthier due to the education just as he or she would be wealthier on receiving shares of stock: The child will have a higher income in the future due to either of these investments. The investments that produce human capital usually occur through education or employment. They can be financed by parents, taxpayers, or the individuals.

The value of an individual's human capital is frequently only minimally related to that person's current income. This is especially true at the normal age at which people marry for the first time. Human capital increases when individuals' expected future earnings rise, and these individuals can have substantial human capital even though their current earnings are low. To go one step further, there can be an inverse relationship between individuals' income and their human capital. People who leave school to find a job usually have higher earnings over the subsequent couple of years than their contemporaries who remain in school. Education, however, is a primary source of higher future earnings. The people who remain in school will usually have more human capital than their higher-income contemporaries who are not in school.

The value of an individual's human capital is based on that individual's anticipated future net earnings. The usual assumption is that those earnings will increase over time.[54] This occurs for a number of reasons. First, their earnings increase as they apply the education and training that they received early to particular occupations. The increases in productivity and earnings tend to be higher for better-educated workers. Second, the earlier education opens up the opportunity for additional training. This additional training often occurs on the job. The time and therefore the investment spent on this additional training will usually be small compared to the time and resources invested in human capital earlier. High school graduates have a minimum of twelve years of essentially full-time education. Without this prior education, workers usually do not qualify for additional training. Although this additional training is important, the critical investments in human capital usually occur early in an individual's life--generally before marriage. An individual's income at marriage is often a poor gauge of that individual's human capital at that time.

Human capital could be formally incorporated into property considered at divorce by modifying the property section of the Uniform Marriage and Divorce Act in a manner suggested in the Appendix. The recognition of human capital may not require complex calculations. Human capital has a value that reflects the individual's expected future earnings. The human capital possessed before marriage is separate property just like any other asset acquired before marriage. When third-year medical students marry, it is reasonable to assume that they will receive their medical degree and pursue a medical career. We do not need to know the exact amounts that they will earn. All we need to recognize is that the investments by parents, taxpayers, and the individual before marriage were substantial. The career pattern was established and a medical career is essentially separate property. Although the funding of the acquisition of this separate property may require compensation to a spouse, the property itself is essentially separate. Alternatively, any human capital acquired during marriage should be treated as marital property.

Adjustments in Property Settlements at Divorce

The value of the spouses' human capital can change during marriage so that an adjustment becomes necessary if there is a divorce.[55] If spouses can expect to have earnings after a divorce that could have been anticipated at marriage, the marriage has not affected their human capital. Consequently, they leave the marriage with that component of their separate property intact. But when the spouses' human capital has increased or decreased during marriage, adjustments are required in the property settlement at divorce. If the expected future earnings have increased, human capital has been created that should be treated as marital property. Alternatively, if the expected earnings have decreased, the individuals' separate properties have been diminished and they should be compensated for this loss.

An Increase in Human Capital. The expected earnings of spouses can increase during marriage for a number of reasons. Their spouse can help them in ways that would not otherwise have occurred. Opera singer Frederica von Stade's husband argued in their November 1990 dissolution proceeding that he was her voice coach and teacher during their seventeen-year marriage. He claimed that he was responsible for her success. The court held that her voice was marital property.[56] Financial assistance can be provided for graduate education that is unobtainable from any other

132 *The Reform of No-Fault Divorce*

source. The individuals' expected earnings and therefore their human capital have increased. Marital property has been created. The increased earnings during the marriage were enjoyed by both spouses, so they are not an issue at divorce.[57]

A word of caution is in order. Even if an individual's earnings are above those of his or her contemporaries at divorce, that is not prima facie evidence that marital property has been created. The earnings of individuals vary for a number of reasons, with the obvious ones being level of intelligence, quality of education, disposition toward work, and willingness to accept risks. Because these characteristics are so fundamental, the usual presumption should be that they were acquired before the marriage and an individual's human capital is separate property.

When human capital was created during marriage, its value can be estimated by discounting the increase in the expected future earnings that are a result of the marriage.[58] This is a process similar to that used by economists to estimate lost profits in commercial cases or lost earnings in personal injury cases. Using a rate of return on similar cash flows, the economist discounts the expected increase in future earnings back to the present.

This process can be illustrated by estimating the value of the professional goodwill created during a marriage. A professional's wife has been instrumental in his meeting people, so that at divorce he can expect to earn more than before he met those influential people. The increase in his earnings is $25,000 per year. Because these business relationships are uncertain and unmarketable, an annual discount rate of 50 percent might be reasonable. Applying this discount rate to the excess earnings would give a value to his professional goodwill of $50,000.[59] It is a marital asset because it was created during the marriage.

A Decrease in Human Capital. Individuals' expected future earnings also can decrease during marriage. The investment process before marriage gives individuals skills. These skills can be used to generate earnings, but if these skills are not used or updated, their value depreciates. Often spouses will decide that their family will benefit from a spouse limiting his or her participation in the labor force to specialize in household production. That traditionally resulted in wives assuming roles as housewives and mothers. This decision can cause their human capital to depreciate. If their marriage is later dissolved, they will find that they no longer can expect future earnings as large as the earnings that they could have expected if they had not limited their participation in the labor force.[60] If the marriage lasts, the wife is compensated for the reduction in her human capital by actions taken for her benefit by the other family members. But if the marriage is dissolved, the wife is often the one who has to incur most of the long-term costs of the decisions that resulted in her specializing in household production and reducing the value of her human capital.

The lack of recognition of the reduction in the human capital of many women during marriage is a significant injustice that occurs due to the nature of the financial arrangements under the current no-fault divorce laws. Many states recognize the contributions of housewives to the acquisition of marital property,[61] but in only a limited number of states, such as California and Colorado, are the courts required to consider the extent a housewife's future earning capacity has been affected by unemployment during marriage.[62] Even in those states this calculation is not made in a systematic manner. This injustice could be reduced by recognizing human capital as property by statute. The human capital possessed by individuals at marriage could be acknowledged as separate property, and the reduction in the value of separate property human capital shared between the spouses at divorce.

As an alternative to a statutory approach, the reduction in the human capital of spouses who specialize in household production could be recognized by the courts as creating implied contracts of indemnification. If their marriage is dissolved, these parties have a right to compensation for the reduced value of their human capital. Their actions fulfilled the requirements of an implied contract. Their limited participation in the labor force conferred benefits on their family through services provided at home. The decisions that produced those actions were made with the expectation of compensation, that is, a sharing of the family's income and services. The persons who worked at home were not acting as volunteers, as marriage is a partnership. To allow the primary income-earning spouse to have the benefits of the other spouse's past services without compensating him or her for the reduction in human capital would result in an unjust enrichment of some spouses at the expense of others. If the sacrifice was made by the wife, this implied contract of indemnification would result in a debt of the couple to the wife if the marriage is dissolved. In effect, the husband would be required, as part of the property settlement, to compensate the wife for half her loss.[63]

The value of the reduced future earnings due to limited participation in the labor force during marriage can be estimated using the discounted present value method described above. Let us assume that a divorced woman can now earn $10,000 per year less than she would be earning if she had never limited her employment during marriage. It will take ten years experience in the labor force for her earnings to reach the level that she could have expected without the limitations. If her loss dropped from $10,000 in the first year to $1,000 in the tenth, her limiting her employment during marriage reduced her human capital by $42,410, assuming a 10 percent discount rate.[64] Her loss is a debt of the marriage to her personally. The effect would be that husbands and wives would share the losses equally.

Being housewives and mothers does not have the same impact on all women's human capital. Women enter marriage with different amounts of human capital. In addition, limiting their employment during marriage has different effects on women's human capital.[65] A third-year medical student has much more to lose from leaving medical school than a waitress has from leaving her job. The third-year medical student may find that she cannot return to medical school if she divorces later in life. The decision to leave medical school has a substantial effect on her human capital. She will now earn substantially less than if she had completed medical school and pursued a career in medicine. But being a housewife and mother many have only a limited effect on the human capital of the waitress. She may be able to find a job after divorce that provides earnings similar to those of women who worked continuously over the intervening period. The marriage did not affect her human capital.

Educational Support. The recognition of individuals' human capital at marriage as separate property also will clarify how educational support should be handled if a marriage is dissolved. The earnings from the separate property human capital of the spouses are usually used during the marriage for current consumption and the acquisition of marital property. The relative contributions of the spouses to the marriage normally are not a concern of the courts at divorce. Most products and services purchased during marriage are for the benefit of both spouses or their children.

This is not universally true. Some of the earnings during marriage from one spouse's separate property human capital may be used to increase the human capital of the other spouse. Education is an obvious example. The spouse providing the funds is making an investment. An initial question is the nature of the property interest created by the investment. The funding can result in either a debt or an equity interest in the student spouse's human capital. Equity funding is essential to the student. As equity does not guarantee a return, it is usually required before debt financing. An equity lender is entitled to a share of the profits of an enterprise. Debt funding comes later when the investment is more secure, and the debt lender is entitled only to a market rate of return on the investment. Given the prior investments in human capital, the funds provided by supporting spouses for graduate or professional education are usually in the form of debt financing. These funds usually replace loans, parental support, or student earnings. If the marriage lasts a sufficient time for the supporting spouse to receive a fair return on the investment, no compensation is necessary.

Alternatively, the marriage may not last long enough for the supporting spouse to receive an adequate return on the investment. Under those circumstances, the beneficiary of the investment should pay the supporting spouse the unamortized amount of the investment plus interest. The investment by the working spouse consists of the student spouse's living expenses and the direct cost of the education. The funds came from the working spouse's separate property and he or she should be reimbursed.

The foregone income of the student spouse is also a cost of the education, and the working spouse incurred half of the cost of this reduced income. The current legal rules that limit the reimbursement for investments in human capital at divorce tend to result in suboptimal levels of investment in human capital during marriage.[66]

On-the-Job Training. On-the-job training also can result in the need for an adjustment at divorce. Economists have identified on-the-job training as an important factor that influences workers' future earnings. To induce an employer to provide on-the-job training that has broad applications, workers often have to accept wages below those offered in other positions. After these special skills are acquired, the current employer has to meet the higher wages that the increased productivity would command from other employers. For example, some of the highest-qualified law graduates accept positions in government agencies that pay less than they could receive in the private sector. These lawyers are not irrational nor are they necessarily altruistic. They often view the experience that they will receive in the government as an investment, as they will ultimately receive a higher income in the private sector if they are familiar with the procedures and standards of the agencies before which they will represent clients. Of course, the lawyers might stay with the government if the government compensation was similar to that available to them in the private sector after they acquire the new skills. Thus one spouse can increase his or her human capital by reducing the family's standard of living temporarily. If the reduction in the family's standard of living was substantial and the family has not received an adequate return on the investment, then indemnification of the other spouse would be appropriate.

Remarriage Prospects. Divorced men find it easier to find new spouses than divorced women. Between ages twenty-five and forty-four, the remarriage rates for men are almost twice as high as for women.[67] Remarriage prospects fall with age.[68] There tends to be a larger difference in age between grooms and brides in remarriages than in first marriages. Victor Fuchs noted a trend toward divorced women remaining divorced for a longer period of time even if they eventually remarry, which he attributed to divorced women having other alternatives to marriage such as better employment opportunities and government transfer programs.[69]

The human capital analysis could be used, with caution, for individuals whose "marketability" declined during a marriage. This might be particularly true for especially physically attractive people. As their physical attraction may find them a higher-income spouse, it can be viewed as a form of human capital. Fault divorce provided some protection for these individuals in that as they became less attractive, their spouses were forced to continue the marriage or pay increased compensation. No-fault divorce removed much of that protection. Lloyd Cohen argued that fault divorce never provided perfect protection, and women traditionally protected themselves by marrying older men.[70] Therefore, the attraction of both spouses probably declines at similar rates. Such unusual cases are probably better dealt with through premarital agreements than statutes.

Child Support

An understanding of human capital can provide insights into the adjustments that are necessary in the current provisions for child support. Efficient outcomes require confronting individuals with the benefits and costs of their actions. The current child support rules tend to underestimate the cost of child custody. The cost of raising a child consists of the direct costs, such as clothing and food, plus the indirect costs incurred by the custodial parent. Custodial parents may have to limit their employment opportunities because they lack the flexibility of employees without child care obligations. As a result, they may have to reject jobs involving extensive travel or overtime. Another cost to the custodial parent is the reduced probability that the custodial parent will be able to remarry. The custody of the children reduces social interaction and may be viewed as a negative attribute by potential new partners. Of course, the costs incurred by the custodial parent have to be balanced against the consumptive value to the parent of having custody. Both costs and benefits are likely to be difficult to calculate, but they should not be disregarded.

The support of children is the responsibility of children's parents. Given the large number of children born to unwed mothers, child support is clearly an issue that goes beyond marriage. Aid to Families with Dependent Children has become an important public program for helping women and children, but it cannot and should not replace the obligations of the parents.[71] Support is an obligation of the marriage. While the marriage lasted, the children were enjoyed by both parents. Some authors argue that child support and the property settlement should be combined,[72] but the two are conceptually separate issues. For the best outcomes, I believe the usual assumption should be that the true costs of custody should be shared equally. If the human capital costs of the custodial parent are recognized, this allocation would tend to require larger financial contributions from the noncustodial parent. All periodic payments such as those for child support must be adjusted to their current costs, which should as a minimum include a cost-of-living adjustment.

Alimony

The introduction of human capital into property settlements at divorce reduces the need for alimony. Alimony has traditionally been just one component of the financial arrangements at divorce, usually not even evaluated on its own, for the spouses are generally more concerned about the overall package than the components. The division of the financial settlements into separate components is as likely to be driven by tax considerations as legal requirements. Alimony has had an ambiguous role at divorce, with the standards being very broad. Alimony decisions tend to be ad hoc with few clearly articulated principles and only occasional disclosure of the underlying reasons.[73] Without a systematic framework for awarding alimony, awards have predictably been highly arbitrary. This arbitrariness has not been a major problem because alimony only has been awarded in a limited number of cases and its duration usually has been limited as well.[74] Under no-fault, alimony, or spousal support, has shifted toward rehabilitation.[75]

Potentially, alimony serves three distinct functions:[76] damages for breach of the marriage contract, repaying the wife her share of the marital partnership assets, or providing the wife with a form of severance pay or unemployment benefits. Alimony thus compensates for property settlements underestimating the losses incurred by many women at divorce. A recognition of human capital as property would provide a more equitable solution to these concerns.

It might be tempting to use alimony or spousal support to deal with a special problem that occurs when even with the recognition of human capital, a divorced woman does not qualify for either a substantial property settlement or child support. A woman with limited human capital at marriage may only qualify for a small adjustment in her property settlement at divorce if the marriage had only a limited effect on her human capital and she could still obtain a job similar to the job that she had before marriage. Say she was, and still is, qualified to be a supermarket clerk. The income generated by her best job may be very low and disproportionate to the husband's, but this concern is best addressed as the society-wide problem of low-income workers rather than an issue in family law.

Mutual Consent Divorce

The incorporation of human capital into the property considered at divorce would still not recognize all the costs incurred by divorced spouses and their children. Many of these costs are difficult to estimate, and the spouses' situations may be unique. Specific performance is the normal remedy for breaches of contracts involving unique items, mainly due to the problems associated with estimating damages under those circumstances. Social welfare might be improved by making the dissolution of marriage agreements subject to specific performance as well. The effect would be to limit divorces to situations in which there is mutual consent by the spouses. Then a divorce would only occur when the collective benefits exceeded the costs.

The opponents of fault divorce do not appear to have given serious consideration to mutual consent divorce, which is fault divorce without the fault, but mutual consent is more likely to produce efficient outcomes than either fault or no-fault grounds. Mutual consent would increase the incentives for the spouses to recognize and place a value on the benefits and costs of divorce. Both benefits and costs are broad concepts that include both financial as well as psychological factors. Some of the costs of divorce beyond human capital that are currently ignored under no-fault divorce are those associated with lost companionship, the search for a new spouse or companions, and the disruption in the lives of the children. As discussed above, these costs can be substantial. Under mutual consent divorce, the party who does not want the divorce would have an incentive to ask for compensation for these costs as a basis for agreeing to the divorce.

One of the attractive aspects of mutual consent divorce is its ability to force the parents to address the costs incurred by their children due to a divorce. These costs go far beyond just maintenance, which is covered by child support. If the divorcing spouses are forced to recognize the full costs of their divorce, some parents might be able to make their marriage work and thereby provide benefits to their children. The parents, usually the mothers, who expect custody of the children after divorce are most likely to recognize the costs that the children will incur. If the children are less happy after divorce, their attitudes will impact the welfare of the custodial parent. These changes in the welfare of the children and of the custodial parent are a cost. The custodial parent has incentives to take these costs into consideration when considering whether to agree to divorce. These companionship, search, and children's costs would be difficult for anyone other than the spouses to estimate and include in any award at divorce.

Mutual consent is not a perfect solution. Like specific performance, it can result in excessive performance if one party wants to ignore the costs of performance.[77] This can occur when a spouse basing a decision on spite is opposed to a divorce under any circumstances. One of the recurring themes of this book is the fundamental rationality of individuals' decisions even when dealing with emotional issues such as marriage and divorce. In most divorces, at least one spouse initially wanted the marriage to continue,[78] but when the collective benefits of divorce exceed the costs, social welfare is increased by a divorce. Under those circumstances, the parties have incentives to construct an agreement that leaves them both better off. The large number of divorces based on mutual consent under the fault grounds illustrates the willingness of spouses to negotiate even under trying conditions.

This point can be illustrated with two examples. A wife who did not initiate the divorce may feel that she is no longer strongly attracted to her spouse, she can find someone just as attractive with a limited amount of effort, and any children would not be adversely affected by a divorce. She might therefore be willing to reach a divorce agreement at a small cost to the party who initially wanted the divorce. Social welfare would be improved by permitting the divorce. Alternatively, she might still be strongly attracted to her spouse, feel that only a long and costly search would find another comparable spouse or situation, and believe that the children would suffer compared with the quality of life that is still possible if the parents stay together. She might under those circumstances ask for a level of compensation that the other spouse is unwilling to pay. In other words, the party who wants the divorce does not value the divorce as much as the other spouse and the children value the continuation of the marriage. In that case, social welfare is improved by continuing the marriage.

Mutual consent can create problems when someone is "driven out" of a marriage rather than "wanting out." It is often difficult for anyone, including the spouses and judges, to separate divorces into these two classes. Being driven out of a marriage raises concerns similar to those addressed with the fault divorce statutes. Under fault divorce, the "guilty" spouse did something that gave the "innocent" spouse a right to dissolve the marriage: The innocent spouse was driven out of the marriage. Mutual consent would not provide a solution for the situation in which one spouse is the victim of acts such as cruelty or adultery, but the "guilty" spouse does not want a divorce. Courts during the fault divorce era showed little skill, however, at making determinations in these cases. Often the grounds given for fault divorce were hypocritical and the marriage had failed for other reasons. And even when the fault grounds could be proven, the reasons why a marriage failed were probably a great deal more complicated than just the acts that established the grounds. Therefore, mutual consent would be no worse than fault divorce was in dealing with these situations.

None of the alternative approaches to divorce procedures produces perfect outcomes. Fault divorce can be hypocritical and ineffective. No-fault divorce, even with a broader definition of property, underestimates the costs of divorce to the divorced spouse and the children. Mutual consent divorce might require the continuation of a marriage when acts that would have constituted fault at an earlier time have occurred. Even when the grounds for divorce are mutual consent, the spouses cannot be forced to live together. Subject to financial obligations to the other spouse and the children, a spouse who felt that he or she was being driven out of a marriage could leave the other spouse. The spouse who left just could not marry someone else. Separation for a long period could be added to mutual consent as a basis for divorce.

Mutual consent divorce gives substantial power to spouses who do not want a divorce. To limit abuse of this power, it might be attractive to permit no-fault divorce when the potential costs of divorce are likely to be low, as they tend to be early in a marriage and when there are no children. Therefore, no-fault divorce might be permitted during the first year of marriage or until the wife becomes pregnant, whichever comes first. Later divorce would only be granted based on mutual consent.

If people considering marriage knew that mutual consent was the only, or one of a limited number of, grounds for divorce, that knowledge might increase the incentive for them to negotiate premarital agreements. Neither fault divorce nor no-fault divorce provided marrying individuals with the opportunity to construct their own grounds for the dissolution of their marriage. With mutual consent divorce, the dissolution of marriage would be based on the parties' criteria rather than those of the state. Under those circumstances, the parties might be more inclined to specify their own grounds at the time of marriage. For example, some might feel that adultery should be a ground for dissolution, others might not.

If society were willing to consider another radical change in the grounds for divorce, it should seriously consider mutual consent. But it is unlikely that this change will occur. The most probable reform of the divorce laws at the present time would expand the definition of property considered under the no-fault divorce statutes to include human capital.

Concerns About Using Human Capital in Property Settlements

Even the reform of the no-fault divorce laws to incorporate human capital might appear to call for a radical change in the existing divorce laws. A review of some of the concerns that might develop should demonstrate that this reform is necessary, but it would not be difficult to implement.

Wouldn't it be difficult to estimate the effect of marriage on human capital?

The estimation of the effect of marriage on the spouses' human capital will be necessary in only a limited number of cases. Many divorces occur after only a few years without the parties having made substantial alterations in their careers.[79] Most of the debate over expanding the definition of property has focused on individuals' income-earning capacity. I argue that the usual assumption at divorce should be that the income-earning careers pursued by spouses during marriage were the ones that could have been anticipated at marriage. Marriage increases the opportunities for specialization by income-earning spouses, but few jobs respond to the specialization made possible by marriage. Thus most income-earning spouses probably do not have a substantially higher income due to their marriage. These spouses benefit from marriage because they receive more household commodities, with less time spent on the production of those commodities. For these reasons, the ordinary presumption should be that income-earning spouses' human capital is separate property.

Consideration of human capital at divorce will be important under three circumstances: when there has been an unanticipated increase in one spouse's expected earnings during marriage, a spouse has made a significant specialization in household production during marriage, or an investment has been made in education during the marriage. At present, these situations are either ignored or handled on an ad hoc basis in most states at divorce. The systematic recognition of the effect of marriage on human capital alone would be a step in the right direction.

The techniques for estimating the effect of marriage on the parties' human capital are similar to those used by economists and financial analysts in personal injury or commercial cases, but several presumptions could facilitate the process. For example, it could be presumed that it takes two years of employment by a student spouse to compensate a supporting spouse for each year of assistance. If there are children and the primary source of the child care has been one parent, it could be presumed that that parent incurred a loss of human capital during the marriage. In both these cases, the compensation has to be estimated, but the presumption would give the parties an incentive to make their own calculations.

Doesn't the recognition of the reduced value of the human capital of people who work at home place an unfair burden on their spouse?

When decisions made during marriage result in reductions in the human capital of spouses, losses exist. At divorce these spouses must expect lower earnings in the future than if they had not specialized in household production. The only issue is who is going to incur the losses. If the losses of human capital are not shared between the spouses, they will be incurred only by the person who worked at home. The shifting of the cost of the reduced human capital from one spouse to the other does not cause it to disappear. Divorce is a costly process, and two households cannot live as cheaply as one. At least temporarily, the standard of living of all family members will decrease if the costs of divorce are correctly allocated.

Will all people who work at home during marriage qualify for an adjustment in the property settlement to reflect the reduction in their human capital?

Not all people who work at home during marriage incur a reduction in their human capital. They have experienced a reduction in their human capital if they can expect earnings after divorce that are less than they would be receiving if they had focused on their best employment opportunities during marriage. Some individuals have the prospect of flat income profiles over their lives because of limited investments in human capital before their marriage. They probably do not have the capacity to experience a substantial depreciation in their human capital during marriage. For example, a woman who at marriage was and expected to continue to be a retail sales clerk may not be left worse off financially by divorce compared with where she would be without a marriage and the resulting absence from the labor force. Her human capital separate property has not been adversely affected by the marriage. Alternatively, many women who work during marriage will have their human capital intact at divorce. The women who had considerable human capital at marriage and then specialized in household production during marriage are the ones who need an adjustment at divorce. These are usually the women with substantial education or an established career at marriage.

Do only women deserve compensation for the reduction in their human capital during the marriage?

Marriage can effect the human capital of both spouses, since they are both capable of making sacrifices. The spouses who limit their employment opportunities during marriage usually are those who specialized in household production, especially child rearing. As employment opportunities increase for women, the parents who raise the children will increasingly be the fathers. In the case of two working spouses, both may make career adjustments to accommodate their marriage. In those cases, there may be offsetting effects. A common stereotype recognizes that an injustice occurs when the wife works to put the husband through medical school. The large number of married women in college would indicate that there are numerous situations in which husbands should be compensated at divorce for providing financial support so that wives can acquire human capital during marriage.

Will only people who work exclusively at home qualify for compensation?

Compensation may be required when decisions were made during marriage that affected the spouses' human capital. This can occur even when both spouses worked continuously throughout their marriage. If decisions were made that resulted in the wife having the expectation of lower future earnings than she would have without the decisions, an adjustment would be appropriate. The wife may have rejected higher-paying jobs with overtime that would make it difficult to pick up the children at day care. Women tend to have less continuous employment and tend to make lower earnings on average than men. It is therefore reasonable for most families to place a higher priority on the husband's income-earning capacity than the wife's. An emphasis on the husband's career during marriage can lead to the need for compensation for the wife at divorce, even if she had substantial employment during marriage. The compensation should normally be based on the loss of human capital experienced by the wife, not the income earned by the husband. Of course, any claim of a career not pursued has to be realistic.

How can a reduction in human capital be funded when there is only limited physical and financial property?

If a reduction in human capital has occurred during marriage, it would be inappropriate to ignore it because of a lack of liquid assets. A loss has occurred and now the issue is who is going to pay for it. Property settlements tend to be a onetime event if physical and financial assets are the primary forms of marital property. Physical and financial assets can usually be sold to enable a division. The courts like the idea of a clean break between the parties. But human capital cannot be sold. Property settlements that recognize human capital may require periodic payments. Some have criticized the current law as contemplating only the special case in which there is substantial marital property to divide rather than the typical case in which there are minor children and not enough property to support them.[80] This concern misses an important point in that the spouses' largest assets are probably their human capital. Their human capital has value because they have the capacity to produce future earnings. These future earnings can be the source of the compensation between the spouses.

Didn't the wives voluntarily make the choice to be housewives and mothers?

Most women who specialize in household production make that choice voluntarily, but based on assurances and the belief that they would be compensated for that choice by love and income from their husband and children. Fault divorce made it difficult for husbands to back out of those agreements without providing their wife with some compensation for the choices she made. No-fault divorce does not provide the same protection and therefore many married women are choosing to specialize less in being housewives and mothers. Some women still overestimate the durability of their marriage. They choose to be housewives and mothers and find themselves in a poor financial situation at divorce. It may have been reasonable for them to expect their marriage to be a long-term relationship. If they are divorced, they should then be compensated for their losses.

Conclusion

No-fault divorce has led to some obvious and some less obvious problems. The response to these problems has been a reform movement among legislators, judges, and academics. The reform has focused on shifting funds to divorced women and children by expanding the concept of marital property to include tangible and intangible assets that had not been considered property in the past. The recognition of pensions and retirement plans as property is long overdue. But the expanded definition of intangible property often has not been based on financial principles, and there has been a tendency for the reformers to focus on the earnings of income-earning husbands as a basis for increasing the financial awards to divorced women. The recognition of human capital as property would provide a more systematic reform of the financial arrangements at divorce. As we have seen, human capital is the income-earning capacity of individuals. The human capital possessed by individuals at marriage should be treated as separate property, but if a spouse's human capital increases during marriage, marital property is created. If a spouse's human capital decreases during marriage, compensation should be required at divorce for the reduced value of this separate property. This framework is useful for correcting the primary problems in the financial arrangements under the current divorce laws because it recognizes the effect of divorce on spouses who increased their specialization in household production during marriage. These spouses sacrifice part of the value of their human capital for the benefit of their family. If their marriage is dissolved, they should be compensated for their losses. This framework also can be used to compensate spouses who fund a student spouse's education. But I must caution against attributing a substantial share of the earnings of income-earning spouses to their marriage. Because of the large investments in human capital before marriage, most individuals' human capital is best treated as separate property.

No-fault grounds for divorce are more desirable than the fault grounds if the financial custodial awards at divorce accurately reflect the effect of marriage on the parties' property and welfare. Even with an expanded definition of property, no-fault divorce does not have the capacity to recognize all the costs of divorce. Some of the costs of divorce, such as lost companionship, search for a replacement mate or living situation, and effects on the children, are difficult to estimate. Social welfare might be improved by the introduction of mutual consent divorce, which would force the parties to estimate all of these costs of divorce and only divorce when the benefits exceed the costs. The implementation of the reforms presented in this book would lead to divorce laws that are more efficient, fairer, and more equitable.

Notes

1. Lynne Carol Halem, *Divorce Reform* (New York: Free Press, 1980), p. 288.

2. Robert H. Mnookin and Lewis Kornhauser, "Bargaining in the Shadow of the Law: The Case of Divorce," *Yale Law Journal,* Vol. 88, April 1979, p. 951, n. 3.

3. The comment to Uniform Marriage and Divorce Act, § 308 (Section 9A, Uniform Laws Annotated, 1973) on maintenance states: "The dual intention of this section and Section 307 (property division) is to encourage the court to provide for the financial needs of the spouses by property disposition rather than by an award of maintenance. Only if the available property is insufficient for the purpose and if the

spouse who seeks maintenance is unable to secure employment appropriate to his skills and interests or is occupied with child care may an award of maintenance be ordered."

4. Mary Ann Glendon, *The New Family and the New Property* (Toronto: Butterworths, 1981), p. 63; Mary Ann Glendon, "Family Law Reform in the 1980's," *Louisiana Law Review*, Vol. 44, No. 6, July 1984, p. 1561 and Joan M. Krauskopf, "A Theory for 'Just' Division of Marital Property in Missouri," *Missouri Law Review*, Vol. 41, 1976, pp. 165-178.

5. Lenore J. Weitzman, "The Economics of Divorce: Social and Economic Consequences of Property, Alimony and Child Support Awards," *UCLA Law Review*, Vol. 28, 1981, p. 1199.

6. Although alimony has become a less important source of financial support for divorced women, property settlements have not increased by a corresponding amount. Suzanne Reynolds has argued that the need standard for division of property has been underutilized because of a lack of a consensus on what constitutes "need." See Suzanne Reynolds, "The Relationship of Property Division and Alimony: The Division of Property to Address Need," *Fordham Law Review*, Vol. 56, No. 5, April 1988, p. 830.

7. Doris J. Freed and Timothy B. Walker, "Family Law in the Fifty States: An Overview," *Family Law Quarterly*, Vol. 18, No. 4, Winter 1985, p. 392.

8. Annual summaries are provided in the American Bar Association's *Family Law Quarterly*. For example, see Doris J. Freed and Timothy B. Walker, "Family Law in the Fifty States: An Overview," *Family Law Quarterly*, Vol. 23, No. 4, Winter 1990, pp. 495-608.

9. Cal. Civ. Code, § 4800.3[b][1] and [c], [c][1], [c][2],[c][3] effective January 1, 1985 [West Supp. 1985, added by Stats 1984, C. 1661, Section 2]. If the divorce occurs at least ten years after the contribution was made, the assumption is made that the contributing spouse has received adequate compensation for the investment and no further compensation is required. See Lenore J. Weitzman, *The Divorce Revolution* (New York: Free Press, 1985), p. 128.

10. Harriet N. Cohen and Patricia Hennessey, "Valuation of Property in Marital Dissolutions," *Family Law Quarterly*, Vol. 23, No. 2, Summer 1989, p. 380.

11. Allen M. Parkman, "The Treatment of Professional Goodwill in Divorce Proceedings," *Family Law Quarterly*, Vol. 18, No. 2, Summer 1984, pp. 213-224.

12. Hurley v. Hurley, 94 N.M. 641, 615 P.2d 256 (1980).

13. Krauskopf, "Marital Property," p. 170.

14. Cohen and Hennessey, "Valuation," p. 367.

15. Hertz v. Hertz, 99 N.M. 320, 657 P.2d 1169 (1983).

16. Freed and Walker, "Family Law: 1990."

17. Glendon, *New Family*, p. 68.

18. Krauskopf, "Marital Property," p. 167.

19. Weitzman, "Economics of Divorce," p. 1220 and Weitzman, *Divorce Revolution*, p. 53.

20. Weitzman, *Divorce Revolution*, p. 184.

21. Ibid., p. 387.

22. Ibid., p. 112.

23. Ibid., p. 390.

24. Ibid., p. 396.

25. Ibid., p. 400.

26. Joan M. Krauskopf, "Recompense for Financing Spouse's Education: Legal Protection for the Marital Investor in Human Capital," *Kansas Law Review,* Vol. 28, Spring 1980, pp. 379-417. She recognized that funds provided by a spouse tend to replace loans, p. 385, but then she argued that an equity interest has been created, p. 401.

27. Ibid., p. 401.

28. Ibid., pp. 384-386, discusses the funds used to finance the education.

29. Mary Ann Glendon, *Abortion and Divorce in Western Law* (Cambridge, MA: Harvard University Press, 1987), p. 82.

30. Ibid.

31. Ibid., p. 92.

32. Glendon, "Family Law Reform," p. 1558.

33. Ibid., p. 1559.

34. Ibid., p. 1565 and Lenore J. Weitzman, *The Divorce Contract* (New York: Macmillan, 1981).

35. Douglas W. Allen, "An Inquiry into the State's Role in Marriage," *Journal of Economic Behavior and Organization,* Vol. 13, 1990, pp. 171-191.

36. Ibid.

37. Almost one out of three persons marrying has been married at least once before, and almost half of all weddings involve at least one person who has been married before. See Victor R. Fuchs, *How We Live* (Cambridge: Harvard University Press, 1983), p. 151.

38. Wallerstein and Kelly note that children recognize when their parents do not have a happy marriage, but an overwhelming majority of the children that they interviewed preferred the unhappy marriage to the divorce. See Judith S. Wallerstein and Joan Berlin Kelly, *Surviving the Breakup* (New York: Basic Books, 1980), p. 10.

39. Ibid., p. 17.

40. Richard A. Posner, *Economic Analysis of Law,* 3d ed. (Boston: Little, Brown, 1986), pp. 79-126.

41. Ibid., p. 230. Contract law can be viewed as filling in the gaps in a contract. Economists assume that the parties would have chosen rules that maximize their joint net benefits, which effectively establishes efficiency as their goal. See A. Mitchell Polinsky, *An Introduction to Law and Economics* (Boston: Little, Brown, 1989), p. 27.

42. Janet K. Smith and Richard L. Smith, "Contract Law, Mutual Mistake, and Incentives to Produce and Disclose Information," *Journal of Legal Studies,* Vol. 19, No. 2, June 1990, pp. 467-488.

43. Polinsky, *Law and Economics,* p. 65.

44. For example, the courts have held that liquidated damages that exceed the expected damages due to a breach create for at least one party a disincentive to perform under a contract. The result would be inefficient. Therefore, the courts review liquidated damage provisions in a contract to make sure that they are reasonable. Lake River Corporation v. Carborundum Company, 769 Fed.2d 1284 (1985).

45. This outcome is based on the Coase Theorem, which was presented in Ronald H. Coase, "The Problem of Social Cost," *Journal of Law & Economics,* Vol. 3, 1960, pp. 3-44.

46. William Bishop, "The Choice of Remedy for Breach of Contract," *Journal of Legal Studies,* Vol. 14, June 1985, p. 299.

47. Posner, *Economic Analysis,* p. 117.

48. Ibid., pp. 117-119. In other legal systems, such as Germany's, specific performance is the general remedy to a breach of a contract. See Bishop, "Remedy for Breach," pp. 299-320.

49. For a thorough discussion of the efficiency-enhancing characteristics of contract law, see Posner, *Economic Analysis,* pp. 79-126.

50. Stephen Sugarman has objected to treating marriage as a contract. He argues that no-fault is like a contract-at-will in which there is no place for the concept of a breach and resulting damages. See Stephen D. Sugarman, "Dividing Financial Interests on Divorce," in Stephen D. Sugarman and Herma Hill Kay, eds., *Divorce Reform at the Crossroads* (New Haven: Yale University Press, 1990), p. 139. We do not talk about "fault," however, when a party unilaterally breaches a commercial contract and subjects itself to damages. The parties anticipated performance, but they recognized each party had a right to breach the contract subject to the requirement of compensation. That is the more appropriate analogy.

51. Harry D. Krause, *Family Law,* 2d ed. (St. Paul, MN: West, 1986), p. 45.

52. Allen M. Parkman, "Dividing Human Capital with an Eye to Future Earnings," *Family Advocate,* Vol. 12, No. 2, Fall 1989, pp. 34-37.

53. A discussion of problems associated with the inappropriate definition of property is contained in Allen M. Parkman, "Human Capital as Property in Divorce Settlements," *Arkansas Law Review,* Vol. 40, No. 3, 1987, pp. 439-467.

54. The standard work on earnings profiles and, therefore, human capital is Gary S. Becker, *Human Capital,* 2d ed. (New York: Columbia University Press, 1975).

55. It has been suggested that rather than incorporating human capital into the traditional notions of property, some of the situations discussed here should be treated as "exceptions" to the equal treatment of the spouses. See Weitzman, *Divorce Revolution,* pp. 104-105. The incorporation of human capital into property is more systematic, however, and would permit equal treatment of the spouses.

56. The court cited a 1980 law that stated that marriage is an economic partnership and included medical licenses and law degrees as marital property. The court held that special skills that generate substantial income should not be distinguished from degrees or licenses. *USA Today,* July 3, 1991, 1D.

57. It is not common for the courts to hold that a spouse has wasted potential income during marriage. Mark Gastineau, a defensive end for the New York Jets football team, was required to pay his wife $100,000 for prematurely retiring from professional football to spend time with actress Brigitte Nielsen, however. *USA Today,* July 3, 1991, 11C.

58. One hundred dollars that I will receive a year from now is worth less than that amount to me at the present time. If the current rate of interest is 10 percent, I can borrow $91 now with the understanding that I will owe the bank $100 in a year. I will be able to pay off the loan with $100, when it arrives. The $100 a year from now has been discounted to its value now, which is $91. The same procedure can be used for a series of payments.

59. The standard formula for valuing an infinite income stream is $V = I/(r - g)$, where V is the value, I is the initial annual income, r is the required rate of return on the investment, and g is the anticipated growth rate of the annual income. In this example, $V = \$25,000/(.5 - 0) = \$50,000$.

60. The determination of the career path of an individual who has limited his or her participation in the labor force is not easy. More people start out intending to become medical doctors than end up graduating from medical school. The courts have to be realistic in determining the career that a housewife would have pursued.

61. Doris J. Freed and Timothy B. Walker, "Family Law in the Fifty States: An Overview," *Family Law Quarterly,* Vol. 22, No. 4, Winter 1989, p. 407.

62. Freed and Walker, "Family Law: 1985," p. 393.

63. If one spouse fraudulently induced the other spouse into incurring this loss, then the full amount of the loss should be levied on the defrauding spouse. For example, a husband might ask his wife to give up a high-paying, but unique, job. The husband has been offered a high-paying job in a new location that would benefit the entire family. The wife's employment prospects are much poorer in that location, however. The husband might assure the wife that the marriage is stable, but if he takes actions that contradict that situation, such as having an affair, it would seem reasonable that he should be assessed the full amount of his wife's loss if there is a divorce.

64. The $10,000 lost during the current year has a discounted value of $10,000. The loss in the second year is $9,000. Because it will occur in the future, it has a discounted value of $8,182. The calculation can be made with the lost earnings in each of the future years. The sum of the discounted values will be $42,410.

65. Knowing that they were going to be absent from the labor force for certain periods, women traditionally went into careers that tended to be less sensitive to absences from the labor force. These careers entailed general skills supported by certification. Teaching and nursing are obvious examples.

66. See Severin Borenstein and Paul N. Courant, "How to Carve a Medical Degree: Human Capital Assets in Divorce Settlements," *American Economic Review,* Vol. 79, No. 5, December 1989, pp. 992-1009.

67. Victor R. Fuchs, *How We Live* (Cambridge: Harvard University Press, 1983), p. 152.

68. Ibid., p. 151.

69. Ibid.

70. Lloyd Cohen, "Marriage, Divorce, and Quasi Rents; or 'I Gave Him the Best Years of My Life,'" *Journal of Legal Studies,* Vol. 16, 1987, p. 293.

71. It has been argued that by reducing the cost of having children outside of marriage, AFDC has contributed to the increase in the number of children born to unwed mothers. See Charles A. Murray, *Losing Ground: American Social Policy, 1950-1980* (New York: Basic Books, 1984).

72. Glendon, "Family Law Reform," p. 1565, argues that the two issues should be combined.

73. Margaret F. Brinig and June Carbone, "The Reliance Interest in Marriage and Divorce," *Tulane Law Review,* Vol. 62, No. 5, May 1988, p. 893.

74. Weitzman, "Economics of Divorce," p. 1221.

75. Weitzman, *Divorce Revolution,* p. 143.

76. Posner, *Economic Analysis,* p. 136.

77. Bishop, "Remedies for Breach," p. 300.

78. Wallerstein and Kelly, *Surviving,* p. 17.

79. The median duration of marriages in the United States was less than seven years in 1986. *Statistical Abstract of the United States, 1990* (Washington, DC: Government Printing Office, 1990), Table 130, p. 88.

80. Glendon, "Family Law Reform," p. 1557.

Appendix

Human capital could be incorporated into a statutory form by amending the community property version of Section 307 of the Uniform Marriage and Divorce Act to delete provisions struck out and add material enclosed in brackets:

Section 307. [Disposition of Property] In a proceeding for dissolution of the marriage, legal separation, or disposition of property following a decree of dissolution of the marriage or legal dissolution by a court which lacked personal jurisdiction over the absent spouse or lacked jurisdiction to dispose of the property, the court shall assign each spouse's separate property to that spouse. It also shall divide community [marital] property, without regard to marital misconduct[.]in just proportions after considering all relevant factors including:

(1) contribution of each spouse to acquisition of the marital property, including contribution of a spouse as homemaker;

(2) value of the property set apart to each spouse;

(3) duration of the marriage; and

(4) economic circumstances of each spouse when the division of property is to become effective, including the desirability of awarding the family house or the right to live therein for a reasonable period to the spouse having custody of any children.

[(a) For purposes of this Act, "separate property" means all property acquired by either spouse prior to the marriage.

(1) Separate property can consist of:
    a. real property
    b. personal property
    c. financial property and
    d. human capital.

(2) Human capital is the value of an individual's expected future net earnings. The anticipated career and, therefore, the human capital of each spouse at the commencement of the marriage is separate property. For a spouse who remains relatively active in the labor force during marriage, the presumption at a dissolution of the marriage is that the career pursued during the marriage was the one that was anticipated at the commencement of the marriage.

(3) If a spouse limits his/her employment or educational opportunities during the marriage so that he/she can no longer expect the future earnings that he/she could reasonably have expected for that period at the commencement of the marriage, the reduction in the value of that spouse's human capital at dissolution will be viewed as a contribution of separate property to the marriage. The value of the contribution will be determined by the difference between the earnings that the spouse could have

expected after the dissolution without the limitations, in contrast to the earnings that the spouse can then expect. The value of the contribution is a debt of the community and an asset of the contributing spouse.

(4) Any funds from a spouse's separate property that were used to finance the education and training of the other spouse will be presumed to be a loan to that spouse. If the enhanced earnings of the student spouse due to the loan have not produced a reasonable return prior to the dissolution, the spouse providing the funds shall be reimbursed an amount that represents the unamortized value of the loan.

(b) For purposes of this Act, "marital property" means all property acquired by either spouse subsequent to the marriage,

(1) with the following exceptions:

a. property acquired by gift, bequest, devise, or descent;

b. property acquired in exchange for property acquired before the marriage or in exchange for property acquired by gift, bequest, devise, or descent;

c. property acquired by a spouse after a decree of legal separation;

d. property excluded by valid agreement of the parties; and

e. the increase in the value of property acquired before the marriage.

(2) Marital property can consist of:

a. real property

b. personal property

c. financial property and

d. human capital.

(3) The human capital acquired during the marriage is the value at the dissolution of the marriage of the increase in the anticipated future earnings of either spouse after the dissolution compared to the earnings during that period that could have been anticipated at the marriage. For a spouse who remains relatively active in the labor force during the marriage, the presumption at a dissolution is that the career pursued during the marriage was the one that was anticipated at the commencement of the marriage.

(c) All property acquired by either spouse after the marriage and before a decree of legal separation is presumed to be marital property. The presumption of marital property is overcome by a showing that the property was acquired by a method listed in subsection (b)(1)a.-e.]

References

Allen, Douglas W. 1990. "An Inquiry into the State's Role in Marriage." *Journal of Economic Behavior and Organization* 13: 171-191.

Arendell, Terry. 1986. *Mothers and Divorce*. Berkeley: University of California Press.

Arnold, Roger. 1986. "Marriage, Divorce, and Property Rights: A Natural Rights Framework," in Joseph R. Peden and Fred R. Glahe, eds., *The American Family and the State*. Pp. 195-227. San Francisco: Pacific Research Institute for Public Policy.

Bahr, Steven J. 1983. "Marital Dissolution Laws: Impact of Recent Changes for Women." *Journal of Family Issues* 4: 455-466.

Baker, Lynn A. 1990. "Promulgating the Marriage Contract." *Journal of Law Reform* 23: 217-264.

Bayer, A. E. 1969. "Marriage Plans and Educational Aspirations." *American Journal of Sociology* 75: 239-244.

Becker, Gary. 1965. "A Theory of the Allocation of Time." *Economic Journal* 75: 493-517.

_____. 1975. *Human Capital*, 2d ed. New York: Columbia University Press.

_____. 1976. *The Economic Approach to Human Behavior*. Chicago: University of Chicago Press.

_____. 1981. *A Treatise on the Family*. Cambridge, MA: Harvard University Press.

_____. 1989. "Family" in John Eatwell, Murray Milgate, and Peter Newman, eds., *The New Palgrave: Social Economics*. Pp. 64-76. New York: Norton.

Becker, Gary S., Elizabeth M. Landes, and Robert Michael. 1977. "An Analysis of Marital Instability." *Journal of Political Economy* 85: 1141-1187.

Ben-Porath, Yoram. 1982. "Economics and the Family--Match or Mismatch? A Review of Becker's *A Treatise on the Family*." *Journal of Economic Literature* 20: 52-64.

Bianchi, Suzanne M., and Daphne Spain. 1986. *American Women in Transition*. New York: Russell Sage.

Billington, Ray Allen. 1974. *American's Frontier Heritage*. Albuquerque, NM: University of New Mexico Press.

Bishop, William. 1985. "The Choice of Remedy for Breach of Contract." *Journal of Legal Studies* 14: 299-320.

Black, Duncan. 1958. *The Theory of Committees and Elections*. Cambridge, UK: Cambridge University Press.

Blakemore, Arthur E., and Stuart A. Low. 1984. "Sex Differences in Occupational Selection: The Case of College Majors." *Review of Economics and Statistics* 66: 157-163.

Blau, Francine D., and Marianne A. Ferber. 1986. *The Economics of Women, Men, and Work.* Englewood Cliffs, NJ: Prentice-Hall.

Blumberg, Grace Ganz. 1985. "New Models of Marriage and Divorce" in Kingsley Davis, ed., *Contemporary Marriage.* Pp. 349-372. New York: Russell Sage.

_____. 1986. "Marital Property Treatment of Pensions, Disability Pay, Workers' Compensation, and Other Wage Substitutes: An Insurance, or Replacement, Analysis." *UCLA Law Review* 33: 1250-1308.

Borenstein, Severin, and Paul N. Courant. 1989. "How to Carve a Medical Degree: Human Capital Assets in Divorce Settlements." *American Economic Review* 79: 992-1009.

Bouton, Katherine. 1984. "Women and Divorce." *New York,* October 8, 1984, 34-41.

Boyer, Helen. 1985. "Equitable Interest in Enhanced Earning Capacity: The Treatment of a Professional Degree at Dissolution." *Washington Law Review* 60: 431-459.

Brinig, Margaret F., and June Carbone. 1988. "The Reliance Interest in Marriage and Divorce." *Tulane Law Review* 62: 855-905.

Brody, Stuart A. 1970. "California's Divorce Reform: Its Sociological Implications." *Pacific Law Journal* 1: 223-232.

Bruch, Carol S. 1982a. "The Definition and Division of Marital Property in California: Towards Parity and Simplicity." *Hastings Law Journal* 33: 769-869.

_____. 1982b. "Developing Standards for Child Support Payments: A Critique of Current Practice." *UC-Davis Law Review* 16: 49-64.

_____. 1983. "Of Work, Family Wealth, and Equality." *Family Law Quarterly* 17: 99-108.

Carbone, June. 1990. "Economics, Feminism, and the Reinvention of Alimony: A Reply to Ira Ellman." *Vanderbilt Law Review* 43: 1463-1501.

Carbone, June, and Margaret F. Brinig. 1991. "Rethinking Marriage: Feminist Ideology, Economic Change, and Divorce Reform." *Tulane Law Review* 65: 953-1010.

Chandler, Jon Andrew. 1981. "A Property Theory of Future Earning Potential in Dissolution Proceedings." *Washington Law Review* 56: 277-288.

Chase, Marilyn. 1985. "Single Trouble: The No-Fault Divorce Has a Fault of Its Own, Many Women Learn." *Wall Street Journal* January 21, 1985, 1.

Cherlin, Andrew J. 1981. *Marriage, Divorce, Remarriage.* Cambridge, MA: Harvard University Press.

Clark, Homer H., Jr. 1988. *The Law of Domestic Relations in the United States,* 2d ed. St. Paul, MN: West.

Coase, Ronald H. 1960. "The Problem of Social Cost." *Journal of Law and Economics* 3: 3-44.

Cohen, Harriet N., and Patricia Hennessey. 1989. "Valuation of Property in Marital Dissolutions." *Family Law Quarterly* 23: 339-381.

Cohen, Lloyd. 1987. "Marriage, Divorce, and Quasi Rents; or 'I Gave Him the Best Years of My Life,'" *Journal of Legal Studies* 16: 267-304.

Coombs, E. Raedene. "The Human Capital Concept as a Basis for Property Settlement at Divorce: Theory and Implementation." *Journal of Divorce* 2: 329-355.

Cooter, Robert, and Mevin Aron Eisenberg. 1985. "Damages for Breach of Contract." *California Law Review* 73: 1432-1481.

Davis, Kingsley, ed. 1985. *Contemporary Marriage: Comparative Perspectives on a Changing Institution.* New York: Russell Sage.

Dixon, Ruth B., and Lenore J. Weitzman. 1982. "When Husbands File for Divorce." *Journal of Marriage and the Family* 44: 103-115.

Duncan, Greg J., and Saul D. Hoffman. 1985. "A Reconsideration of the Economic Consequences of Divorce." *Demography* 22: 485-97.

Egge, Karl A., and Robert L. Bunting. 1985. "Divorce Settlements: How to Divide Human Capital Assets." *Trial* August 1985, 27-29.

Eisler, Riane Tennenhaus. 1977. *Dissolution, No-Fault Divorce, Marriage, and the Future of Women.* New York: McGraw-Hill.

Ellman, Ira Mark. 1989. "The Theory of Alimony." *California Law Review* 77: 3-81.

England, Paula, and George Farkas. 1986. *Households, Employment, and Gender.* New York: Aldine De Gruyter.

Espensade, Thomas J. 1979. "The Economic Consequences of Divorce." *Journal of Marriage and the Family* 41: 615-625.

Ferber, Marianne A., and William Sander. 1989. "Of Women, Men, and Divorce: Not by Economics Alone." *Review of Social Economics* 47: 15-24.

Fineman, Martha L. 1986. "Illusive Equality: On Weitzman's *Divorce Revolution*," in Howard S.Erlanger, ed., "Review Symposium on Weitzman's *Divorce Revolution*." *American Bar Foundation Research Journal* 1986: 781-790.

Foote, Caleb, Robert Levy, and Frank E. Sander. 1976. *Cases and Materials on Family Law.* 2d ed. Boston: Little, Brown.

Freed, Doris J. 1972. "Grounds for Divorce in the American Jurisdictions." *Family Law Quarterly* 6: 178-212.

Freed, Doris J., and Timothy B. Walker. 1985. "Family Law in the Fifty States: An Overview." *Family Law Quarterly* 18: 369-471.

_____. 1989. "Family Law in the Fifty States: An Overview." *Family Law Quarterly* 22: 367-521.

_____. 1990. "Family Law in the Fifty States: An Overview." *Family Law Quarterly* 23: 495-608.

Freiden, Alan. 1974. "The United States Marriage Market." *Journal of Political Economy* 82 Pt. 2: s34-s53.

Friedman, Daniel. 1989. "The Efficient Breach Fallacy." *Journal of Legal Studies* 18: 1-24.

Friedman, Lawrence M. 1973. *A History of American Law.* New York: Simon and Schuster.

_____. 1984. "Rights of Passage: Divorce Law in Historical Perspective." *Oregon Law Review* 63: 649-669.

Fuchs, Victor R. 1983. *How We Live.* Cambridge, MA: Harvard University Press.

_____. 1986. "Sex Differences in Economic Well-Being." *Science* 232, April 25, 1986, 459-464.

_____. 1988. *Women's Quest for Economic Equality.* Cambridge, MA: Harvard University Press.

Fulop, Marcel. 1980. "A Brief Survey of the Literature on the Economic Analysis of Marriage and Divorce." *American Economist* 1980: 12-18.

Glendon, Mary Ann. 1981. *The New Family and the New Property.* Toronto: Butterworths.

_____. 1984. "Family Law Reform in the 1980's." *Louisiana Law Review* 44: 1553-1573.

_____. 1987. *Abortion and Divorce in Western Law*. Cambridge, MA: Harvard University Press.

_____. 1989. *The Transformation of Family Law*. Chicago: University of Chicago Press.

Glick, Paul C., and Arthur J. Norton. 1973. "Perspectives on the Recent Upturn in Divorce and Remarriage." *Demography* 10: 301-314.

Glick, Paul C., and Graham B. Spanier. 1980. "Married and Unmarried Cohabitation in the United States." *Journal of Marriage and the Family* 42: 19-30.

Goddard, John Leslie. 1968. "The Proposal for Divorce Upon Petition and Without Fault." *Journal of the State Bar of California* 43: 90-102.

Golden, Lawrence J. 1983. *Equitable Distribution of Property*. Colorado Springs, CO: Shepard's/McGraw-Hill.

Goldin, Claudia. 1989. "Life-Cycle Labor-Force Participation of Married Women: Historical Evidence and Implications." *Journal of Labor Economics* 7: 20-47.

_____. 1990. *Understanding the Gender Gap*. Oxford, UK: Oxford University Press.

Grossbard-Shechtman, Shoshana A., and Shoshana Neuman. 1988. "Women's Labor Supply and Marital Choice." *Journal of Political Economy* 96: 294-302.

Gunning, J. Patrick. 1984. "Marriage Law and Human Capital Investment: A Comment." *Southern Economic Journal* 51: 594-597.

Gunter, B. G., and Doyle Johnson. 1978. "Divorce Filing as Role Behavior: Effect of No-Fault Law on Divorce Filing Patterns." *Journal of Marriage and the Family* 40: 571-574.

Haas, Theodore F. 1988. "The Rationality and Enforceability of Contractual Restrictions on Divorce." *North Carolina Law Review* 66: 879-930.

Halem, Lynne Carol. 1980. *Divorce Reform*. New York: Free Press.

Hannan, Michael T. 1982. "Families, Markets, and Social Structures: An Essay on Becker's *A Treatise on the Family*." *Journal of Economic Literature* 20: 65-72.

Haurin, Donald R. 1989. "Women's Labor Market Reactions to Family Disruptions." *Review of Economics and Statistics* 71: 54-61.

Hauserman, Nancy R. 1983. "Homemakers and Divorce: Problems of the Invisible Occupation." *Family Law Quarterly* 17: 41-63.

Hayes, James A. 1970. "California Divorce Reform: Parting is Sweeter Sorrow." *American Bar Association Journal* 56: 660-663.

Hersch, Joni. 1991. "The Impact of Nonmarket Work on Market Wages." *American Economic Review* 81: 157-160.

Hewlett, Sylvia Ann. 1986. *A Lesser Life: The Myth of Women's Liberation in America*. New York: William Morrow.

Hoffman, Saul D., and Greg J. Duncan. 1988. "What Are the Economic Consequences of Divorce?" *Demography* 25: 641-645.

Jacob, Herbert. 1986. "Faulting No-Fault," in Howard S. Erlanger, ed., "Review Symposium on Weitzman's *Divorce Revolution*, *American Bar Foundation Research Journal* 1986: 773-780.

_____. 1988. *Silent Revolution: The Transformation of Divorce Law in the United States*. Chicago: University of Chicago Press.

_____. 1989. "Another Look at No-Fault Divorce and the Post-Divorce Finances of Women." *Law and Society Review* 23: 95-115.

Johnson, William R., and Jonathan Skinner. 1986. "Labor Supply and Marital Separation." *American Economic Review* 76: 455-469.

———. 1988. "Accounting for Changes in the Labor Supply of Recently Divorced Women." *Journal of Human Resources* 23: 417-436.

Kay, Herma Hill. 1968. "A Family Court: The California Proposal." *California Law Review* 56: 1205-1248.

———. 1987a. "Equality and Difference: A Perspective on No-Fault Divorce and Its Aftermath." *University of Cincinnati Law Review* 56: 1-90.

———. 1987b. "An Appraisal of California's No-Fault Divorce Law." *California Law Review* 75: 291-319.

Kiker, B. F. 1980. "Divorce Litigation: Valuing the Spouse's Contribution to the Marriage." *Trial*, December 1980, 48-50.

King, Allan G. 1982a. "Human Capital and the Risk of Divorce: An Asset in Search of a Property Right." *Southern Economic Journal* 49: 536-541.

———. 1982b. "Divorce Settlements: The Value of Human Capital." *Trial*, August 1982, 48-51.

Klein, Benjamin, Robert G. Crawford, and Armen A. Alchian. 1978. "Vertical Integration, Appropriable Rents, and the Competitive Contracting Process." *Journal of Law and Economics* 21: 297-326.

Krause, Harry D. 1986. *Family Law*, 2d ed. St. Paul, MN: West.

Krauskopf, Joan M. 1976. "A Theory for "Just" Division of Marital Property in Missouri." *Missouri Law Review* 41: 165-178.

———. 1978. "Marital Property at Marriage Dissolution." *Missouri Law Review* 43: 157-198.

———. 1980. "Recompense for Financing Spouse's Education: Legal Protection for the Marital Investor in Human Capital." *Kansas Law Review* 28: 379-417.

———. 1989. "Theories of Property Division/Spousal Support: Searching for Solutions to the Mystery." *Family Law Quarterly* 23: 253-278.

Kressel, Kenneth. 1985. *The Process of Divorce*. New York: Basic Books.

Krom, Howard. 1970. "California's Divorce Law Reform: An Historical Analysis." *Pacific Law Journal* 1: 156-181.

Kronman, Anthony T. 1978. "Specific Performance." *University of Chicago Law Review* 45: 351-382.

Laine, Charles R. 1985. "Distribution of Jointly Owned Private Goods by the Demand-Revealing Pocess: Applications to Divorce Settlements and Estate Administration." *Public Choice* 47: 437-457.

Landes, Elizabeth. 1978. "Economics of Alimony." *Journal of Legal Studies* 7: 35-63.

Lazear, Edward P., and Robert T. Michael. 1988. *Allocation of Income Within the Household*. Chicago: University of Chicago Press.

Leigh, J. Paul. 1985. "Divorce as a Risky Prospect." *Applied Economics* 17: 309-320.

Levy, Robert. 1969. *Uniform Marriage and Divorce Legislation: A Preliminary Analysis*. Chicago: American Bar Association.

Lichter, Daniel T., and Janice A. Costanzo. 1987. "How Do Demographic Changes Affect Labor Force Participation of Women?" *Monthly Labor Review*, November 1987, 23-25.

Lillard, Lee A., and Linda J. Waite. 1990. "Determinants of Divorce." *Social Security Bulletin* 53, February 1990, 29-31.

158 *References*

Lommerud, Kjell Erik. 1989. "Marital Division of Labor with Risk of Divorce: The Role of "Voice" Enforcement of Contracts." *Journal of Labor Economics* 7: 113-127.

London, Kathryn A. 1991. "Cohabitation, Marriage, Marital Dissolution, and Remarriage: United States, 1988." U.S. Department of Health and Human Services, Advanced Data No. 194, January 4, 1991.

Melli, Marygold S. 1986. "Constructing a Social Problem: The Post-Divorce Plight of Women and Children," in Howard S. Erlanger, ed., "Review Symposium on Weitzman's *Divorce Revolution.*" *American Bar Foundation Research Journal* 1986: 759-772.

Michael, Robert T. 1978. "The Rise in Divorce Rates, 1960-1974: Age-Specific Components." *Demography* 15: 345-347.

_____. 1985. "Consequences of the Rise in Female Labor Force Participation Rates: Questions and Probes." *Journal of Labor Economics* 3: s117-s146.

_____. 1988. "Why Did the U.S. Divorce Rate Double Within a Decade," in T. Paul Schultz, ed., *Research in Population Economics* 6: 367-400.

Mincer, Jacob, and Haim Ofek. 1982. "Interrupted Work Careers: Depreciation and Restoration of Human Capital." *Journal of Human Resources* 17: 1-24.

Mincer, Jacob, and Solomon Polachek. 1974. "Family Investments in Human Capital: Earnings of Women." *Journal of Political Economy* 82 Pt. 2: s76-s108.

_____. 1978. "Women's Earnings Reexamined." *Journal of Human Resources* 8: 118-134.

Mnookin, Robert H., and Lewis Kornhauser. 1979. "Bargaining in the Shadow of the Law: The Case of Divorce." *Yale Law Journal* 88: 950-997.

Mott, Frank L., and Sylvia F. Moore. 1978. "The Causes and Consequences of Marital Breakdown," in Frank L. Mott, ed., *Women, Work, and Family.* Pp. 113-136. Lexington, MA: Lexington Books.

Mueller, Dennis C. 1989. *Public Choice II.* Cambridge, UK: Cambridge University Press.

Murray, Charles A. 1984. *Losing Ground: American Social Policy, 1950-1980.* New York: Basic Books.

O'Connell, Mary E. 1988. "Alimony After No-Fault: A Practice in Search of a Theory." *New England Law Review* 23: 437-513.

Oldham, J. Thomas. 1989. *Divorce, Separation and the Distribution of Property.* New York: Law Journal Seminars-Press.

O'Neill, June. 1990. "Women and Wages." *American Enterprise* 1: November/December 1990, 25-33.

Parkman, Allen M. 1984. "The Treatment of Professional Goodwill in Divorce Proceedings." *Family Law Quarterly* 18: 213-224.

_____. 1986. "The Economic Approach to Valuing a Sacrificed Career in Divorce Proceedings." *Journal of the American Academy of Matrimonial Lawyers* 2: 45-56.

_____. 1987. "Human Capital as Property in Divorce Settlements." *Arkansas Law Review* 40: 439-467.

_____. 1989. "Dividing Human Capital With an Eye to Future Earnings." *Family Advocate* 12: 34-37.

_____. 1992. "Unilateral Divorce and the Labor-Force Participation Rate of Married Women, Revisited." *American Economic Review* 82: 671-678.

Peters, H. Elizabeth. 1986. "Marriage and Divorce: Informational Constraints and Private Contracting." *American Economic Review* 76: 437-454.

Polinsky, A. Mitchell. 1989. *An Introduction to Law and Economics,* 2d ed. Boston: Little, Brown.

Pollak, Robert A. 1985. "A Transaction Cost Approach to Families and Households." *Journal of Economic Literature* 23: 581-608.

Posner, Richard. 1986. *The Economic Analysis of Law,* 3d ed. Boston: Little, Brown.

Preston, Samuel H., and John McDonald. 1979. "The Incidence of Divorce Within Cohorts of American Marriage Contracted Since the Civil War." *Demography* 16: February, 1-25.

Price, Sharon J., and Patrick C. Mckenry. 1988. *Divorce.* Newbury Park, CA: Sage.

Reppy, Susan W. 1970. "The End of Innocence: Elimination of Fault in California Divorce Law." *UCLA Law Review* 17: 1306-1332.

Reppy, William A., Jr. 1989. "Major Events in the Evolution of American Community Property Law and Their Import to Equitable Distribution States." *Family Law Quarterly* 23: 163-192.

Rheinstein, Max. 1972. *Marriage, Stability, Divorce and the Law.* Chicago: University of Chicago Press.

Riley, Glenda. 1991. *Divorce: An American Tradition.* Oxford, UK: Oxford University Press.

Ross, Heather L., and Isabel V. Sawhill. 1975. *Time of Transition: The Growth of Families Headed by Women.* Washington, DC: Urban Institute.

Sandell, Steven H., and David Shapiro. 1978. "An Exchange: The Theory of Human Capital and the Earnings of Women." *Journal of Human Resources* 8: 103-117.

Sander, William. 1985. "Women, Work, and Divorce." *American Economic Review* 75: 519-523.

Schoen, Robert, Harry N. Greenblatt, and Robert B. Mielke. 1975. "California's Experience With Non-Adversary Divorce." *Demography* 12: 223-244.

Schoen, Robert, and Verne E. Nelson. 1974. "Marriage, Divorce, and Mortality." *Demography* 11: 267-290.

Schoen, Robert, William Urton, Karen Woodrow, and John Baj. 1985. "Marriage and Divorce in Twentieth Century American Cohorts." *Demography* 22: 101-114.

Schwartz, Alan. 1979. "The Case for Specific Performance." *Yale Law Journal* 89: 271-306.

Schwartz, Leonard Charles. 1982. "Divorce and Earning Ability." *Detroit College of Law Review* 1982: 69-80.

Scott, Elizabeth. 1990. "Rational Decisionmaking About Marriage and Divorce." *Virginia Law Review* 76: 9-94.

Singer, Jana B. 1989. "Divorce Reform and Gender Justice." *North Carolina Law Review* 67: 1103-1121.

Smith, James P., and Michael P. Ward. 1985. "Time-Series Growth in the Female Labor Force." *Journal of Labor Economics* 3: s59-s90.

Spanier, Graham B. 1985. "Cohabitation in the 1980s: Recent Changes in the United States," in Kingsley Davis, ed., *Contemporary Marriage.* Pp. 91-112. New York: Russell Sage.

Sugarman, Stephen D., and Herma Hill Kay, eds. 1990. *Divorce Reform at the Crossroads.* New Haven: Yale University Press.

Swan, George Steven. 1986. "The Political Economy of American Family Policy, 1945-85." *Population and Development Review* 12: 739-758.

Sweet, James A. and Ruy Teixeira. 1984. "Breaking Tradition: Schooling, Marriage, Work, and Childrearing in the Lives of Young Women, 1960-1980." Center For Demography and Ecology, University of Wisconsin Madison, CDE Working Paper 84-13.

Walker, Timothy B. 1971. "Beyond Fault: An Examination of Patterns of Behavior in Response to Present Divorce Laws." *Journal of Family Law* 10: 267-299.

Wallerstein, Judith S., and Joan Berlin Kelly. 1980. *Surviving the Breakup.* New York: Basic Books.

Weiss, Yoram, and Robert J. Willis. 1985. "Children as Collective Goods and Divorce Settlements." *Journal of Labor Economics* 3: 268-292.

Weitzman, Lenore J. 1981a. *The Divorce Contract.* New York: Macmillan.

_____. 1981b. "The Economics of Divorce: Social and Economic Consequences of Property, Alimony and Child Support Awards." *UCLA Law Review* 28: 1181-1268.

_____. 1985a. *The Divorce Revolution.* New York: Free Press.

_____. 1985b. "The Divorce Law Revolution and the Transformation of Legal Marriage" in Kingsley Davis, ed., *Contemporary Marriage.* Pp. 301-348. New York: Russell Sage.

_____. 1986. "Bringing the Law Back," in Howard S. Erlanger, ed., "Review Symposium on Weitzman's *Divorce Revolution.*" *American Bar Foundation Research Journal* 1986: 791-797.

Welch, Charles E., III, and Sharon Price-Bonham. 1983. "A Decade of No-Fault Divorce Revisited: California, Georgia, and Washington." *Journal of Marriage and the Family* 45: 411-418.

Wheeler, Michael. 1974. *No-Fault Divorce.* Boston: Beacon.

_____. 1980. *Divided Children.* New York: Norton.

Williamson, Oliver E. 1975. *Markets and Hierarchies: Analysis and Antitrust Implications.* New York: Free Press.

Wright, Gerald C., and Dorothy M. Stetson. 1978. "The Impact of No-Fault Divorce Law Reform on Divorce in American States." *Journal of Marriage and the Family* 40: 575-580.

Zalokar, Nadja. 1988. "Male-Female Differences in Occupational Choice and the Demand for General and Occupation-Specific Human Capital." *Economic Inquiry* 26: 59-74.

About the Book and Author

Since 1970, all the states adopted no-fault divorce statutes, which have had the unexpected effect of producing dire financial conditions for many divorced women and their children. In this important study, economist and lawyer Allen Parkman shows how no-fault divorce has systematically operated against the interests of these women and children.

With rare economic and legal insight, Parkman argues that by changing the grounds for divorce without changing the laws that define and allocate property at divorce, the legal system created substantial injustices. The key mistake, he suggests, was in accepting a definition of property that did not include the income-earning capacity--human capital--of the individuals involved. Using human capital theory, Parkman criticizes current divorce law and presents a framework for reform that would reduce the injustices introduced by no-fault divorce. He concludes that a thorough reform, however, may require the changing of the grounds for divorce to mutual consent.

This book is essential reading for scholars, professionals, and, indeed, for anyone interested in the health and future of the family and the well-being of women in contemporary U.S. society.

Allen Parkman, Ph.D, J.D., is the Regents' Professor of Management at the University of New Mexico. His articles on family law have appeared in numerous journals, including the *American Economic Review*, the *Family Advocate*, the *Family Law Quarterly*, and the *ABA Journal*.

Index

Adultery 1, 16, 17, 56, 139, 140
Aid to Families with Dependent Children 59, 83, 136
Alimony 5, 37, 38, 80, 81, 83, 86, 93, 113
  California laws 54
  effect of no-fault divorce 2, 82
  human capital and 137
  marriage rate and 37
  premarital agreements and 97
  removal of fault grounds 5
Asymmetric contributions 37

Bargaining power 45, 64, 76
  married women and 82
Becker, Gary S. 27, 36, 45, 78
Brody, Stuart A. 57
Brown, Edmund G. 55, 60
Bruch, Carol S. 83
Business goodwill 7
  defined 115

California
  deliberations on no-fault divorce 54
  divorce rate 78
  Family Law Act 4, 61, 80, 113
  introduction of no-fault divorce 54
  legislative report on no-fault divorce 58
  no-fault divorce in 1
  no-fault divorce proceedings 56
  pensions 90
California Commission on the Status of Women 58
California State Bar 56
Career assets 117
Case law 53, 93

Catholic church 14-17, 58
Child custody 64
  California laws 54
  cost of 136
  cost to custodial parent 7
  negotiations and 76
  standards 57
Child support 5, 38, 81, 84, 89, 118, 129
  California laws 54
  cost of 118
  criteria for 112
  effect of no-fault divorce 2, 82, 113
  human capital and 136
Cohabitation 15, 64, 94
Cohen, Lloyd 32, 136
Colorado 133
Commission on the Family 4, 55, 57, 58
Commissioners on Uniform State Laws 58
Common law states 19, 20, 88, 89, 113
Community property 20, 38, 80, 88, 113, 130
  basis for unequal shares 57
  California laws 55, 56
  economic analysis and 5
  equal division of 80
  pensions and 89
Comparative advantage 28, 32, 66
Contraceptives 33, 59, 60, 75
Contract law 123-125, 128
Costs of divorce 63, 86, 122
  for divorcing spouses 121
  ignored by courts 45
  ignored by no-fault divorce 111

mutual consent and 138
psychological costs 118
recognizing all the 123
subjective costs 7
Council of Trent 14
Cruelty 1, 17, 54, 56, 77
    common fault ground for divorce 18
    under mutual consent divorce 139

DeBurgh v. DeBurgh 55
Degrees 98
    as property 7, 114
    professional 89, 93
Desertion 1, 16
Divorce rate 8, 21, 59, 71, 75, 78
    between 1965 and 1975 59
    California experience 78
    causation 72
    effect of no-fault divorce 45, 75
    gains from marriage and 74
    recent trends in 72
Duncan, Greg J. 82

Economic analysis
    basic assumptions of 25
    divorce and 35
    marriage decision and 27
    no-fault divorce and 3
    nonmarket activities and 25
    of child support 7
    of introduction of no-fault 58
    property and 38
Education
    family welfare and 65
    human capital and 39, 130
    incentives created by no-fault divorce
        2
    marriage and 98
    no-fault divorce and 71
    parental involvement in 103
    spousal support in California 114
    spousal support of 134
Efficiency
    as the goal of human action 120
    contract law and 123
Equal division
    community property and 20

-property in California 5
Equitable distribution 20, 89
    common law states 113
    New York laws 86

Family court 55-57, 60
Family Court Act 55
Fault divorce
    after World War II 17
    California during 55
    California laws 54
    divorced men's view 61
    grounds 1
    hypocrisy of 63
    long-term contract 32
    negotiated settlements 18
    perjury and 2
    property settlements 6
    protection provided by 38
    second best and 46
    specific performance and 64
    when contested 5
Feminists 118
Fertility rate 38, 74, 75
Financial condition of divorced women
        5, 42, 71, 79, 82, 84, 88, 103
    groups affected 116
Freiden, Alan 35
Friedman, David D. 43
Fuchs, Victor R. 59, 74, 99, 100, 135

Garrison, Marsha 86
Glendon, Mary Ann 76, 83, 119
Glick, Paul C. 94

Hayes, James 56, 57, 61, 63
Hayes, Janne 61, 62
Hoffman, Saul D. 82
Human capital 2, 7, 45, 65, 87, 93, 98,
        102, 111, 117, 122, 130-138
    as property 130
    at divorce 7
    at marriage 41
    changes during marriage 131
    concerns about the use of 140
    decreasing during marriage 42, 132
    defined 6

education and 65
effect of marriage on 38, 40
effect on the labor force participation
  of married women 96
employment and 96
how acquired 39
increasing during marriage 41, 131
marriage and 40
on-the-job training and 135
timing of investments in 92

Implied contract 133
In re Marriage of Brown 90
Incentive to marry 31, 33, 71, 94
Income-earning capacity 2, 6, 31, 65
  as property 130
Incompatibility 1, 43
  in colonial America 17
Indemnification 133
Innocent party 4, 16, 17, 55, 57
Interrelated laws 5
Irretrievable breakdown 1, 43, 58
  California laws 54

Jacob, Herbert 83

Kay, Herma Hill 58
Krauskopf, Joan M. 115, 118
Krom, Howard 57

Labor force participation rate 59, 73, 88,
  94, 96, 129
  married women 96
Landes, Elizabeth 36, 37
Licenses 7, 89, 93, 114, 116
Los Angeles 61, 82
  property awards in 80
  spousal support in 81
Loss of companionship 111

Marital property
  California laws 5, 80
  common law states 19
  defined 5
  degree or licenses as 93
  economic perspective of 40
  education and 134

expanded definition 91
no-fault divorce and 64
pensions as 89
trend in the distribution of 6
U.S. laws 19
Marriage contracts 18, 21, 120, 129
Marriage laws 13, 15, 22, 32, 128
Marriage rate 94
Marriage-specific investment 96
Married Women's Property acts 19
Matrimonial Causes Act of 1857 17
Melli, Marygold S. 84, 85
Michael, Robert T. 36, 59
Migratory divorce 17
Mutual consent
  as a basis for divorce 2, 137-139,
    140
  fault divorce and 1
  grounds for divorce in New York 86
  specific performance and 127

Negative sum game 103
Negotiations
  change due to no-fault divorce 45
  costs of 77
  economic analysis of 44
  for custody 81
  under fault divorce 5, 79
Nevada 17, 64
New York 86
No-fault divorce
  California laws 54
  costs of divorce and 37
  defined 1
  divorce rate and 72
  education and 98
  effect of 1
  financial condition of divorced wom-
    en and 79
  impact of 71
  introduction of 1, 53
  labor force participation of married
    women and 96
  limited negotiations 5
  marriage rate and 94
  political process and 43
  problems with 2

proponents of 58
quality of family life and 101
quality of life for married women and
    99
reemphasized legal standards 18
reform of 111
second best and 63
transaction costs and 77
unexpected results of 2

On-the-job training 42, 88, 95, 103, 135
Opportunistic behavior 32, 65, 124, 128

Pensions 7, 114, 117
  civil service 90
  federal 90
  military 90
  nonvested 89
  vested 89
Peskin, Janice 73
Peters, H. Elizabeth 1, 4, 78, 82, 83, 96
Polinsky, A. Mitchell 125
Political process 3, 26, 42, 43, 53, 62
Premarital agreements 20, 21, 120, 136,
    140
Production possibility frontiers 29, 33
Professional goodwill 41, 91, 92, 114-
    116, 132
Property 6
  degrees 93
  goodwill of an individual 91
  licenses 93
  pensions 89
Property settlements
  effect of no-fault divorce 82
  encouraged under no-fault divorce 112
Public Choice
  defined 43
  introduction of no-fault divorce and 60
  predictions from 43

Quality of family life 71, 101
Quality of life for married women 99

Reform in the courts 114
Remarriage prospects 135

San Francisco
  property awards in 80
Search
  divorce and 35
  for a new mate or situation 7, 123
  preferred spouse and 35
Search costs 8, 111, 123
Second best 46
  introduction of no-fault divorce and
    63
Separate property
  at divorce 38
  common law states 19, 89
  community property states 20
  defined 5
  educational support from 134
  human capital as 6, 131
  Spanish law 18
Singer, Jana B. 86
Smith, James P. 96
Social security 91
Spanier, Graham B. 94
Specialization
  based on joint decision 100
  benefits of 28
  child care and 31, 65
  costs of 33
  during marriage 28, 31, 41, 72
  effect of higher wages 59
  no-fault divorce and 78
Specific performance
  as a contract remedy 124
  as a preferred remedy 126
  fault divorce and 64
  marriage agreements and 128
  mutual consent divorce and 137
Spousal support
  California laws 54
  fault divorce and 1
  no-fault divorce and 79, 112, 113
Statutory law 53
Sugarman, Stephen D. 87

Transaction costs 75-78

Uncertain outcomes 36, 37, 60
Uniform Marital Property Act 20

Uniform Marriage and Divorce Act 20, 21, 54, 131
Uniform Premarital Agreement Act 21
Unjust enrichment 133

von Stade, Frederica 131

Ward, Michael P. 96
Weitzman, Lenore J. 1, 4, 57, 58, 79-87, 89, 92, 116-118, 120
Women's earnings 87

Zero sum game 103